Authentic Though Not Exotic

Authentic Though Not Exotic: Essays On Filipino Identity

Fernando Nakpil Zialcita

ATENEO DE MANILA UNIVERSITY PRESS

ATENEO DE MANILA UNIVERSITY PRESS
Bellarmine Hall, Katipunan Avenue
Loyola Heights, Quezon City
P.O. Box 154, 1099 Manila, Philippines
Tel.: (632) 426-59-84 / Fax (632) 426-59-09
E-mail: unipress@admu.edu.ph
Website: www.ateneopress.org

Cover design by Ernesto Enrique
Book design by JB de la Peña

Bagong Taon on the cover by Arturo Luz
Illustrations by Fernando N. Zialcita

The author and publisher would like to thank the Ateneo Art Gallery
and Mr. Arturo Luz for permission to reproduce his painting on the cover.

The National Library of the Philippines CIP Data

Recommended entry:

Zialcita, Fernando N.
        Authentic though not exotic : essays on
Filipino identity / Fernando N. Zialcita.
– Quezon City : ADMU Press, c2005.
        1 v

        1. Culture. 2. Group identity – Philippines.
I. Ateneo de Manila University Press. II. Title.

HM101 306 2005 P051000155
ISBN 971–550–479–5

For my mother and father,
   at whose table these musings began.

Contents

Introduction

An Identity under Question

ENJOYING A FOREIGN DISH means more than ingesting food; it is an acknowledgment that the Other has a value worth welcoming into one's being. During the last decades of the twentieth century, the cuisines of Thailand, Vietnam, Bali, and Singapore gained international acceptance and prestige. So have other expressions of their culture. As recently as the 1960s, Southeast Asian arts were classified as either "Farther Indian" or "Chinese"; these labels have since been dropped and the unique features of each style appreciated. May we expect that the same respect will eventually be accorded our Filipino arts, specifically those created in the Christianized, Hispanized lowlands?

In the realm of taste, as in other realms, such respect is closer now than before, but still remote. Part of the problem is presentation. Ordinary Filipino restaurants, both here and abroad, do not make their offerings visually attractive. As even Filipinos complain, "Everything looks brown!" And, because our restaurateurs skimp, they will not serve the *sawsawan* [dipping sauce] in a saucer but instead stock it in a bottle on the table. But as serious, as this lack of concern for the customer, is the question of self-respect. While Filipinos love their cuisine, when asked about its characteristics, some

1

answer, "There really is no Filipino cooking. It's Spanish, it's Chinese." Or worse, according to a Filipina who runs a Thai restaurant, "*Kare-kare*[1] like the rest is bastardized cooking."

Some Filipinos' tendency to denigrate, without basis, their major cultural symbols shows in other realms, and works against us. During the Asian Pacific Economic Cooperation conference held in Subic in December 1996, the participating heads of states were photographed wearing barong Tagalog made for the occasion. This should have been a glorious hour for our designers, and for the Philippines as a whole. It was not to be. Local writers repeated the legend of how the shirt came about. Supposedly the wicked Spaniards compelled Filipinos to wear their shirttails out to mark their low status, and obliged them to use a transparent fabric so as to expose their weapons (Ramos 1996, 11). Thanks to this cliché, the *Bangkok Post* trumpeted that the Filipino national shirt was a "slave shirt" (Cunanan 1996, 6). Thanks again to this cliché, some Filipinos, like an uncle of mine, now refuse to wear the barong Tagalog.

While studying and teaching in the U.S., a frequent insinuation I met was "Oh, the Philippines? You mean tree houses/little bamboo huts/Smokey Mountain"? I countered this by showing books on our houses in wood and stone from the 1800s to the 1930s and on our baroque churches. For large, free-standing structures either in timber or stone that attempt to symbolize the cosmos and Man's place within it indicate a sophisticated level of social development. They require a variety of highly specialized skills from masonry to mathematics, a managerial class to coordinate thousands of artisans, and speculative thinkers. Such structures first appeared in the Near East three millennia before Christ; then in India and China; and, during the first millennium after Christ, in other Asian countries. Examples are the temples of Nara and Kyoto, the sacred city of Angkor, and the vast stupa of Borobudur. However, in the lowlands of Luzon and Visayas, available data indicate that such stone structures with cosmic symbolism would appear only from the early seventeenth century onward in the form of churches.[2] The native artisans who built these eighteenth–nineteenth-century churches had a good knowledge of the Golden Mean, as shown by a recent, unpublished study by the Spanish architect Santiago Porras. Often, their designs and their details are exquisite. But many educated Filipinos feel alienated. They deride these designs as products of "forced labor."[3] I have heard architects dismiss this stone legacy as "a colonial imposition."

Equally downgraded are other highlights of our cultural heritage. While a tour operator agrees on the need to showcase the Philippines' Spanish-influenced arts, he speaks of them "as bastardized Spanish." Another friend, who conceptualized a tour for the modern art collection of the GSIS, the Central Bank collection of pre-Hispanic gold jewelry, and the museum of San Agustin, says that "Modern art and pre-Hispanic old jewelry are us Filipinos. Those baroque saints and carvings have no connection to us." Has she ever attended processions and seen how important these baroque-garbed saints are in fostering municipal solidarity? I wonder. During one 12 June celebration at the East-West Center in Honolulu, I invited practitioners of Filipino martial arts to perform before an international audience. However, a visiting Tagalog asked me why I featured *eskrima*. "Why not Maranao martial arts?" Unconsciously he thought "eskrima," because derived from the Spanish word *escrima*, was less authentic. He should have listened to a young German expert in martial arts explain our martial arts, which he teaches. Unlike Indian and Chinese martial arts whose center of gravity is the navel, "Your eskrima has the heart as the center."

When describing outstanding artifacts of their own culture, I hear educated Filipinos use adjectives such as "bastardized" and "mongrel." Sometimes they use kinder, but still condescending, adjectives such as "imitative" or "derivative."

Anxieties about Identity

Identity simultaneously includes and excludes. To define yourself as part of a group is to distance yourself from those who are outside it

(Hall and Gay 1996, 4–5). Identity has several dimensions. Depending on the situation, you may choose to affirm an identity based on, for instance, any of the following: family, religion, class, gender, or nation. Preoccupations with a national identity began with the birth of the nation-state during the 1789 French Revolution. Previously, the state's legitimacy derived from its association with a ruler endowed with semidivine attributes. Supposedly, the king had a healing touch and, depending on the country, enjoyed titles such as "His Most Christian Majesty" (France), "His Catholic Majesty" (Spain), "Son of Heaven" (China), or "God-King" (Java). But with the downfall of thrones, henceforth, the state drew its legitimacy from the "will of the people." But what was the "people"? The old term "nation" was redefined to designate a group separate from others because of its distinct language, history, traditions, and mission. Thus, though the French revolutionists fought against the Bourbons, they pursued with more vehemence the latter's goal of unifying the various linguistically divided peoples of the realm by using just one administrative language. And they now deemed it important to endow the "people/nation" with a heroic past and the promise of a glorious future.[4]

During the same period, the German scholar Gottfried Herder (Ergang 1956) claimed that each people [*Volk*] had a spirit [*Geist*], manifest above all in their unique language and literature, which needed to be studied and respected. He deemed it unnatural for Germans to slavishly emulate outsiders like the French; he believed it more natural to develop institutions and learning that accorded with the *Volksgeist*. Herder's ideas spread worldwide and inspired studies on popular culture in all its dimensions. They challenged other peoples to define their "national" characteristics.[5]

Today, however, the notion of a "national culture" is under attack, for what is called a "nation" is not monolithic. It brings together peoples who differ from each other in religion, ethnicity, social class, and gender. Moreover, the "national," if it indeed is real, constitutes only one dimension of an individual's reality. Indeed even "culture" itself is under scrutiny. Herder's notion of culture, which he referred to as Volksgeist, now seems too restrictive. According to Wolfgang Welsch (in Featherstone and Lash 1999, 95), it assumes a social uniformity which does not exist. People differ in lifestyle according to social class and gender preference. Modern cultures are themselves "multicultural." Herder envisioned a culture that was pure because it unflinchingly excluded the foreign. Members are supposed to experience "insensibility, coldness, blindness," even "contempt and disgust" (ibid.) toward outsiders. Herder's vision of cultural identity leads to political conflicts and wars, according to Welsch.

But the preoccupation with a national identity is inevitable. For the global village continues to be divided into nation-states, each protective of its interests and each eager to maximize its gains.[6] In competing for prestige, identity is crucial, and with it, heritage. In the European Union, for instance, the member states insist on the use of their own particular language even though one working language would be more efficient. At stake are pride, millenial traditions, and potential influence. Or consider China which waged a bitter Communist revolution against feudal landlords and Western capitalist imperialists. Recently, the People's Republic mounted an expensive world-class production of the vaguely anti-Chinese opera of Puccini, *Turandot*, at Beijing's Forbidden City. No doubt officials calculated that projecting the magnificent palaces of former feudal despots through an ambivalent foreign opera would attract tourism and trade. Rather than scrap the concept of national identity as useless, we could make it more complex and more supple.[7]

Preoccupations with a national identity have intensified among us, educated Filipinos, since independence in 1946. We believe that the diverse peoples of the islands should have a common vision and a sense of pride in their heritage. At the same time we have to define our role vis-à-vis Asia, Southeast Asia, the World Powers, and other nations. Moreover, we are obliged to articulate our uniqueness when planning tourism campaigns, attracting investors, selling finished products on the world market, or even when just entertaining foreign visitors.

It is not easy to affirm a Filipino identity. Like many other nation-states, the Philippines is culturally diverse. Many Filipinos, particularly in the hinterlands, still preserve the animism and other ways of our ancestors in the face of Hispanization and Islamization in the lowlands. Other Filipinos in Sulu and Mindanao embraced Islam by the fourteenth to the fifteenth centuries and through it constructed states that resisted Spanish aggression. The majority embraced Christianity; it accepted Hispanic and, subsequently, American practices. Such are the groups anthropologists call "lowland Christian Filipinos." Hispanization is present in varying degrees according to region and social class. It is more vivid in urban areas, particularly the metropolis, than in the countryside, among the bourgeoisie than among the workers. While the Spanish language did not penetrate down to the peasant, Christianity did so, along with music, cookery, visual styles, vocabulary, and social customs from Spain and parts of Spanish America. The lowland Christian majority often looks down on the two other Filipino groups. Paradoxically, it is they, rather than the other two, who are angst-ridden when attempting to define their cultural identity, as shown by examples above.

One reason for this angst may be that internationally there seems little respect for lowland Christian Filipino culture. We should take note of this because self-confidence and respect by others reinforce each other. If we are confident about our identity, others take notice of this and respect us. On the other hand, if others respect us, then our self-confidence deepens.

There is indeed a fund of respect for our culture in the Spanish-speaking world. Hence, in these essays, I refer with pleasure to our ties with Spaniards and Spanish Americans. Conversing with ordinary Spaniards, Mexicans, Colombians, and Argentines, who were not in academe, I met a number who had read on our history, on our presidents, on Rizal, and who wanted to know more. Nothing beats the experience of hearing a Mexican shopkeeper talk about Rizal or a Colombian seaman mention events from Philippine history and exclaim that "we have a common history." Superbly crafted books and articles that discuss the contributions of the Philippines to Mexico and Spanish America via the galleon trade are published in Madrid and Mexico D.F. But these are not the people or the publications most educated, English-speaking Filipinos encounter. Their world consists rather of Anglo-Americans[8] and English-speaking Asians, many of whom look down on the lowland Christian Filipino as an oddity because they cannot pigeonhole him that easily into either "Asian" or "Western." Even my Catholic students from Indonesia and Japan are puzzled when I bring them to the heritage towns of Paete and Taal: "Why is there so much Spanish in your culture? What is truly Filipino?" Since few Filipinos speak Spanish and since most of the foreigners and foreign publications they meet are English-speaking, they become anxious about their identity. Or else their preexisting anxiety is reinforced.

Puzzlement by non-Spanish speaking foreigners at the very least, disdain at worst: This shows in the scant attention artifacts of lowland Christian Filipino culture get in international overviews of national cultures. A book on national costumes from around the world (Kennett and Haig 1994) discusses and illustrates those of the Cordillera peoples rather than those of the lowland Christian majority. Two books on Southeast Asian textiles (Fraser-Lu 1988, Maxwell 1990) emphasize in both print and photograph the textiles of the Cordillera and merely glance at the textiles of the Ilocanos, Tagalogs, and Visayans. And yet the op-artlike weavings of the Ilocos are surely significant; while piña which is woven from pineapple fibers is unique in the world. The latter deserved colored photos—which it did not get. Even when a Filipino composes in the vernacular languages, he cannot be sure that he will be deemed original and truly authentic. A miniencyclopedia on world music (Broughton et al. 1994, 438–39) downplays popular Filipino music—written mostly in Filipino—for being influenced by American and Spanish models.[9] A recent overview of contemporary Asian architects by Hasan-Uddin Khan (1995) discusses Chinese, Japanese, Indian, Malaysian, Thai, and Indonesian architects. It devotes only a short paragraph to the Philippines. Though it acknowledges that Leandro Locsin and "Bobby" Mañosa did "some interesting Modernist architecture in the 1970s," nonetheless, they "do not appear to have contributed to the dialogue of Asian architecture in the past decades" (ibid., 44). The substance of this "dialogue" is not defined. The minimal space given to these two architects is an anomaly in a book attempting a regional perspective. Locsin won an international award for Outstanding Architect of the Pacific early in his career; moreover, he designed the palace of the sultan of Brunei. Both Locsin and Mañosa have focused on creating an architecture that is both contemporary and responsive to tropical conditions. What is more, they have spoken in public about the need for such. Mañosa has done commissioned work for companies in East Asia. These are ignored by the author. Even in the Third World, we Filipinos are marginal.

Other examples abound. The Discovery Channel series on Asian martial arts, aired in 1999, made no mention of any of the Filipino martial arts even though these attract many non-Filipino American students in Hawaii and on the West Coast. Like the National Geographic Channel, this channel will feature the Philippines only if the material is from the supposedly "tribal" uplands or if it is something as kinky as Good Friday crucifixions. When asked by Discovery Channel to appear as commentator on Good Friday bloodletting, I asked why the rest of our Holy Week celebrations was ignored. They never answered me. While living in Hawaii in the early 1980s, I approached an officer of a reputable university press to propose that they market my book, *Philippine Ancestral Houses, 1810–1930*, and other such books on the Philippines, for I was sick and tired of all the negative stereotypes Americans had. The interview was revealing. She admired the book design but bluntly commented that when American libraries buy books they emphasize those Asian countries that the State Department gives priority to, namely "Mainland Asia." Curiously, this includes Japan and Indonesia, both archipelagoes, but leaves out the Philippines! Moreover, "If it were a book on tribal Filipinos, it would sell; but not this type of book." Better yet, she said, would be books on Southeast Asia where the Philippines and other countries would be chapters. I did not tell her that in such a book, inevitably, the Philippines would play second fiddle to its more admired neighbors and that the culture of the lowland Christian majority would most likely be ignored. Subsequent books on Southeast Asian art, like those on textiles mentioned above, confirmed my fears.

Lowland Christian Filipinos may be English-speaking but their culture is less known and less appreciated among the English-speaking public in Asia, Europe, or the Anglo countries, than either the Tibetan or the Laotian. In the global competition for national prestige, the Ilocano, Tagalog, or the Visayan competes with one arm tied behind—partly, because of insecurities about our worth; but partly, too, because of the game rules that outsiders have imposed.

What would be wrong if the Tagalog or the Visayan projected instead the art of his tribal brothers? Nothing indeed. We Tagalogs and Visayans, should project our own pre-Hispanic, tribal heritage as well. But, for us Tagalogs or Visayans, this is only one segment of our heritage. To ignore our peasant and urban heritage, just because of the obvious Spanish influence, does violence to our identity. Moreover, for all the attention that the artifacts of hitherto tribal peoples now command internationally, the fact remains that in the U.S. and elsewhere, aboriginal culture continues to be looked down upon. A week after I first arrived in Honolulu in 1974 as a student, my White American roommate invited me to meet his friends and his parents. I wore an intricately embroidered piña barong Tagalog. His father, it turned out, had been to Manila several times. But this budding familiarity did not deter his father from asking me abruptly in front of others, "But what about the headhunters?"

Part of the stigma attached to Filipino cooking in the U.S. derives from its supposed association with "tribalism." While Northern Vietnamese and Southern Chinese eat dogs and cats, in Hawaii Filipinos are singled out for eating dog meat. My American-Chinese dentist, in all innocence, once remarked that "Filipinos eat raw meat; that is their diet." He did not know that even in isolated upland hamlets, such a diet is uncommon.

Because I am a Manileño who loves *adobo*, the barong Tagalog, the embroidered piña, baroque art, the fiesta, jotas, and Rolando Tinio's Tagalog poems that draw freely from the Spanish word chest, I have written this collection of essays in order to answer the following questions: Why do lowland Christian Filipinos experience an unease when reflecting on their Hispanized heritage? How has this unease been fed by current ways of reading history and culture? What might be an alternative way to read history and culture?

This unease stems from the way we (and outsiders) read our history and culture. It is partly attitudinal, partly methodological. Key major symbols fuse together native and Hispanic elements. Consider that most popular of Filipino dishes, the adobo. Chicken and/or pork is seasoned with pepper and salt, marinated in vinegar and soy sauce together with bay leaf (laurel) and plenty of garlic, and then cooked. Pickling has indigenous roots; soy sauce is Chinese-Japanese. When told that adobo comes from *adobado*, the Spanish for "pickled" and that the liking for bay leaf and garlic is very Mediterranean, friends react with, "Then it is not Filipino!"—instead of finding out how its taste differs from the peninsular adobado.

Their unease increases when they discover that the *harana*, or evening serenade, derives from the Spanish *jarana*, that the well-loved tinikling combines the pan-Southeast Asian bamboo dance with the beat of the jota, that our martial *eskrima* counts in Spanish and names its passes in Spanish,[10] or that a full one-fourth of Tagalog words, including well-loved ones like *pamilya, karinyoso, nobya, compare*, are Spanish in origin.[11]

Filipinos love their way of life. However, problems appear when they reflect on their identity and try to explain this to themselves, to fellow Filipinos, or to outsiders. This is not helped by the readiness of biased Anglo-Americans and fellow Asians who scorn the Filipino for not being truly Asian. These problems and biases stem from (1) the demonization of Spanish influence, (2) a limited menu of binaries for interpreting culture, and (3) reductionist interpretations.

A Demonized Influence

For centuries, many Christians, including Spanish Catholics, blamed the Jews, not only for the death of Christ, but also for the various calamities that befell them. A similar blame game is happening today. Almost any major problem of the Filipino today is attributed to "colonial" influence, particularly the Spanish. Even the traffic problem in Philippine cities is blamed on Western colonialism (Baetiong 1999);[12] likewise the popular belief in *aswang*, witches who sever themselves in two before hunting for victims (Caruncho 1999).[13] Or, lately, even natural disasters! At the open forum of the conference in June 2003, on Spanish-Filipino relations, a teacher from Taguig City said that some of his townmates blame the country's earthquakes, fires, typhoons on the fact that it is named after a bad Spanish king. Given all these, how then can Filipinos take pride in their supposedly "corrupted" culture?

Two things can be noted about this demonization: (1) In key popular accusations, no empirical evidence is offered. (2) In some other cases, no attempt is made to situate an event, practice, or institution within its historic and cultural context.

No doubt the social order that prevailed between 1565 and 1898 distributed power unequally. Power was concentrated at the upper levels of the state and the Church. This, of course, is what we would find in any state in any part of the world before the spread of liberal democracy in the nineteenth century. In addition it was a colonial system. It gave more rights to those who came from the Spanish peninsula; there was no popular representation; abuses were rampant. Moreover, it united religion and the state and thus gave one religion and its officials a monopoly on truth. Still, not every accusation made today about that period can be accepted, in the name of nationalism and anticolonialism, without supporting evidence.

Where is the evidence? Examples of accusations without evidence are the following: (1) that the barong Tagalog was the result of racial discrimination, and (2) that all churches during the Spanish period were built with "forced labor."

Supposedly the Spaniards wanted to humiliate the *indios* by denying them the right to tuck in their shirt. Moreover the fabric had to be gauzy so as to expose weapons. But, to date no such law or ordinance has been brought forward as proof![14] In truth the Spaniards did not have to impose a ban. Indian traders then as now wore their loose long sleeved *kurta* over their equally loose pants. So likewise did the Chinese traders. If one lives in the tropics, isn't it more convenient to free one's shirttails? As for the gauze, filmy textiles let the air through. Thus jusi and piña. Since women wore see-through blouses made of these—despite churchmen's protests—there was no reason why the men could not either. I shall go back to these examples in the essays.

Another allegation is that stone monuments, like the walls of Intramuros and the churches, were built with "forced labor." Again the issue turns on proof. Father Merino (1987, 50–51) cites a sixteenth-century document, "Quentas de la muralla para su Magestad," which lists in detail the wages paid the workers who built these walls: P50 in gold a month for the maestro, one *tomin,* or gold real, per week, plus a rice ration, for the peon. The maestro was not European. Merino believes him to be a native, rather than Chinese, because he, like the rest of the workers, had no family name.

Turning to the churches, accounts by Isacio Rodriguez, OSA (1976), and Pedro Galende, OSA (1987), of how such major churches, like San Agustin in Intramuros or the monastery of Guadalupe in Makati, were built at the turn of the sixteenth century share a common theme: shortages of funds, inadequate revenues from estates, and the need for donations. When the construction of the present cathedral of Vigan began in 1790, funds did not suffice. Bishop Blaquier, OSA, mentions in 1799 that the parishioners contributed sand, water, gravel, lime, stones, and wood "but not everything." Monetary contributions were also solicited from wealthy Spaniards living outside the Ilocos. Skilled workmen were hired and paid for using the parish income.[15] Indeed his predecessor, Bishop Ruiz, OSA, became destitute from spending his own limited stipend on the project. He appealed to the king (Scharpf 1985, 35).

> I only ask for the alms Your Majesty may wish to give me, while taking note of the present condition of the enterprise, the amount I have spent on it, and what else needs to be spent. Rest assured that the last maravedi Your Majesty gives me shall be spent on the church, and not only this, I shall also spend whatever I can save from my expenses as in fact I have done till now.

He had no money to order masses with to be said on his behalf after death.

Writing in 1803–1805, Joaquin Martinez de Zuñiga, OSA, said that when a new church of solid materials had to be built in the islands, the parish priest "obliged the indios to assemble together with the materials." But what would "obliging" mean? The parish priest "paid for the masons, carpenters, nails, tiles, and other materials that could not be found in the towns. In these payments, he made use of the rights that pertained to the church and at times his own stipends." Zuñiga even claims that this is "how all the churches of the Philippines have been made" ([1803–1805] 1897, 203).[16]

At the heart of this demonization of Spanish influence is a moralistic approach to the social sciences widely popular in the Philippines. History and culture are seen as a struggle between good and evil. Historians are expected to paint the pre-Hispanic past as a wondrous Golden Age to be restored. Should one point out the intervillage wars and the slaving raids that occurred, one gets criticized for being "colonial." Anthropologists and sociologists are likewise expected to describe only "ideal" Filipino values, preferably those that imply self-determination, rather than actual values that operate in everyday life. Portraits of rural villages are expected to glow with harmony, fellowship, and *bayanihan.*[17] Sociology and anthropology are confused with moral social philosophy.[18] But the two could never play such a role. They merely wish to understand and interpret a given pattern of behavior in all its complexity.

No Sense of Context. A serious failing of some present evaluations made of the Spanish period is that they float in limbo because they do not look at either the historical or the cultural context of the person, event, or pattern under review. They do not consider what was possible and what was not in past period. They judge the past exclusively in terms of present standards. They are "presentist." True, we cannot help but look at the world from a given perspective; we are most familiar with our present values and norms. Nonetheless, a trained scholar should realize that previous generations may have had different values and norms. For the sociologist Anthony Giddens (1982, 30), people act on the basis of knowledge that is available to them at a particular time and place. There are unforeseen consequences to human actions. We are humans, not omniscient gods! Grossberg (in Hall and Du Gay 1996, 100–1) adds that we experience the world from a particular position in space. Our capacity for taking charge of our lives "to make history," for negotiating with others to our best advantage, depends on our access to particular kinds of places.

Without this cultural and historical relativism, we cannot appreciate the achievements of our own ancestors, whether pre-Hispanic or Hispanized. Unknowingly, we belittle them for not anticipating our present fashions. This may be one reason why many are reluctant to depict our indigenous ancestors in Luzon and the Visayas in loincloth rather than in sarongs. They think it shameful. On the contrary, within the context of a non-Moslem, non-Christian society in the tropics, wearing a loincloth makes perfect sense.[19]

It is claimed that the Spaniards were so perverse that they deliberately kept Filipinos ignorant.[20] Renato Constantino (1978, 36), whose writings on nationalism and anti-imperialism are influential, speaks of the "Spanish legacy of ignorance." Moreover, the accusation is that the Spaniards forced Filipinos to render forced labor on state-sponsored projects. Many do not realize that the educational system in nineteenth-century Philippines was actually ahead of that of other Asian countries of the period. Or that corvee labor has characterized even societies in independent, noncolonial states.

Today free public education on at least the primary level forms a basic pillar of public policy in nation-states all over the world because of several reasons. Industrialism requires skilled, literate labor to run the machines. Moreover the merchant class is now dominant; they know that education confers advantages in trading (Cipolla 1969).

But the situation differed in the eighteenth century on the eve of the revolutions that led to the victory of capitalism and industrialism. Since most states then were monarchies whose subjects were mostly farmers handling simple tools, understandably the educational system even in Western Europe concentrated on educating the elite, namely, the clergy, nobility, and merchants. The situation changed radically with the triumph of bourgeois-led liberal democracy and industrialism. For understanding current issues and, especially, for operating machinery, literacy was needed. During the nineteenth century, Western nation-states made public schooling compulsory (ibid.). In 1857, the Spanish government made it mandatory to open public schools in major towns in the Spanish peninsula (*EUIEA* 1925, 1,738). Shortly after, in 1863, they did the same for the Philippines "with compulsory attendance for the pupils, and Sunday schools for adults" (Corpuz 1989, 500). Even before this decree, however, many parishes, for instance in Cebu, already had free elementary schools (Fox and Mercader 1961). According to the French traveller Jean Mallat (1846, 1:386), "The three R's were more widely taught in the Philippines than in most of the country districts of Europe." What the 1863 Decree did was to "set up a national system under government control"—independently of the Church (Fox and Mercader 1961, 28). Reviewing nineteenth-century Asia as a whole, the Swedish economist Gunnar Myrdal (1968, 3:1632–34) singles out the Philippines and Japan for the attention paid by their governments to education. This had no parallel in other Asian countries of the time.

During the nineteenth century, Church and state in Catholic countries fought with each other over who would control the educational system. Churchmen saw the secular schools as breeding grounds for atheists and subversives, secularists scorned the church-controlled schools for fostering superstition. This conflict was repeated in the Philippines. Unfortunately, because this social context is often ignored by discussions of education under Spain, a simplistic interpretation of Spanish educational policy has become popular.

An awareness of historical context can also explain why corvee labor remained in force up until the 1880s in the Philippines, and for that matter in other state societies, including those that were not colonies (Robles 1969, 239–42; Lasker 1949; Webber and Wildavsky 1986). To continue its activities, a state must have a stable source of revenues. While simple societies with no states do not levy taxes, states do so in monetary form, in kind or in labor. Significantly, pre-Hispanic datus charged high interest rates: *ganda*, 100 percent per annum; *ibayiw*, any loan at 100 percent; and *dalawa-lima*, at 150 percent (Scott 1992, 83).[21] This gave them a pool of debtors who paid their debts by working on their creditors' fields or helping in house construction for a set number of days. Such a pool was needed because the Tagalog freemen (*timawa*) were bound to the datu only by contract rather than by obligation (ibid., 92).

The Spaniards introduced a regular and obligatory system of taxation as a basic pillar of the state. One important tax was the duty required of all male inhabitants of age to work on roads and bridges for forty days in a year. A fee could be paid in exchange. However, before 1880, all native functionaries and Spaniards were automatically exempt (Robles 1969, 64, 70). There were abuses in the extraction of corvee labor, as well as of other taxes. Thus the mutinies or the flight to the hills. But there could not have been a system of taxation, particularly in the noncapitalist countryside, that relied solely on monetary payments. Stories by Ilocano farmer-friends about life in the 1930s to the 1940s suggest that the circulation of money was limited even under the capitalist Americans. Farmers bartered their products when they needed outside products like salt. When a farmer contracted a debt to another peer, he promised that his sons would work for the latter for a set number of days. In England and Scotland during the sixteenth to the nineteenth centuries, all able-bodied male inhabitants had to contribute days of labor in maintaining the roads (McCrea 1971). Marx observes that the universalization of monetization in nineteenth-century Europe accompanied capitalism's triumph. Previously, even in the most developed economy of the ancient world, the Roman, monetization was limited: Taxes and payments were in kind. Thus, the historical uniqueness of the bourgeois-dominated world (Marx [1857–1858] 1973, 103). To my mind, the Spaniards can be faulted for automatically exempting Spaniards and native functionaries from corvee. The first has a colonial import for it made one ethnic group dominant over another; the second reinforced the division of society into two strata: those in mental occupations and those in manual.

In the construction of Bohol churches, it appears that pre-nineteenth century projects extended wage labor only to particular individuals like the headman. In the nineteenth century this would be expanded to benefit carpenters, masons, painters, but not those working on the church as part of their *polo* [corvee labor] duties. Nonetheless nineteenth-century inventories include expenses for food allocations [*raciones*], rice, refreshments, tobacco, and lunch (Jose 2003, 55–56). Here again, context is important both temporally and spatially. Monetization increased during the nineteenth century. At the same time its spread throughout the islands was uneven. It would have been more available in metropolitan and more commercial areas like Cebu than in poorer areas like Bohol.

Sometimes, it is not just the social and cultural context that is ignored. An author's words are interpreted in isolation from his other overall message. A classic example of this is how poor Sinibaldo de Mas ([1842] 1963) is misrepresented. Supposedly he advocated that indios should not be educated and that they should be obliged to wear a different costume. In fact he advocated the exact opposite. Sent to Manila to do a report on conditions in the islands, he proposed two options: either retain the colony or prepare it for independence. If Spain wanted to retain the colony, then it was imperative to keep the indio in his place by not educating him and by even compelling the use of a separate costume. However, if Spain wanted to let go, it should educate the indio and treat him as an equal. He concludes by saying that he preferred granting independence. "Why deny other peoples the benefit that we seek for our own motherland?" (De Mas [1842] 1963, 89, 194).[22] Strangely enough, Corpuz's (1965, 37) popular history of the Philippines quotes De Mas's words about keeping the indio in place while ignoring both the hypothetical "If" and De Mas's own liberal preference. He thus makes it appear that De Mas was recommending not teaching Spanish, and then adds that it suited the Spanish priests to be the intermediary between natives and Spaniards. He says that because of this official indifference, only a few Filipinos, unlike Spanish Americans, speak Spanish.[23]

Though Carlos Quirino (1978) provides an accurate reading of De Mas,[24] it is Corpuz's misreading that has become the accepted gospel truth.

A second reason for this unease about identity is that the unconscious binary contrasts used in interpreting data are just two. Other fruitful contrasts are overlooked.

A Limited Menu of Binary Contrasts

Following Levi-Strauss, there are anthropologists who claim that the mind thinks spontaneously in binaries when interpreting data. I notice that much of current discourse about Filipino history and culture is shaped by two binaries: (1) colonial versus noncolonial/anticolonial, and (2) Asia versus West.

Beyond Colonial versus Noncolonial. "Colonial" is equated with subservience and lack of freedom, "noncolonial/anticolonial" with assertion and freedom. I agree that this theme is important. The Philippines has been dominated by foreign powers, and continues to be so today, particularly by the U.S. However, there are other themes that also matter and that cannot be reduced to it.

For instance, there is the binary: "kin-based community" versus "community broader than the kin." We complain that Filipinos are individualistic; many seem unable to think of a common good on the level of a city, a province, or the nation. Comparing ourselves to the Japanese and the Thais, we think this individualism is all because of colonialism. But is this really true, were we united as a people before 1565? My opening essay in this collection shows this was not the case and articulates some of the obstacles. Today loyalty to the kin above all other loyalties persists in many circles, though not in all. We should be careful of reducing this to either Western influence or to colonial residues.

Another ignored binary contrast is: "the state (as a form of political organization) versus the nonstate." The "nation" [*bansa*] has become part of ordinary discourse. But not the "state" [*estado*]. And yet major problems we have concerning both identity and other domains are related to this contrast. The origin of the state in the Philippines and its challenges past and present need to be highlighted. We should beware of calling the pre-1565 barangay a "city-state" or an "ethnic state."

The nature of the state[25] is discussed at great length in the first essay where it is a key variable. Let me point out a major feature. The state is a political organization that can mobilize not just a small locality or a group of families, but thousands, because it has a continuous formal government existing everyday. Such a government exists because a stable source of revenue through taxation exists. And this revenue comes about because this political organization controls the use of weapons within its jurisdiction, and hence the instruments of coercion. In contrast, nonstates, like those that existed in our inaccessible uplands down to the middle of the twentieth century, claim the allegiance of only a locality, be this a lineage or interrelated lineages. Kinship is often the bond that links all together. Since adult males often carry weapons as their right, the existing government has limited powers. It cannot exact obedience to laws that contradict the interests of particular adults, for instance, surrendering part of their income to support a formal government.

Filipinos look with envy at Meiji Japan for modernizing overnight in the face of Western imperialism. Looking at themselves, they blame their disunity on colonialism. They forget that despite civil wars and struggles between shogun and emperor, Japanese leaders by the 1880s were aware of the bonds that linked all together regardless of kin, class, and regional differences in speech. They had at least a millennium and a half of living together under a state led by one monarch. Can we say this of Filipinos in the 1880s or of Filipinos before 1565? Surely not.

Today the Philippine state must compete vis-à-vis other nation-states. It has to improve its infrastructure, attract investments and offer more products. To do all these, it has to project internal stability. This image, in contrast to its neighbors, it does not have. Nor is this state able to collect enough taxes. Part of the problem indeed is an attitude of dependency on the U.S. But on the grassroots level, it may be that our long nonstate tradition continues to influence many into avoiding taxes and into carrying weapons.

Finally, another binary that is glossed over is "predemocratic versus democratic state." Democracy matters because every individual has rights as a human being and as a citizen. But there seems to be a double standard when we look at the past. When critiquing the Spanish record before 1896, we assume that the Thais, Chinese, Japanese, or even the people of Sulu and Maguindanao, who lived under their unconquered monarchs, had more rights then than our eighteenth-century ancestors. While we lived in a midnight, supposedly our neighbors flourished in the sun of freedom and can, therefore, be proud of their traditions. Given that our neighbors lived in predemocratic monarchies, we may wonder how much sun they enjoyed.

Beyond Asia versus West. The Filipino's achievements are often not appreciated enough either by himself or by others because they do not seem "Asian" enough. But what is "Asia"? What is "Southeast Asia"? These are discussed by two essays.

How true is it that while other Asians have retained their original culture, the Christian Filipinos have lost theirs? The problem is that "authenticity" is confused with "exoticism." And exoticism is identified with being non-Western. The more non-Westernized a culture, supposedly, the more authentic it is. Such a definition by its very nature works against the lowland Christian Filipino.

If, however, we define authenticity as continuity with major patterns in early Austronesian culture, we may be pleasantly surprised.[26] Filipinos, Malaysians, Indonesians, Micronesians, and Polynesians belong to what is called the Austronesian family of languages. Associated with this family is a complex of cultural traits that anthropologists have identified on the basis of studies of prehistory and of the culture of peoples that escaped Christianity, Islam, Confucianism, and Buddhism until fairly recently. Some traits are the following: veneration of ancestral spirits; reverence for particular rocks, mountains, trees, bodies of water, and animals such as the snake and crocodile; a fondness for pigs and dogs; for men, the use of tatoos and loincloth; for women, a wraparound skirt; in kinship, equal rights among men and women in inheriting and transmitting property. Both Islam and Christianity frown on the veneration of ancestral spirits and on reverence for aspects of nature. Islam despises both pigs and dogs as dirty, but Christianity does not. Both Islam and Christianity have discouraged tattooing and the use of loincloth as indecent. But while Islam considers the exposure of men's thighs as indecent, Christianity does not. Both Christianity and Islam insist on covering women's breasts. Some groups in Islam take the further step of covering a woman's figure, including her hair, and even her face. But Christians let their women roam around with exposed hair, shoulders, arms, and thighs. Islam favors giving men a larger share of the parental inheritance. In contrast equal inheritance by both men and women is likewise a tradition in Western Christian societies, including Spain.

Traditional dancing in the Cordillera brings male and female performers together. This, too, is the case among lowland Christian Filipinos who often equate dancing with moving in rhythm with a partner of the opposite sex. In the tinikling, a man and a woman weave in and out of bamboo canes that players clap together in rhythm. Is this the case in the *singkil*? When danced correctly, the singkil should employ only female dancers, according to Usopay Camar, a Maranao scholar. In the Bayanihan version, made by Christian Filipinos for the stage, a prince stands on stage brandishing a kris. This mixing of the sexes goes against Moslem tradition as practised among the Maranao. Moreover, a Moslem man does not display his sword in front of women, nor bare his chest (Camar 1970, 45–51). We turn to the tinikling. The Visayans, according to the dance scholar Edru Abraham (1993), used a Spanish dance form (the quick-paced jota with its complex footwork), when they choreographed their own version of the bamboo dance (which is found all over Southeast Asia), and composed a melody to accompany it. The Spanish jota, like the dances of the Ifugaos and the Kalingas and unlike those of the Maranao, encourages men and women to dance together. Who indeed is closer to the original, hypothetical Austronesian culture: the Christian Visayan or the Moslem Maranao?

There is thus a binary contrast that many are unaware of: "Austronesian" versus "non-Austronesian." And still another: "authentic versus nonauthentic." The "exotic" is not the same as the "authentic." The exotic is what is unfamiliar—from the point of view of the outsider. This in itself does not guarantee that the exotic self is true to either its past or to its convictions.

Is Rizal "authentic"? For the Euroamerican, his ideas and his language are certainly not exotic. How about Emilio Jacinto and Andres Bonifacio? They may have written in Tagalog, but they were influenced by Freemasonry and by Christianity. Are the three less authentic than the isolated mountain villager who conforms to the Euroamerican's stereotype of a true Asian? In the case of all three, they believed in their vision and sacrificed everything for it. "Authenticity" has another meaning. Existentialism defines it as a choice consciously made and acted out. It is fidelity to one's self in relation to one's concrete circumstances. The concerns of Rizal, Jacinto, and Bonifacio were certainly far removed from those of our Austronesian ancestors or of our cousins in the uplands.[27] But then they lived in a major, international port city of the nineteenth century that headed an entire archipelago. The authentic should not be confused with the exotic.[28]

A third reason for our unease about our culture and history is a prevailing "reductionism" whose oversimplification can be dangerous.

Reductionist Interpretations

The claim that all Spanish influence is evil injures our sense of national identity. So likewise is the notion that Filipinos lost their culture and ended up as mere copycats. Almost anything with a Spanish name is now suspected as being non-Filipino even if it is original. The mestiza dress with its butterfly sleeves; the wood-and-stone house with its sliding shell windows; the adobo which pickles meat in garlic, vinegar, and soy sauce; the many lively jotas: Anything that carries a Spanish term or seems faintly Spanish stirs doubts among educated Filipinos. "How can these be Filipino if they are not indigenous?" On the other hand, despite the value placed on the indigenous, few seem to bother to read the voluminous anthropological ethnographies on our brothers and sisters in the non-Hispanized parts of the Philippines during the early part of the twentieth century, or the detailed accounts by the early European travellers on sixteenth-century Philippine societies. I have gone through many academic papers that tend to fantasize when alluding to indigenous, non-Hispanized culture because they ignore these accounts and ethnographies. As a result they fail to realize how strong and persistent indigenous ways are even in the lowlands, and that these modify the foreign.

Moreover, notions of culture in the Philippines tend to be static: Many use "culture" [*kultura/kalinangan*] and "race" [*lahi*] interchangeably. In January 2003, the permanent exhibit at the National Museum entitled *History of the Filipino People* was translated as *Kasaysayan ng Lahi*. History of the Race! This is a dangerous confusion that any basic textbook in introductory anthropology critiques. For anthropologists today, culture refers to systems of beliefs and values communicated through symbols, especially language. Because symbols are invented by a community and can be acquired through learning, symbols can change. They can also be imported from or exported to other communities. On the other hand, physical characteristics, like skin color, are inherited genetically. They have nothing to do with behavior; nor can they be changed. And yet in 1999, the *Philippine Daily Inquirer* ran a series of articles extolling achievements of Filipinos, over the past two millennia, which show the "nobility of the Filipino race."[29] I shall discuss this and other issues raised above in the essays.

There is no metaphysical principle—nor biological law—which mandates that members of a culture should borrow only from a given culture rather than from another. People often assume that the Filipino would have been better off borrowing from his neighbors in Asia and Southeast Asia rather than from the West. And yet while the Chinese kinship system is patrilineal—that is, property is transmitted only through the sons, especially the eldest son—the Spanish system is bilateral. Surely the Filipino cannot be faulted for feeling more at home in a system spiritually closer to his, even if it came from farther away.

Because culture is an open symbolic system, we can assume that the Filipino could not have merely blindly borrowed from the West. He must have transformed what he got and given it new unsuspected meanings. This I discuss in an essay. Consider religion. Two of the most popular Virgins in the islands, those of Manaoag and of Antipolo, are associated with trees. This is significant because we know that our ancestors revered trees as abodes of spirits. How did trees get associated with Mary, given that the Church kept tight control over representations? The image of Our Lady of Peace and Good Voyage was made in Mexico and brought over in a galleon in 1626. Hence the brown features. Installed in Antipolo, a story circulated that the image would disappear and appear instead on a tree. The church authorities took this as a sign that the Virgin wanted her shrine to be built elsewhere.[30] We can assume that a subtle negotiation took place: between the native consciousness insisting on a meaningful location, the tree, and the foreign priests equally vehement about the church enclosure as the location. Moreover, precisely because Filipinos read their own meanings into icons and rituals, the oppressed—as Reynaldo Ileto (1979) tells us—saw themselves as Kristos defending the poor against the priests and the bureaucrats. Anthony Giddens (1982, 28 ff.) says it is not a question of choosing between Marx and Heidegger, between an image of man upon whom material forces act and one which posits him questing for meaning. Both are needed to complete the picture.

Static, too, are our notions of history. I hear appeals to "return to our glorious past" or to "return to our indigenous past." There is value in such appeals, for an aggressive colonialism, whether Spanish or American, has made many shy about their indigenous heritage. There is value, too, in returning to the use of the vernacular languages, for these carry our indigenous heritage. Indeed I must confess to an unease in using English in discussing identity. Whenever possible, I prefer to use the vernacular because this forces me to rethink abstract concepts in a clear, concrete way. Also there is genuine communication. But the reality, however, is that in both the Visayas and Mindanao, the colleagues I wish to reach complain when the discourse is completely in Filipino.

We need a dialectical interpretation of both culture and history. Interpretations of the shift from one culture to another or from historical context to another could benefit from that use of *Aufhebung* found in both Hegel and Marx. Often people think in terms of "Either . . . or," that is, a choice between the colonial and the anticolonial, the indigenous or the Western, the pre-Hispanic or the Hispanic. I believe it is really a case of "Yes . . . but . . . ." Yes, to certain features of Westernization; no to others and at the same time going beyond them to work out a better order. Alternatively, it is also a case of "No . . . but . . . ." Karl Marx does indeed show that the triumph of one class over the other is a case of "Either . . . or": the proletariat replaces the bourgeoisie. But the transformation of capitalism into socialism is a case of "Yes . . . but . . . ." Or a "No . . . but . . . ." More precisely of how one set of social relations is transformed into another.

I mention Marx because since the 1970s, interpretations of him by some nationalists have influenced many Filipinos—even those who would never consider themselves Marxist in any way. But it is easy to misinterpret Marx if one uses a mechanical, rather than a dialectical, approach. Consider Marx's example of how forces within nineteenth-century capitalism lead to the negation of capitalism itself. Thus in *Capital 3*, the emergence of companies that sell stocks to the public is regarded as an omen. As an enterprise grows, the capitalist may no longer be able to fully finance all its capital needs. He must sell stocks to the public. The total profit he henceforth receives takes the form of interest, as mere compensation for owning capital that now is entirely divorced from the process of reproducing wealth. Such a company constitutes a transition in the conversion of the process of production from an individual into a social one. "This is the *Aufhebung* of the capitalist mode of production within the capitalist mode of production itself" (Marx [1894] 1978–1981, 569).[31] That capitalist invention, stock companies, is retained but its individualistic, exploitative character is reduced through the sale of stocks; at the same time it is transformed into something other than itself: a publicly owned company. For Shlomo Avineri (1968, 37)—in orientation a Social Democrat rather than a Leninist—Marx's "*Aufhebung* means abolition, transcendence, and preservation." Marx is not saying that capitalist institutions must be forcibly extinguished, nor capitalists exterminated.

Unfortunately, translations of this tricky German concept have sometimes chosen the easy way out by using only "abolition." This dangerous simplification by rigid interpretations of Marx has led to massive purges of supposed enemies of the people in totalitarian states.

Aufhebung, or supersession, happens continually in our own daily lives. "One's early beliefs . . . are sublated in one's later, more measured beliefs or one's early drafts in one's final draft" (Inwood 1992, 283).

Philippine history and culture can be read as a series of Aufhebung. Consider, for instance, the encounter between indigenous religion and Christianity. The former venerated trees as abodes of spirits. Most likely, such veneration involved only those from a locality or from a cluster of villages rather than an entire region, for relations between barangays ranged from trade to armed conflict. In contrast Christianity's advocacy of various cults, such as of Mary, were supralocal. The Church was for all believers. Nonetheless elements from the indigenous religion, such as the tree, were retained. This now became the abode of a new spirit, the Mother of God. Still later—as Reynaldo Ileto (1979) and others suggest—ordinary people saw new meanings into cults such as this. The oppressed saw in the verses of poems imbued with Christian doctrine an ideology that justified their revolt against the rich, the educated, and even against the priests themselves.[32]

Using Aufhebung has the added advantage of allowing us to cross the gap between the Actual and the Ideal, the Is and the Ought. From our current perspective, a previous form of behavior or a past institution may seem narrow and repressive. However, elements in it may lead to a more rational way of acting and thinking. Or else, those elements may have value, seen from another perspective. They could thus be retained and at the same time transcended. Neither indigenous society nor colonial society can be normative from our present, democratic perspective which stresses human rights. But some of their practices, like their architecture, literature, and music, have value. The same can be said for paganism and for pre-Vatican II Catholicism. In Singapore, at a 1996 conference for French-speaking Southeast Asian professors, I heard a French scholar lecture eloquently on how the notion of the Mystical Body of Christ enabled the subjects of the kings of France to realize, over the course of centuries, that, despite differences in language and custom, they formed one body politic. When I asked him afterwards if he was a practising Catholic, he answered, "I am an atheist. Besides, I know how intolerant the French Church was until the 1950s. But I appreciate its contributions to French culture." I dream of finding Filipino atheists and agnostics who regard our baroque churches, together with the rice terraces or the farmer's house, as a basic component of their heritage.

The Essays

These essays were written for various conferences and periodicals at different times, and so did not at the start constitute a single narrative. A common thread, nonetheless, is the need to look at lowland Christian Filipino culture, with its mixture of the indigenous and the Hispanic, in a more positive light.

Part 1 deals with one frequent charge, namely, that Hispanization and Westernization subverted the indigenous sense of community by introducing the serpent of individualism. I question whether the notion of private ownership of strategic resources came in only with Spain by looking at both the early Spanish chronicles and twentieth-century ethnographies written by anthropologists on upland peoples. I also question whether our persistent problems in transcending the good of our kin group are due to Spanish influence. Again I examine the same sources mentioned above. Indeed there are institutions created during the Spanish period that we use today to create a suprakin sense of common good. One such institution is the "state" which admittedly is ambivalent because its basic instruments, like taxation, have been oppressive. A third essay examines the accusation that during the 1896 Revolution the more Hispanized sector of society, the elite, rejected the emerging vision of a national community.

Part 2 responds to the accusation that lowland Christian Filipino culture is "elitist" and "derivative." At issue is not culture, in general, but rather what we can call "civil culture." Such cultures are prestigious worldwide. But along with the benefits are costs. The elitism that Filipinos associate with Spanish influence, for instance, in education, has, in fact, been true of all civil cultures until democracy's advent. There is a Christian Filipino civil culture that differs from the Spanish and has its own achievements. True, it has inconsistencies and contradictions but this does not mean that it is "schizophrenic" and "bastardized," as many educated Filipinos claim it to be. Culture consists of symbols which are inherently arbitrary.

Part 3 examines appeals to joining "Asia" and "Southeast Asia" and shows that though we should indeed participate in both, we should realize that both concepts were invented by Westerners and that their content tends to exclude Westernized peoples like us. We Filipinos should reexamine these concepts. Looked at from another angle, the Hispanized Filipino, whether farmer or urbanite, has practices, for instance in costume, religion, or architecture, that continue his Austronesian heritage and, at the same time, link him to Chinese, Japanese, and Arabic traditions.

Notes

1. This delicious dish combines beef, vegetables, and banana blossom in a thick ground peanut sauce with bagoong as the dipping sauce. It was probably inspired by curry [*kari* in Indonesian], but it is not spicy and has different characteristics such as the use of annatto [*atswete* in Tagalog], which came in from Mexican Indians.

2. In Mindanao and Sulu, such structures may have appeared earlier, by the fifteenth century, thanks to the introduction of Islam. In Luzon, the Ifugao rice terraces, carved onto the mountains by hand and drawing water from watershed to ponds, constitute an engineering marvel. However, in my text, I refer to stone structures that symbolize the cosmos. Moreover, their date remains unresolved at present: 2,000 years ago or only during the past 500 years? Maher (1974, 56) excavated charcoal associated with a constructed terrace surface and concluded on the basis of a radiocarbon analysis of charcoal fragments that it dated back three thousand years ago. On the other hand Keesing (1962, 323), studying the patterns of migration to the Cordillera says that the Ifugaos entered their present homeland only during the Spanish period. Originally lowlanders, they fled Spanish impositions.

3. This uneasiness about the Filipino's cultural heritage affects even Catholic Church officials. At a conference in Cagayan de Oro in 1996 on cultural heritage, a young theologian said that in the Ilocos, people are happy when a colonial church finally collapses. "They are expensive to maintain. And they are symbols of colonialism." He subscribes to the popular belief that they were built with "forced labor." Given the fact that even educated, practicing Catholics see Spanish period churches as symbols of "slave labor," tourism officials lack the enthusiasm needed to promote them. When tour guides do bring people to ancient churches, they focus on the imagined evils of the priests. Thus the guide at Sarrat, Ilocos Norte, routinely tells visitors at the ruins of the convent that "That lone column of brick in the patio was a guillotine where the friars would execute their enemies." When I tried to explain what a guillotine is, and that it is French rather than Spanish, he ignored me.

4. Shortly after the fall of the Bastille in 1789, the newly formed National Assembly formed a commission to inventory all assets that should form the nation's property and to protect all works of art within France (Bermond 1999). This set a precedent for other nation-states.

5. It was the Briton, Edward Tylor ([1871] 1958), who defined "culture" as we now use it, that is, as a society's repertoire of knowledge and practices that is *acquired through learning*. But Herder's ideas were an obvious inspiration to the

German-born and educated American anthropologist Franz Boas who conceived of a people's culture as the outcome of a few key ideas. Through his students, Alfred Kroeber and Ruth Benedict, his influence on subsequent anthropologists has been immense (Voget 1975).

6. Both the nation-state and the relations between the local and the global are discussed by new anthropological writing (see Foster 1991, Alonso 1994, Kearney 1995).

7. Mickunas (1994) distinguishes between "archaic" nationalism and "modernizing" nationalism. The former claims that individual members of a nation bear the national spirit of an original people. It emphasizes a return to a narrowly defined mythic past via sacral rituals and places. Nationalism in nineteenth-century Germany and Eastern Europe, and in the present-day Middle East and the republics of the former Soviet Union exhibits these archaic tendencies. In contrast "modernizing" nationalism bases nationality on the recognition of basic individual rights within a democratic system. While it upholds a dominant myth, it can tolerate other myths within its borders. Mickunas regards the U.S., France and, to a certain extent, Britain as examples of this second type of nationalism—which he evidently prefers.

8. To qualify: Some of the individuals, I know, who showed a keen appreciation for Hispanized Filipino culture were Britons, Australians, and Anglo-Americans. However, these few were in academe.

9. It did not evaluate particular groups like the Apo Hiking Society, River Maya, or Joey Ayala's Bagong Lumad. It had praise only for Freddie Aguilar—perhaps because his international reputation simply cannot be ignored.

10. The Visayan instructors in Hawaii led their students with *uno, dos, tres,* and so on and named particular steps with poetic names such as *de abanico* [fan-like]. Willey (1994, 23) describes other Hispanic components.

11. This is based on the study of Quilis (1984).

12. The urban planner Palafox argues that the Spaniards introduced the plaza complex which concentrated major activities around the plaza where the homes of the wealthy were located; at the same time they compelled the peasants to live away from the center close to their fields. Unfortunately this argument ignores the persistent efforts by the Spanish authorities to settle all Filipinos under the church bells [*bajo las campanas*] (Reed 1978, 15). The ordinary farmer resisted this as impractical because it meant a longer walk to the fields. The argument also ignores the fact that in traditional preindustrial cities all over the world, the dwellings of the wealthy do indeed congregate in the center because of proximity to many services (Sjoberg 1960). Nor does the argument mention obvious reasons why traffic is a mess in present-day Filipino towns: Private ve-

hicles are preferred to mass transport; buses and jeepneys use the highways as their terminals; vendors sell right on the roads. Surely, all these are not due to colonial influence.

13. The tale of the bloodsucker who divides in half is found in other Southeast Asian countries. The Cambodian version features a severed head that flies at night with its entrails exposed (Ramos 1990, xviii–xix). Note, too, that the name for witch in Flores, Indonesia, is *suangi*.

14. De la Torre (1986, 15) mentions this supposed Spanish restriction but merely concludes that "These allegations, though, deserve further study."

15. When repairs had to be made in 1845, Father Bumatay, whose family name is Ilokano, withdrew money from the cathedral treasury (King 1991, 14).

16. To be sure the borderline between corvee labor for the government and voluntary labor for the church, at times, disappeared as when the townspeople of Majayjay were exempted by the government in 1660 and in 1707 from rendering taxes in the form of personal services for a given period so that they could repair their crumbling church. The task of reinforcing the walls with an extra width in a small town of only four thousand inhabitants provoked protests which apparently were resolved after a town meeting. At the same time it is noteworthy that the same report mentions that twelve carpenters who worked on the reconstruction of the church in 1716 were paid out of a general fund created from fines on absentees (Palazon 1964, 13–14).

17. In the 1990s, I participated in a weekly seminar that lasted for several months. Its theme was "community." The organizers were uncomfortable when I pointed out that what this means for the farmer may differ from what it means for an NGO worker and that even in the non-Hispanized upland villages, conflicts occur between villages.

18. Just four years ago, a newspaper ad placed by a well-known private, religious school announced an opening for a sociology teacher. Qualifications needed? The applicant had to have a degree in "Law, Political Science, or Philosophy." There was no mention of sociology.

19. Many Filipinos will not look at the animist, non-Moslem Filipinos of the Cordillera or Mindanao highlands as a possible image of what they were before Christianization. In the recent grand parade of 12 June 1996, the first tableau represented pre-Hispanic shamans. Having seen other parades and festival tableaux that represent the pre-Hispanic past, I was not surprised to see the same mistake repeated. The actors should have been tattooed all over and in loincloth. Instead they had some body paint on their arms to suggest tattoos, but none on their chests and backs. And they wore batik sarongs.

20. An example of this position is that of Abella's (1977).

21. He bases his analysis on Pedro de San Buenaventura's *Vocabulario de lengua tagala el romance castellano presto primero* [Vocabulary of the Tagalog Language with Castilian Romance (given first)] printed by Tomas Pinpin and Domingo Loag in Pila, Laguna, 1613.

22. The Spanish original reads: *Porque negar a otros el beneficio que para nuestra patria deseamos?*

23. Maria Cristina Barron Soto, a historian connected with the Universidad Iberoamericana in Mexico, offers a contrary view. The Spanish language spread in the Americas because of (1) Spanish migration and (2) nationalism. Where there were more lay Spanish migrants, the language became established as the everyday tongue. Where there were less of them, American Indian languages kept their ground. And yet despite heavy Spanish migration, only 20 percent of Mexicans spoke Spanish in 1821. Spanish gained ground following independence because Mexico's leaders found it more effective in promoting unity than any of the many, actively used Indian languages. She claims that though Spanish migration to the Philippines was minimal, had the Malolos Republic prevailed, it would have promoted Spanish as the instrument of national unity. However, the Americans triumphed over the Malolos Republic and successfully imposed English through the educational system. (Unfortunately, as this book goes to press, I do not have a copy of her published article.)

24. But prejudices die hard. One caption made by the editorial staff for a photo accompanying Quirino's article contradicts his text. It says that "Sinibaldo de Mas suggested that natives had to dress differently to distinguish them from the Spaniards. Native *principales* are shown wearing their shirts out." Would a course on remedial reading have helped the caption-writer?

25. The nature of the state and its formation is a major topic in political anthropology. The extensive bibliography on this is referred to in the opening essay.

26. To understand what Austronesian cultures were like before the advent of outside influences, I have used Bellwood's (1985) classic study and various ethnographies on upland peoples of the Philippines and Indonesia. A good starting point are the summaries of various ethnographies per ethnolinguistic group made by the Human Relations Area Files for Taiwan and the Philippines (Lebar 1975) and for Indonesia (Geertz 1963).

27. An American author, whose name escapes me, once claimed that Rizal was more "European" than Filipino. The remark betrays an extremely static notion of culture. It is saying that sophistication and being Filipino do not go together. But Filipinos who claim that only the ancestral bamboo-and-thatch house is truly Filipino, and dismiss as foreign all urban structures since the sixteenth century, are not far removed from this American.

28. When some Filipinos try to imagine what their ancestors were like before Legazpi, they look at Malays, Sumatrans, Javanese, and Balinese of today, or the Taosug and the Maranao. Filipinos who visit Indonesia lament that whereas they have retained their culture, we have lost ours. This assertion has no basis.

29. Thus, too, the publishing house that produced the ten-volume *Filipino Heritage* of 1978 called itself "Lahing Pilipino."

30. Wendt (1998) has a similar interpretation of the way Filipinos reinterpreted Christian images and rituals. He mentions the cult of Antipolo in particular.

31. The original German text reads: *Es ist dies die Aufhebung der kapitalistischen Produktions weise innerhalb der kapitalistischen Produktionsweise selbst* (Marx [1894] 1967, 454). My interpretation relies heavily on that of Shlomo Avineri (1968). Because I am fond of Hegel, I find this approach more relevant. Also, Marx criticized Hegel's content rather than his method because it did not deal with material, economic forces at work in society. The different levels of "contradiction" in Hegel, particularly Aufhebung, are analyzed by Grégoire (1958, 65–66) and Inwood (1992, 283).

32. *Aufhebung* is also used by Nick Joaquin (1989) when he shows how the infrastructure laid by friar and conquistador gave the Filipino revolutionary materials with which to create a sense of community broader than that of kinship and village. But both Joaquin and Ileto have been misunderstood. I heard a writer with Maoist commitments scoff at Ileto for interpreting Philippine history "as salvation history." On the other hand Nick Joaquin is pilloried by many for praising the Hispanic past and for supposedly being blind to its dark side. They forget that his father was an official in Aguinaldo's army and that the major heroes of his fiction are colonels and generals of the 1896 Revolution. One of the best eulogies ever written of the Propaganda and the Revolution is the concluding page-long paragraph of Joaquin's *A Question of Heroes* (1977).

PART I

Constructions of Community and Identity

Toward a Community
Broader than the Kin

Kung ang pagibig ay wala ang mga Bayan ay dili magtatagal.
If love is absent, countries will not last.

—Emilio Jacinto, ca. 1895–1896

SOME TEACHER-FRIENDS in the Ilocos confide that when they visit an unfamiliar hamlet, even within the same municipality where they reside, they carry small bottles of consecrated coconut oil[1] as protection against sorcery. One supposed sign of hexing is stomach disorder. When I would mention wanting to visit, say, another hamlet a few kilometers down the road, friends would warn me that it harbored sorcerers [*mannamay*]. However, in that hamlet-down-the-road, friends there would be concerned that I had been staying in that hamlet-up-the-road. They feared it for its sorcerers! This suspiciousness toward outsiders, even of the same ethnicity and language, has characterized non-Ilocanos as well at certain times in their history. Maximo Ramos (1971, 48), the folklorist, relates a 1930s tale from the Tagalog-speaking town of Lucban, Quezon. Teachers came from all over the province for a seminar. The townspeople claimed that during that week, black-winged creatures with human heads and torso but no lower bodies flew at night. After the seminar ended, peace returned. Bicolanos have also had a similar tendency to accuse the stranger of witchcraft (Lynch 1963, 151). So do rural dwellers in Samar according to my sociologist colleague Leslie Lopez (2002) who hails from that province.

Often assumed is that a broad sense of community has been present in our culture from the very beginning. Supposedly, Filipinos have always believed in the equality of all human beings, have respected each other's personhood, and have cared for each other even as mutual strangers. Allegedly under the impact of Western colonialism, society split into classes; Visayans, Tagalogs, and Ilocanos fought each other; and people thought only of their own individual selves. Many see erasing Western influence and returning to indigenous ways as the solution.[2]

However, as data above show, suspicions occur even *within the same ethnic group* and *within the same municipality*. June Prill-Brett, a Bontoc-born anthropologist, told me that a dividing line between the Cordillera peoples, who were not Hispanized, and the Ilocanos is the way each deals with conflict. While Ilocanos hurl sorcery accusations against another village, Cordillerans in the recent past would war against the other village. Edward Dozier, an anthropologist of American Indian background, talks of the prevalence of feuds between Kalinga villages during the early part of the twentieth century. When Dozier (1966, 60) had to go from a Kalinga village to another just 50 feet away, his boy-companion backed off. The boy feared he "might be the victim of revenge for an unsettled fight several weeks before between two youths." One of them was his first cousin. During my extended stays in the Ilocos, I personally found the relations between the barangays to be peaceful, though at times laden with suspicions.[3] Other colleagues, however, paint a different picture. Raul Pertierra (1988, 66) says that teenage boys in the Ilocos municipality he studied would conduct "organized raids against other barangays." Presumably this resulted in brawls. Minda Cabilao-Valencia (2001), a sociologist who taught at Batac, Ilocos Norte, in 1982–1985 and 1988–1990, reports that colleagues warned her not to go to particular barangays where feuds were taking place.

Are these patterns of suspicion and conflict true only of Filipinos? Accounts of peasant life in nineteenth-century France report that peasants kept pretty much to their own village. It was too expensive to go out, and many roads were muddy trails. When they would go to a town on a pilgrimage and/or to market, brawls often broke out between peasants from different villages at the slightest provocation. Besides, the men liked physical fights (Weber 1976, 383–4).

Discussions of community are often colored by assumptions regarding the "*bayanihan* spirit." Many assume that bayanihan is commonly practised by farmers all over the Philippines, and that they must, therefore, have a deep sense of community.[4] My own observation of Ilocano farmers has been that the dyadic exchange of unpaid labor largely occurs among close kin, friends, and neighbors to favor one individual. It has nothing to do with the interests of the barrio/barangay as a corporate whole. This, too, has been the observation of the sociologist Gelia Castillo (1981, 452). Moreover, farmer-friends tell me that bayanihan is relevant only for particular tasks. For building a house of bamboo-and-thatch, one should indeed throw a party to compensate those who assisted with their unpaid labor. But such a compensation will not do for building a house of hollow blocks and metal roof. My farmer-friends prefer skilled labor and willingly pay for it. Similarly, they prefer to pay for farm labor when transplanting rice shoots because this task has to be done quickly. In contrast if they were to invite their relatives and friends to help them for free for, say, two days, then they would be obliged to reciprocate each of them with two days of unpaid labor away from their farm. On the other hand there are indeed other life-situations in the hamlets, where my farmer-friends willingly help their relatives and neighbors (who are often the same) with unpaid labor. Examples would be a death in the household or preparations for a wedding feast. But this warm intimacy can go hand in hand with sorcery accusations against the Outsider.

Both nationalism and modern democracy assume the importance of the broader community, a community that transcends ties of kinship and locality, a community that is abstractly conceived yet real. Both assume the importance of the Anonymous, Faceless

Stranger: the person or persons whom one will never know face-to-face but whose welfare must be considered because they are fellow citizens. In a democracy there is another key idea: that the individual, regardless of background, is a rational being capable of making decisions on his or her behalf. Consequently even the ragpicker is an end in himself rather than a means to someone else's end. But these notions have not appeared at all times and in all places.

"Kindred" and "kindness" come from the same root according to the anthropologist Edward Tylor ([1871] 1958, 10). "Kindred" refers to those kinspersons that an individual believes he or she can rely on within a bilateral kinship system. So Bituin feels close to two paternal first cousins plus a maternal uncle and two second cousins. On the other hand Tala, her sister, is drawn to four paternal first cousins and three maternal first cousins. Though sisters, their kindreds differ in size and composition. Originally the kindred constituted the basic social organization of the Anglo-Saxons, as of other Germanic peoples up until the fifth to the sixth centuries. Thus, says Tylor, benevolence, cooperation, and nonviolence—in other words "kindness"—were reserved for the kin but not for those outside it, for the latter were potential enemies. In case of conflict with others, no other group but the kindred could be expected to help the individual. The kindred, too, has constituted the moral universe of many Filipinos, whether in the lowlands or in the uplands.

Who is regarded as the Insider in the indigenous notion of community among Filipinos? Who is the Outsider? What role might the state and the Church have played during the sixteenth to the nineteenth centuries in facilitating a "We" that was broader than the kin? Finally, in building a broader "We," are we obliged to choose between the indigenous and the Western? These are the questions I wish to explore.

By "indigenous" here, I mean two peoples: (1) non-Moslem Filipinos of pre-seventeenth-century Luzon and the Visayas; and (2) non-Hispanized, non-Moslem Filipinos who, down to the middle of the twentieth century, lived in relative isolation in the uplands.

In this essay, I look at the role of the state during the late sixteenth to the nineteenth century. I am interested in the interaction between Spanish and indigenous traditions. I argue that in the non-Moslem areas of Luzon and Visayas, our first experience of living in a wider polity, the state, took place under Spanish rule. This explains why particular Spanish/Western institutions continue to play an important role in constituting our sense of community today. Contrary to what some Filipino nationalists and our Asian neighbors say, we are not "colonial-minded" in retaining these. I say this with full awareness of the ambivalent role of the state. On the one hand democracy and, to a certain extent, nationalism were conceptualized in opposition to the monarchy. On the other hand, despite itself, the pre-twentieth-century state created the conditions that made these new forms of consciousness possible by articulating the "I" and broadening the "We." It has been both Enemy and Facilitator. I base my interpretations on both historical accounts and on field data drawn from years of living among farmers for extended periods of time.

The points I wish to make are the following:

1. The notion of the community broader than the kin is not a cultural given. Historically, it has been a response to the appearance of particular social institutions. Two of them are the state and the translocal, or ecclesiastical, cult.

2. Patterns of behavior and institutions from the Spanish period are stigmatized today as "colonial." But in fact some such patterns of behavior and institutions foster a broader sense of community. Conversely, some indigenous patterns of behavior and institutions work against a broader sense of community.

3. It is more realistic to look at Filipino notions of community as the product of a dialectical interaction between indigenous traditions and foreign imports. The foreign imports act upon the indigenous but are themselves transformed.

Paul Hutchcroft (1998), a political scientist, says that the Philippine state is weak because it is unable to control the oligarchs.

John Sidel (1999) shows that once elected into office, even politicians of modest backgrounds entrench themselves in the state apparatus and amass fortunes for their families. In a sense, my essay constitutes a preface to their work.

Community and Polity

We should define some terms: community, communalism, communtarianism, state, and nonstate.

A popular term is "community." But its denotation is often not clear. Many would agree that community refers to a group of people bound together by mutual sympathy. This sympathy shows in the positive interactions among them, their preference for doing things together and their favorable feelings toward fellow-members as against outsiders. The nature of this "group," however, is far from obvious. A kin group, whose members do things together and seek each other out, forms a community. But so can other bigger groups like a town. According to Ferdinand Toennies (1971)—who popularized the term *Gemeinschaft* [community]—even the large and impersonal business organization can become a community given the right conditions. For community, taken as mutual sympathy, is above all a felt relationship. Despite its huge size a nation, in the celebrated expression of Benedict Anderson (1983), is an "imagined community." To complicate matters, each type of community or mutual sympathy exerts a particular claim that differs from those of other types. It may collide with them. Thus a man may uphold his kin's interests at the expense of his obligations both to his town and to the nation. Conversely, his commitment to the nation may overshadow his commitment to the family. "Communitarianism" involves active participation in a community. But merely invoking this without qualification will not clarify social problems, for there are different forms of communitarianism.

We must also caution against singling out "individualism" as the villain, for there are different ways to assert the self. While one type of individualism, which we can call "selfish," looks at other people only as fodder for personal ambition, another type of individualism, the "affirmative," asserts the right to make decisions on matters that affect one's life. Most likely the reader of this essay believes in communitarianism. But surely he or she will not cede to any group the right to choose either a spouse and a career. And yet in many societies, one is expected to give up this right "for the sake of the community." There is no dichotomy between certain forms of communitarianism and individualism. Wanting to choose for one's own life can go hand in hand with a genuine respect for the rights of even strangers.

There are different types of polities. "Nonstate societies" can be contrasted with "state societies." One type of nonstate I would call the "autonomous locality" (see fig. 1). This small settlement does not exceed a few households which are linked together by kin ties.

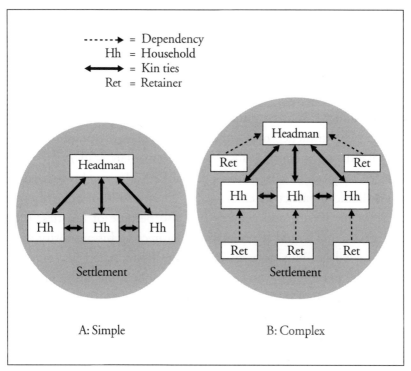

Figure 1. Two Types of Autonomous Localities

The locality can be either a hunting-and-gathering band, a farming hamlet, or a fishing village. Though such a locality may have close ties with its neighbors, it is often independent of them. A headman settles disputes within the settlement and may represent it in important matters vis-à-vis another settlement. In other respects, such a headman's way of life differs little from that of the rest; moreover his influence is normally confined to his settlement and its own immediate surroundings. Relations between settlements may alternate between trade and intermarriage on the one hand, and conflict on the other (Sahlins 1968). In more powerful and complex autonomous villages, particular households acquire retainers either through force or through heavy loans.

Even more complex politically is the chiefdom (fig. 2). The paramount leader may be the scion of the most prominent or the most wealthy family in an area. He exacts tribute either sporadically or, in other cases, on a regular scheduled basis. Despite his preeminence, he does not exercise either a monopoly on force or on the resolution of conflicts. Since weapons proliferate, his followers are likely to resort to armed self-help should peaceful negotiations to a conflict break down. Nonetheless he may intervene if these conflicts escalate and weaken the polity. Aside from his village of residence, he exercises influence over other nearby villages. But because his commands are mediated through the immediate leaders of those villages, they can be rejected by a particular leader and his followers. Even should a particular chief profess loyalty to him, not only because of his wealth and bravery but also because of kin ties, that particular chief would likely insist on protecting his authority over his own village. Nor does an internally differentiated bureaucracy exist. The paramount chief's rights and obligations are replicated by each local chief in his own community. The links between levels of authority are thus personalistic rather than functional. The paramount relies on personal charisma and on kin ties to maintain the loyalty of local chiefs (Carneiro 1981; Flannery 1972; Wright 1977, 1984). Given these factors, Junker (2000, 66) says that a

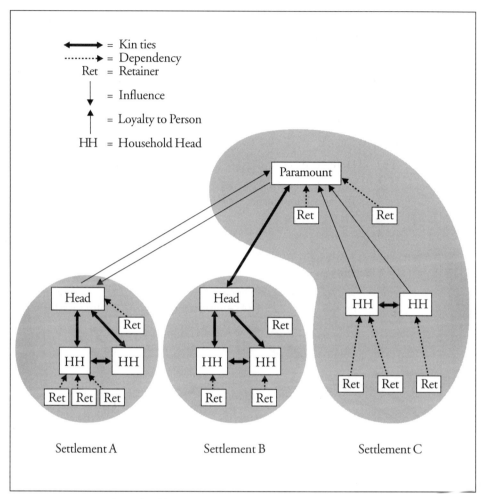

Figure 2. The Chiefdom

chiefdom "is typically highly unstable, characterized by rapidly shifting regional political configurations and intense competition between leaders at various levels in the political hierarchy." Even "complex" chiefdoms have limited levels of authority: only "two levels above the individual village or community leader." As a chiefdom incorporates more and more villages, it may split apart unless it mutates into a state.

Even in its premodern form, the state represents a more comprehensive and tighter organization (fig. 3). Many and various groups fall under its sway. The villages with their leaders form clusters, each under the authority of a district head. In turn all the district heads

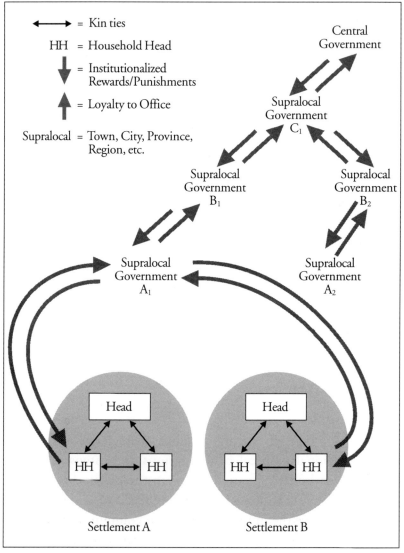

Figure 3. The Predemocratic State

answer to an institutionalized bureaucracy under the authority of a ruler. There are at least three levels of authority above the individual village leader. The organization can thus incorporate more and more villages; at the same time it can multiply levels of authority: district, city, province, region, and others. This increase is possible because (1) a formal bureaucracy exists and runs on a daily basis and (2) the state's monopoly on the use of force can extract taxes and compel submission to its laws (Carneiro 1981; Flannery 1972; Wright 1977, 1984; Junker 2000, 66). Henceforth "surveillance activities" are "stored" in the state as it watches over its members and seeks to control their behavior (Giddens 1982, 5). The state's emergence goes beyond the political. First, villages and entire ethnic groups, which have merely coexisted and may even be at war with each other, are brought together under a single government (Sahlins 1968, Krader 1968). Second, kinship's importance diminishes in a state when it ceases to be the major basis for organizing society. Ideologies, etiquettes, and protocols emerge to indicate how the individual should relate to people outside his small circle of familiars. Among them are ecclesiastical cults which will be discussed below. Third, genuine city life becomes possible within a state because the latter can draw on the surplus of rural producers. A city (or any urban center) is not a settlement that just happens to be larger than a farming village. Aside from being a settlement of substantial size and population density, a city shelters a variety of nonagricultural specialists, such as artisans, merchants, bureaucrats, and teachers. It is the preferred residence of the literate elite and indeed of the key leaders in the political, military, economic, and religious hierarchy (Sjoberg 1960).

Directly and indirectly, the state and the city form a seedbed for a future broader mutual sympathy.[5] Compelled to live and work with strangers, the urban resident must balance kin interests with those other groups he is in. "Urbanity" in English refers to a broader, more tolerant spirit and to an etiquette that watches out for the feelings of Perfect Strangers. So likewise does the Spanish term *urbanidad*, which has been adopted by the Tagalogs.

But these benefits come with costs. Though social stratification on the basis of wealth and power does exist in a nonstate society, this intensifies within a state, for particular groups can gain access to its concentrated power and use this to dominate others. Thus, while the state is an effective apparatus for resolving conflicts between settlements, it may not be so in dealing with class conflict. Indeed, it can exacerbate it. Moreover, the concentration of power within the state, specifically the ruling body, has led to despotism. Through the development of more sophisticated forms of surveillance, despotism became, in the twentieth century, totalitarianism (Giddens 1982). For the state has not watched only over the strictly political and administrative; it has also eyed and modified kinship, dress, amusement, house styles, and other aspects of culture on the excuse that all these affect public order.

Another factor influencing notions of community is the translocal, ecclesiastical cult. In the decentralized nonstate society, cults tend to be purely local in orientation. But as polities grow in size and organizational complexity so, too, do cults. They reproduce the pyramids of the political order. High priests emerge to guide ordinary priests. Meanwhile scholars develop ideologies that transcend the kin. Thus the father-son relationship becomes, in Confucianism, the foundation for the more abstract relationship between sovereign and subject. Similarly, the family in Catholicism supposedly serves as the cornerstone for society as a whole: While caring for his or her family, the individual must comply with obligations to others outside this small circle. The fortunes of ecclesiastical cults and the state are intertwined. The former could not have emerged in a context other than the state; moreover, their ideologies often legitimize power-relations within the state. Confucianism enjoined respect for the emperor as the Son of Heaven. In the past, even as Catholicism emphasized its autonomy from the state, it extolled the state's legitimacy for as long as the latter respected its institutions.

Through the state and the translocal ecclesiastical cult, the individual learns to live and work with those who are not his or her kin: his or her sympathies and allegiances thus widen. However, there are limits to this. For state officials, the foreigner, or the noncitizen, is an outsider who may be dangerous; for leaders of an ecclesiastical cult, the noninitiate is the suspicious outsider. Such prejudices have led to bloody conflicts. Still, the milieu of both state and ecclesiastical cult is broader than that of nonstate societies. It offers relationships other than kinship and neighborship.

All over the world, at various points in time, the state and the ecclesiastical cult have widened the sense of community among hitherto kin-based groups. For instance, this took place in the Huang-ho Valley of China around 1900 B.C., in the Red River Valley of Vietnam around the first century B.C., in Japan's Yamato Plain around the fourth century A.D. I must point this out, for many fear that Filipinos have a "fatal flaw" that keeps them from acting together.

For this essay, I have chosen to compare the experiences of France and the Philippines. French history clearly shows that the community-beyond-the-kin did not exist from the beginning. As in the Philippines, this emerged in response to the state. But why France? Why not some Asian country? I wanted to go beyond that popular but meaningless contrast between "Western individualism" and "Asian/indigenous communalism." I also wanted to go beyond that other, but more meaningful, contrast between "colony" and "noncolony" by comparing state formation in the Philippines, a colony since 1565, and France, a noncolony within the past millennium and a half. It is often forgotten that coercion and conflict assist at the birth of the predemocratic state.

France: An Invented Community

Various Celtic states existed in the Massif Central, that rugged mass of mountains in the center of France when Julius Caesar and his troops entered in 58 B.C. (Champion et al. 1984, 316–17). These plus the Celtic chiefdoms on the northern plains were defeated by Caesar and unified into a new province of the Roman Empire, Gaul. As is well known, the western part of the Roman Empire collapsed in the fifth century under pressure from Germanic tribesmen who initially came as settlers, eventually as conquerors. One of the several Germanic ethnies were the Franks. As the conquerors of Gaul, they became the new aristocracy while their domain was called "Francia."

Kin-Centered Communities. Of interest to us is that initially these invaders lived in loosely organized nonstate societies. Though they modified the structure of the collapsing state society that they conquered, they in turn were modified by it. Over the course of centuries, the imperatives of running a state and participating in a universal Church, such as the Catholic, opened a broader set of allegiances. The Philippine case was the reverse: Nonstate societies in Luzon and Visayas were conquered and baptized into the same universal Church by a people with a long state tradition. As in France, a broader sense of community eventually took root. Despite separation in time and space, the fifth-century Germanic peoples and the sixteenth-century peoples of Visayas and Luzon share organizational similarities as nonstate societies.

Among the Germanic peoples, whatever political body existed to control the many kindreds (*Sippe*) was initially weak.[6] Chiefdoms, rather than states, were the norm.[7] By the fifth century A.D., local assemblies, which all able-bodied men were expected to attend, no longer made the decisions. The Franks descended on Gaul as separate tribes headed by leaders, with a war leader chosen for the occasion. Before the fifth century, they did not have a king.[8] But authority over the various competing kindreds was weakly exercised. Thus when an individual committed a crime or demanded justice, he sought help from the kindred rather than from a body above it. Because the Sippe took care of his needs, its interests took priority over his. Virtue was equated with fulfilling one's duty toward the kin (De Vries 1956, 175 ff.). So identified was the individual with his kindred that a conflict between individuals became a conflict between kindreds: Any of the culprit's relatives could be punished by the aggrieved party even if he had nothing to do with the crime. Thus extended feuds were common.[9]

Germanic society was not egalitarian. There were lord masters (called *principes* by the Latin sources) who prided themselves on their lineage. Below were freemen, the semifree and, at the base, the slaves who were attached to their master's household (Lopez 1985, 7; Much 1959, 103, 231).[10]

After the Salic Franks seized the Roman administrative apparatus, a supreme ruler, the king, appeared. But the king's hold over his subjects was shaky. Ordinary subjects swore allegiance to their immediate lords: the dukes and the counts. The latter in turn pledged their loyalty to the king as his personal followers. However, since the king's personal followers had their own lands and did not depend on the king for their income, they were virtually autonomous and could resist the king's encroachments. Only in the original Frankish enclave, the Ile-de-France ["The Frankish Isle"], where Paris was located, was the king's authority supreme (Bloch 1961, 423). Tribal influence weakened the state apparatus inherited from the Romans, for the Germanic tribesmen did not understand the need for regular taxes. Both the king and the lords relied on their estates and on war booty to pay their followers. The king thus had a weak hold on the lords who were economically independent of him (Pfister 1913b, 140; Wallace-Hadrill 1959, 111–12; Bloch 1961, 297). Nor did he exercise a monopoly on the legal use of violence. The kindreds continued to punish culprits or anyone related to them. In addition to feuds, plunder and violent manners characterized life in France down to the twelfth century (Bloch 1961, 411 ff.). The early French monarchy was a puny chiefdom grappling with a mighty scepter.

An Enlarged Sense of Community. But the challenge did compel the monarchy to flex its muscles. Three patterns run through French history from the ninth to the nineteenth centuries.

First, the king and, below him, the local lord increasingly asserted their authority over the kindreds in case of conflict. The Salic

Law of the Franks, codified in the sixth century, specified the fine [*wergeld*] that should be exacted according to the victim's status. In effect the codification enabled the king's court to impose its authority over the contending parties (Pfister 1913a, 300–2). But this process took centuries to realize. Ordinary laymen and churchmen organized peace movements during the twefth and thirteenth centuries to compel the king to assert his authority (Bloch 1961, 2:412). At the same time, liability became individual rather than kin-based as the king's courts increasingly restricted the kinsmen's traditional rights to seek vengeance on any of the culprit's close relatives (ibid., 128). This helped create a sense of answerability, not to the kin, but to the king who represented the wider society. It also fostered the individual's importance, for he alone was held liable.

Second, the French rulers sought to weaken the nobility's power by enlarging the royal domain to include all of France. This, too, took centuries to achieve, for the nobility resisted and, at times, revolted. After regular taxation was reinstitutionalized from the twelfth century onwards, the king's resources gradually surpassed those of any individual within his realm (ibid., 425). However, only in the second half of the seventeenth century was the monarchy, under Louis XIV, able to tame the nobility by obliging them to live at his palace as harmless, pensioned courtiers. Lords learned to doff their hats before the king's bed, ladies to genuflect (Reinhard 1954, 475).

Third, what was called France expanded over time to include non-French speaking realms because the kings pushed their domain to the so-called natural boundaries, the seas, the mountains, and the Rhine River. In the process, they acquired non-French speaking lands: Provence in the fifteenth century, Britanny in the sixteenth, German-speaking Alsace in the seventeenth, Italian-speaking Corsica in the eighteenth, Savoy and Nice in the nineteenth. Eugen Weber (1976, 485 ff.) defines the formation of metropolitan France as a "colonial empire shaped over the centuries." As recently as the nineteenth century, peoples in the west and southwest of

France protested their "colonization" by the "French," meaning the northerners.

There has not always been a France. Contemporary French scholars argue that "France ought not to have existed" (Braudel 1986, 1:104). French unity "is nothing more than a wrapper, a superstructure, a wager [*pari*]. Its land mass was cut in half by the turbulent Loire River and the rocky Massif Central. Conflict between kindreds divided localities; peasant villages closed in on themselves; cities jealously guarded their privileges against outsiders; many regions spoke languages other than French; and, within a given language, local dialects multiplied because of poor communication. So much diversity has resulted in a lack of cohesion" (ibid.). French authors claim that the history of France down to World War II has been characterized by a running theme: frequent and variously disguised civil wars (ibid.). According to Fernand Braudel (1986, 94), it was necessary "to invent France."

The invention responded to initiatives by the monarchy. For administrative efficiency, the kings propagated "French," or more exactly its polished Parisian variant over other languages spoken in the realm: Flemish, Breton, Alsatian German, Gascon, Catalan, Provencal, and Italian. The kings also cultivated a court ceremonial, etiquette, costume, and style that was copied not only throughout their realm but in the rest of Western Europe as well. Alternative traditions thus became merely "provincial" while to be French meant following fashions of the court. Being French also meant being a member of a universal Church, Catholicism, for this was the court's official creed. Through Baptism, the faithful entered a universe where both familiars and benevolent strangers were deemed brothers and sisters in Christ.

Centralization by the crown intensified in the eighteenth century. First, as capitalism replaced feudalism, the state's revenues increased. It could now supervise more closely the linkages between economic centers within France. Local particularism gave way to standardization, for instance, to a common monetary unit and common measurements. Second, advances in military and administrative techniques required expertise. In response, the state opened schools that admitted even the bourgeoisie and that stressed secular rather than religious formation; gradually the state replaced the Church as the chief educator (Smith 1987, 131–33). "France," as a mental landscape, became increasingly homogenous.

An unintended consequence of the kings' actions was that the French became unified—in response to their abuses. Because there were few checks, the kings acted arbitrarily. So likewise did the noble and bishop within their domains. Eventually, however, by 1789, the notion that the king, as the people's representative, was accountable to them took hold of the public.

Until the French Revolution and long after, "penury, shortages, famines, food riots, revolts" were the peasants' lot (Braudel 1986, 3:159). Often, however, these uprisings erupted only within a locality, sought changes only in personnel and policy, and ended in failure. The peasants supported the clergy and the nobility with tithes, taxes, and corvee labor (Furet and Richet 1973, 17, 41). The bourgeoisie had its own grievances. The clergy and nobility, whose holdings accounted for two-fifths of France, were not taxed while the hardworking and educated bourgeoisie were. Though they formed the Third Estate in the Estates-General, they were always outvoted by the clergy and nobility who together made up only 2 percent of France.

As is well known, the 1789 French Revolution was indeed unique in its attempt to overthrow the existing system and replace it with a just one. Because it obstructed reforms, the monarchy gave the underprivileged classes—the bourgeoisie, the urban workers, and the peasants—a common object of hatred. Bourgeoisie and urban workers rallied together in 1789 and referred to themselves as the "nation," as all of France. On 17 June 1789, the Third Estate asserted that it alone represented the nation; it formed a "National Assembly" (Miquel 1976, 267). Suffrage was extended to all property owners, then in 1848 to all Frenchmen, and in 1945 to all Frenchwomen.

Though this new order contradicted the former, it became possible through it. Territorial boundaries won by the kings—for their own personal ambitions—were retained as factual givens, while the revolution continued to centralize the administration. Instead of a country divided into enclaves governed by the nobility with unique local laws, Paris appointed prefects to apply a uniform set of laws, the Napoleonic Code; it imposed a single standard of weights and measures, the metric; it demanded military service of all. In 1833, compulsory education took effect with French as the sole vehicle. The ordinary man's notion of community began to include all those within that abstraction called "France" (De Bertier de Sauvigny and Pinkney 1983). At the same time the individual's rights became more defined when the Constitution, the new basic law, recognized freedom from warrantless arrest, the right to speak out and the right to choose representatives. As the "We" expanded, the "I" became more self-aware. However, this optimistic picture of the triumph of liberalism is incomplete without the shadows. According to Foucault (1977, 16, 213), it was the liberal state that increased surveillance over the individual. Using techniques from the nascent human sciences, it sought to control, not only the prisoner's body, but his mind as well.

Yet, the consciousness of a broader We was not always manifest on the village level. Nineteenth-century French peasants were divided from each other by languages and, within each language, by dialects (Braudel 1986). Roads in the back country were few, many were muddy trails. There was little reason to leave the village to visit another. Not surprisingly at market towns, peasants from one village picked up fights with those of another for the sheer fun of it (Weber 1976, 383–84). The latter were seen as aliens rather than as brothers in a national community.

The Invention of the Philippines

No single polity embraced the islands that would be known as the Philippines. Let us concentrate on Luzon and the Visayas. In Sulu and Mindanao, the sultanate of Sulu, a state, had formed by the fifteenth century and would engender a broad sense of community among its members. In Luzon and the Visayas, however, there were thousands of small polities independent of each other.

Many Polities, Many Leaders. The dominant type of polity in the Cordillera Mountains was what I would call the "autonomous locality." Down to the twentieth century, this likewise has been the case among peoples in the northwestern Sierra Madre and in the non-Moslem hinterland of Mindanao.[11] During the twentieth century, anthropologists carefully documented the way of life of particular localities in the uplands. Some patterns cut across particular ethnic groups. The leader was a headman who had no taxing powers and had effective power to settle disputes only among his kin and allies who generally lived in small hamlets close to each other. For instance, until the 1970s, the Ilongots of northeastern Luzon lived in groupings [*bertan*] of several settlements. The bertan was the maximum political unit; its population ranged from 64 to 307 individuals (Rosaldo and Rosaldo 1972, 103–4; R. Rosaldo 1980, 223–28). The ideal, one not always realized in practice, was to marry within the bertan (R. Rosaldo 1980, 223 ff.). Somewhat larger were autonomous localities in other parts. For instance, among the Kalinga, the protective circle was the "region" [*boboloy*], or cluster of hamlets, where closely related kin intermarried and settled. The population of one "region," Mabaca in 1959, was 612 people (Dozier 1966, 55). By the 1960s, as hostility between regions decreased, solidarity within a region decreased.

Though this political system may seem idyllic and worthy of Rousseau, problems arose in case of disagreements between nonkin. Leaders could not compel the disputants to come to an agreement, they could only persuade them. Violent conflict between many localities, even of the same language group, was common in parts of the Cordillera.[12] Among the Bontoc in the 1900s, the neighboring settlement was usually, but not always, friendly. The second settlement away was usually an enemy (Jenks 1905, 176). Friendly relations among the Tinguian of the same period seldom extended beyond the second or third settlement. Strangers beyond, including women carrying water from the river, were considered fair game (Cole 1922, 374).[13] Various factors led to bloody conflict. Blood was associated with regeneration. When an illness, epidemic, or crop failure struck the Kalingas in the early twentieth century, the men went outside their cluster of hamlets to hunt for a head as a remedy (Dozier 1966, 56). Since intersettlement warfare was common among the Bontoc, a man who had killed another was regarded as brave and manly (Jenks 1905, 175). Among the Ilongot of the mid-twentieth century, the adolescent often (though not always) signified his entry into manhood by beheading another (R. Rosaldo 1980, 142). In some places, the mourning ritual for a relative had to end with a killing (ibid., 157–58, 286, 288). The relative may have died from an attack, an accident, an illness, or old age. Regardless, there was pressure on the surviving family members to commit a killing. For instance, among the 1900s Tinguian, the family members of the deceased "were barred from wearing good clothing" until they had slain an outsider as victim. How many victims depended on the number of fingers that seemed to point as the dying stiffened. The custom was called *sibrong* (Cole 1922, 372). Cotabato Manobo informants recount that in the mid-twentieth century, while the women wailed over the deceased relative, the male mourner would slay the first nonkin he met (Tianero 2002, 85). Should conflict erupt, anyone outside the small circle of kin-related allies could be the victim. For the unit of liability was not the individual culprit alone but his kindred or any member of his hamlet. Barton's Ifugao informant, Ngidulu, related how the kin of a woman, who was kidnapped and sold, retaliated by going to the kidnappers' village and carried away one of the small boys to sell (Barton 1938, 28). Because no suprakin authority existed to demand or even coerce satisfaction from the culprit, one easy solution was to hold responsible even those kin-members who were not directly involved in the conflict. Responsibility for an individual's misdeed was communal: It was kin-based; and so was satisfaction.[14]

Unresolved interkin conflicts could, therefore, degenerate into un-ending feuds. According to Dozier (1966, 56), it was dangerous to go outside one's cluster of hamlets because of the "backlog of unavenged killings" (see also Cole 1922, Jenks 1905, R. Rosaldo 1980).

We should not conclude, however, that relations between au-tonomous localities must necessarily be violent. Notable exceptions are the upland peoples of Mindoro (Kikuchi 1984, Conklin 1957), the Sulod of Panay (Jocano 1968), and the Tiruray of Western Mindanao (Schlegel 1970) who all have a tradition of peaceably settling disputes between the nonkin. Indeed they have been vic-timized by other powerful groups like Christians and Moslems. Still, even among, for instance, the peaceable Mindoro peoples, suspi-cions existed between localities.

Let us turn to the sixteenth century. "In all these islands," declares Morga ([1609] 1910, 191), "there were no kings or lords who ruled over them. . . . rather there were lord masters (*principales*)." Quite possibly Spanish authors, who were the subjects of a monarch with explicit coercive powers, did not see that some lords were paramounts with more influence and prestige than other lords.

Being in thinly populated and forested areas, upland Visayan and Tagalog polities of the sixteenth century were most likely au-tonomous localities. However, in the lowland and coastal areas of sixteenth-century Luzon and the Visayas, where interisland and in-ternational trade was important, the polities were larger, more complex, and more hierarchic. Plasencia in 1589b ([1903], 174) has reported that among Tagalogs, the lord master exercised author-ity over a following, called the barangay, which consisted of 30 to 100 households. Tagalog barangays clustered together from 4 to 12 in number (Chirino [1604] 1969). Each barangay was independent of the other; but at times the lords deferred to the wealthiest among them (Plasencia [1589b] 1903, 174).[15] Among the Visayans, the group of followers was called *haop, sacop,* or *dolohan.* This group was coextensive with the *parentela,* or kin group (Alcina [1668a] n.d., 4:27). The Visayan lord-master did not recognize anyone as his superior (Alcina [1668b] n.d., 4:54; Loarca [1582] 1903, 174, 175).[16] But Laura Lee Junker (2000) points out that settlement patterns in her archaeological site in Negros Oriental suggest an emergence over time of a central settlement with a number of subordinate settlements. Such chiefdoms were loosely centralized around the figure of a paramount. An enterprising lord-master influenced not only nearby villagers, but even those residing in the distant upland forests particularly if they craved expensive imported goods in exchange for their forest products. She says that chiefdoms may have appeared in the islands by the first millennium A.D., or even earlier. Most likely, allegiances other than to the immediate kin would germinate in a chiefdom.

The lord-master was called datu among the Tagalogs and Visayans. He hailed from an important and wealthy family. Though he often inherited his post and, like his wealthy kin, did not engage in farming, he was productive. Often the Visayan datu traded and practiced as a skilled blacksmith (Alcina [1668b] n.d., 3:104). His closest allies came from his kin; below them were followers in varying degrees of dependency. Some of the latter were freemen who, in the case of the Tagalogs, merely owed service to the datu on occasion. Other followers, who had their own houses and fields, owed tribute. The amount depended on various factors, such as indebtedness or punishment for an offense. At the bottom were chattel slaves who could be bought, sold, or even sacrificed to accompany the lord on his journey to the next life.[17] The lord led his men to war, protected his followers from their enemies, and excluded outsiders from barangay lands.

Armed conflict between barangays could erupt for various reasons. There was no suprakin, suprabarangay authority that could impose its will. The paramount may have had influence within his chiefdom, nonetheless his influence was mediated by subordinate chiefs who were jealous of their authority within their particular barangay. Moreover, there were several chiefdoms. Barangays thus raided other barangays—either distant or unknown—to acquire followers and to kidnap victims that could accompany their dead (Alcina [1668] n.d., 3:256; Boxer Codex [1590] 1960; Morga [1609] 1910, 193). Writing to his superiors in Rome, the Jesuit Pedro Chirino ([1604] 1969, 89, 328) reports of the Tagalogs and Visayans:

> If the deceased had been killed violently, in war or in peace, treacherously or in some other way, mourning clothes were not removed, nor the interdict lifted until the sons, brothers or followers had killed others, not only of enemies and homicides, but also of other strangers who were not friends.

The victim did not have to be a culprit or even a relative of the culprit; it sufficed that he or she was a stranger. Among sixteenth-century lakeside-dwelling and wet rice cultivating Tagalogs, there appears to have been another source of conflict: land. For this reason their settlements were enclosed by bamboo thickets and deep moats guarded by towers (Conquest of the Island of Luzon [1572] 1903, 158).

Two historically recorded examples of chiefdoms in sixteenth-century Luzon and the Visayas were Manila[18] and Cebu. Soliman, Moslem lord of Manila, sought to monopolize the trade between the lakeshore towns and the Chinese ships by levying a tax. But this ploy must have been recent. According to the 1570 anonymous author (Relation of the Voyage to Luzon [1570] 1903, 94), "Moros" came out in their boats to complain to the first Spanish visitors that Soliman had plundered their towns, while the Chinese traders said that he had taken away their boats' helms and had seized the best of their goods without paying. North of the Pasig, a confederation of Moslem villages was indeed emerging. Islam, a religion with a long state tradition, inspired a community that transcended small, local allegiances. In this confederation a chief, who had slightly more prestige because of his wisdom and ability in war, could and did draw military aid from other villages in times of crises (Reed 1978, 5–6). Still, the alliance between Manila and Tondo was recent. Until then they had been enemies (De San Agustin [1698] 1975, 330), most likely because of trade rivalry.[19] Centralizing efforts, likewise ridden with conflict, were at work in Cebu, a non-Moslem coastal settlement of comparable size. Unwisely, Magellan got involved in a rivalry between would-be paramounts, Lapulapu and Humabon. While Manila and Cebu were chiefdoms rather than states, Soliman's alliances with the princely houses of Sulu and Brunei gave him advantages that most likely would have accelerated the process of state formation.

Can Manila and Cebu be called cities? Robert Reed (1967, 1971, 1978), a geographer who examined the emergence of urbanism in the Philippines from a cross-cultural Southeast Asian perspective, doubts this, if "city" is defined as a settlement where most of the populace specializes in nonagricultural pursuits. Such centers appear once a nonfarming group of people that firmly controls the surrounding food-producing countryside, precisely through the state.[20]

Thus though the various Philippine groups spoke languages belonging to the Austronesian family and shared many common cultural patterns, it is highly improbable that the various island peoples were then aware of belonging either to a single archipelago or to an archipelagowide community. We hear claims that "if the Spaniards had not come, we would have eventually formed a confederation to span the entire archipelago." But where does the archipelago begin and end? The Batanes? But Taiwan used not to be Chinese, and it is home to hill peoples who are Austronesians like us. Tawi-Tawi? But the sultans of Sulu used to claim suzerainty over northern Borneo. We also hear it said that pre-Christian, pre-Islamic Filipinos "were apparently aware of objective communalities like a well-defined territory, common racial stock, common parent language" (Cruz 1989, 58). The Tagalogs, however, reminded Goiti that they "were not like the tattooed [*pintados*] Visayans" (Relation of the Voyage to Luzon [1570] 1903, 95). Conversely, the Visayans called both the Borneans and Tagalogs "Chinese" because they, rather than the Chinese, brought over Chinese porcelain to trade (Scott 1994, 75). Moreover, as was pointed out above, bitter conflicts did rage even between localities in the same ethnolinguistic group. The nonkin, even from the same small island, was a potentially dangerous Outsider. The Tagalog value of *pakikipagkapwa-tao*, or oneness with the other, was most likely practiced largely within the small circle of kin within a village or a cluster of hamlets.

Can we say that a "fatal flaw" kept our ancestors from forming larger and more cohesive polities? Not if we pay attention to the material infrastructure. Aside from being an archipelago, the Philippines has a mostly mountainous terrain. Down to the middle of the twentieth century, much of the land, especially the mountains, was covered with forests. Even on the same island, communication other than by boat has been difficult. In addition, population levels had been low. The total population of Luzon and Visayas in 1591 A.D. was around 668,000 (Doeppers and Xenos 1998, 3). The density of persons per square kilometer was a low 4.0 versus a high 30.3 for Java, 79.7 for Bali, and 59.5 for Japan of the same period (Junker 2000, 62). As will be pointed out in the next essay, given the thick forest and the hilly terrain, the more practical form of cultivation was shifting cultivation [kaingin, *huma*] rather than the more laborious wet rice agriculture [*tubigan*]. In Luzon, the latter was practiced in marshlands and lakeshores that were under water.[21] It was more widely practiced in Central Java, Bali, and Central Japan of the same period through extensive irrigation networks. The hegemony of shifting cultivation reinforced the low population density because it encouraged small, dispersed settlements with a limited number of children per mother.[22] In such a setting it was difficult for an ambitious chief to control other chiefs with regular taxes and laws. Either the lower chief or his followers could easily run away to the forested hills.[23]

The idea of a broader community called the Philippines was born both in response to and as a result of Spanish impositions. So likewise, even the sense of community on the municipal level.

An Imposed Unity. The Spanish state asserted its authority by using procedures that were standard practices among states of that period, whether Asian or European. It imposed a common set of laws with the assistance of a bureaucracy and a military arm. However, the Spaniards could not have achieved this unification by themselves. The newly built fort of the Spaniards in Cebu was attacked continually by the Visayans. Yet by day two principales and thirty followers came and were fascinated by the splendor of the Catholic mass, especially since "they were admitted into the church" (De San Agustin [1698] 1975, 193). At the Spanish outpost on the island of Panay, two principales came to ask for help against the people of coastal Mindoro who raided them and inflicted damage. Juan de Salcedo warred on their enemies, and triumphed. The conquered principales promised to become vassals of the Spanish king and offered gold for their ransom. This Salcedo shared with the Panayeños. At the same time he entered into a blood compact with one of the principales (ibid, 320–21). Because there was no Philippines then, the Spaniards were seen by some as protectors against enemies coming from other villages or islands. True, the Spanish Empire was hierarchically structured. But the principales, too, assumed hierarchy as a structural principle within their own world. As warriors, they admired military prowess. At the same time, the Spaniards showed some humaneness. Indeed they, too, went looting and killed those who resisted. However, making sacrificial victims of the defeated was not part of their religion. In addition, they entered into blood pacts with the principales, welcomed them into their own magnificent ceremonies through Baptism, and gave them seats of honor in the church. They also offered material rewards, such as a share of the booty and, later on, of encomiendas. The unification of "Filipinas" was just as much the work of the native allies.

While provincial offices and above were held by the Spaniards, most of the municipalities were run by native Filipinos themselves. The mayor [*gobernadorcillo*] was elected by the heads of the barangay from among themselves. Objectively speaking, the Spaniards did dominate the native Filipinos, but sectors among the latter may not have been aware of being so dominated. This would change in the late eighteenth and nineteenth centuries.

For the poor, there must have been benefits to be reaped from cooperation with the Spanish rulers. Raids to secure victims to accompany a dead ruler had victimized ordinary people. Slave ownership and slave-raiding were banned by Philip II (Scott 1991) even though other Catholics, like the Portuguese, practiced this in South America. The indigenous custom was to charge a variety of interests: 100 percent per annum or 20 percent per month, or even to keep adding more every day to the debt owed so "that he (the debtor) will not be able to repay it and so becomes a slave" (Scott 1992, 83). Missionaries, like Plasencia in 1588–1591 ([1903], 180–81), condemned it. In addition, the missionary ministered to the sick, opened hospitals for the poor, and, when touched with fervor, "served the poor, washed their hands and kissed these hands, while on his knees" (Chirino [1604] 1969, 174). Christianity preached that only the sinner was responsible before God. Punishment should fall only on him, and spare his innocent kin even if they were related by blood.[24]

On the other hand, measures taken by the Spaniards caused suffering. The Spanish monarchy exacted tribute and taxes to support the state's operations. Where money was not available, its officials demanded conscript labor for public works.[25] The harshness with which this was imposed caused suffering, death, and most likely a decline in population during the early part of the seventeenth century.[26] The Spanish monarchy propagated an official creed, Catholic Christianity, in order to give both ruler and ruled a shared ideology. But in the name of this new religion, idols were burned and traditional indigenous practices banned. Some of these coercive measures made the islanders realize that they shared a common condition—they were being oppressed by an intruder. Initially scattered revolts sought a return to traditional religion or

protested against the imposition of tribute and corvee.[27] Gradually
the revolts became better organized, and became regional rather than
merely the affair of a village (Constantino 1975). By 1896, these
revolts had coalesced into a revolution fighting for a liberal, democratic republic.

Spanish influence thus has two faces. On the one hand, the
Spanish state became the enemy of democrats and nationalists by
the late nineteenth century. On the other hand, it brought in symbols, values, and an organization whose unforeseen consequence was
an expanded sense of community where notions of democracy and
nationalism germinated. This other face is ignored by current nationalist writings. They assume that we have always been one people
because of similarities (see, for instance, Mahajani 1971).

A Broader "We." Ever perceptive, Nick Joaquin (1989, 82) pointed
out that the boundaries we regard as sacred are the product of actions taken by Spanish officials and their Tagalog-Pampango allies.
During the early part of the seventeenth century, the Philippines
included Taiwan, the Moluccas, and the Marianas. Koxinga's
threat, the seventeenth-century Dutch Wars, and late nineteenth-
century-American intervention resulted in amputation. The
republic's boundaries, like those of other states, are thus invented;
they did not have to be. Moreover, according to Joaquin (1989,
78), our archetype of the Filipino with his plow-and-carabao is
the result of successful missionary efforts in propagating the plow
[*arado*] in order to create clustered, permanent communities. Reed
(1971, chap. 3; 1978, 7, 16) underscored the significance of
this technological innovation that made urban centers possible.[28]
Once in place, the physical plan of the new urban centers encouraged a broader sense of community. The huge church
dominated the town. Here were celebrated the major events in
the life-cycle of the residents, regardless of their kin affiliations:
christenings, weddings, fiestas, and funerals. In front of the church
opened a central plaza for all to enjoy regardless of family and

status.[29] After death, Christians were buried, not in or by their houses as in indigenous practice, but rather in a cemetery for all Christians. The basis for a notion of the "public," of a community beyond the kin, was in place.

Simultaneously, the individual's worth was acknowledged. No longer could the individual be sacrificed to follow the wealthy master into the next life, nor legally sold to cover a usurious debt, nor be liable for a crime committed by a relative. Christianity taught that the individual, not the kin group, entered paradise, and that entry was on the basis of merit. In the indigenous cosmos, those who died rich kept their high status in the next life if accompanied by their slaves. Hence, as discussed above, the need to kidnap victims from faraway places, and kill them. Those who died poor remained poor.[30] In contrast, Christianity preached that eternal status rested on moral merit rather than on wealth. Its central icon was the bloodied figure of a man nailed to a cross.

Under Spain, the barangay and the *sakop* evolved into the barrio, a territorially bounded settlement that was now the foundation of an overarching political structure. Barrios made up a municipality with the town center as its heart; municipalities constituted a province, provinces all together formed the captaincy general that was the Philippines under Spain. The administrative pyramid brought together tiny far-flung villages and hamlets into a larger whole. It enabled ordinary people to begin imagining an abstract community, be this "Katagalugan" or "Filipinas."

The needs of the older deities fostered enmity between localities. The Bagobo god Mandarangan who resided in Mount Apo sought human sacrifice. Preferred victims were the Bilaans, even though they resembled the Bagobos in culture and physical appearance (Gloria 1987, 13–14). In contrast, the Christian God sought a change of heart and welcomed, through Baptism, new followers. New icons, like the Sto. Niño, transcended language and locality. We should explore how these icons brought together formerly mutually hostile villages; for instance, how devotion to the Virgin of

Antipolo overcame the rivalries that divided sixteenth-century lakeshore Tagalogs from each other.

At the start, the sense of community among Hispanized Filipinos most likely centered on loyalty to the Church and to the Spanish monarchy (Cruz 1989, 58–59). It excluded pagans and Moslems in the same way the sense of community among Moslems in Maguindanao originally excluded Christians and pagans. This new sense of mutual sympathy constituted an advance over the narrow, kin-centered one; revolts against Spain on a regional basis became feasible. In 1762, Diego Silang mobilized thousands of Ilocanos to protest against Spanish taxes, and to revolt. Significantly, one of his first moves was to participate in Vigan's Holy Week procession which, then as now, attracted the populace.[31] Just as significant is that his Tinguian allies had a hard time acting together because of rivalries (Routledge 1979, 21). Unlike Ilocanos, Tinguians lived in hamlets independent of each other with no districtwide public rituals and no hierarchy of command (Cole 1922). During the nineteenth century, the community of baptized Filipinos was reinterpreted in secular, nationalistic terms. This was an unintended consequence of increasing centralization and modernization by Spain. Together with tax and tariff codes operative in the Peninsula, the civil code entered the islands; it reduced differences between regions and brought creole, mestizo, and *indio* together, for they all had to pay similar obligations according to income (Robles 1969, 72, 242). A law in 1857 mandated primary schools in Spanish towns, a law in 1863 mandated the same for every Filipino town (ibid., 219–20). Regardless of region, the educated now conversed with each other via a common tongue, Spanish.

A consciousness of being not creole, not mestizo, not indio but of being Filipino, with interests different from those of the Peninsular, took hold. It intensified when the authorities, who saw how the creoles in Spanish America had led the revolutions, discriminated against the island-born by filling high positions in Church and state, particularly in Tagalog areas, with Peninsulars. Father Burgos had more Spanish than native blood (Villaroel 1971, 1–2). Despite this or precisely because of this, together with Fathers Gomez and Zamora, he was executed in 1872 on false charges of lighting up a mutiny. Eventually 1896 erupted. Emilio Jacinto (J. Santos 1935, 30), philosopher of the Katipunan, declared that all human beings were "magkakapantay sapagka't iisa ang pagkatawo ng lahat" [all human beings are equal because they share a common humanity]. Significantly, this alumnus of a Dominican school based this claim on the Gospel.

Interaction with the state thus resulted in parallel transformations in France and the Philippines. Nonstate peoples outgrew a moral universe centered on the kindred and accepted one which centered on the monarchy, eventually on the republic. It helped that the king's subjects felt oppressed by him and his officials.[32]

But believing in a moral universe broader than the kin is not easy. Once in power in 1986, some prominent activists, who had struggled against Marcos and his ambitious family, hesitated to press for laws outlawing political dynasties. Some even continued the old practice of enriching themselves and their kin. The reasons for this continued devotion to the kin to the exclusion of the public are many; exploring these will take us far afield. I simply wish to point out that this value persists among conscienticized, city-based Filipinos, and definitely on the barangay level.

We should revise our current notions that rural residents, because more indigenous and less exposed to Westernization/Hispanization, are more "communal." Earlier, I mentioned suspicions between hamlets in the Ilocos. A hamlet [barangay] is divided into neighborhoods called either *sitio* or *purok*. Often neighbors in a purok are relatives through blood and marriage, and are not necessarily related to those in other purok. Physical markers—fields, bamboo groves, streams—mark off a purok. A resident can spend most of the time in the purok/sitio without meeting others in other purok/sitio within the same hamlet. This isolation can create mental fences. In their study of child-rearing in the Ilocos, the Nydeggers

(1966, 154) noticed that parents encouraged their children to mix only with those of their own sitio and to shun those from another sitio within the same barrio. Sometimes when announcing that I was going to another purok down the trail, my landlord would mutter that there were "some bad people there."

In centuries past, settlements must have been even more isolated. For this reason, traditional yet disruptive customs persisted. According to the Ilocano scholar and nationalist Isabelo de los Reyes (1890, 235), in pagan times, the Ilocanos, too, like their upland siblings the Tinguians, practised *sibrong*, also called *panagtutuyo* upon the death of a beloved. As late as the 1880s, courts in the Christianized Ilocos tried cases involving sibrong (Scott 1982, 25). Fear gripped the residents of Bangui, Ilocos Norte, in 1907 when a local leader was placed in his coffin, for "his right hand had suddenly raised up with four fingers extended" (Cole 1922, 373). Custom dictated that any four individuals should thus be killed. Though memories of this hopefully extinct custom survive only in scare tales told to disobedient Ilocano children today,[33] they do help create a climate of distrust toward those from distant, unknown neighborhoods.

But the violent conflicts that erupt occasionally between hamlets in the Ilocos today no longer result, it seems, from the once-hallowed ritual. More often, they are stoked by ambitious politicians who seek a monopoly on votes. It seems that 400 years of exposure to Christianity has opened spaces, both physical and spiritual, which enable strangers to meet regularly face-to-face and interact as fellow humans. Christmas and fiestas connect the nonkin. At Christmas time, rural residents roast tubular rice cakes [*tupig*] that they share with passing strangers. They hold dances on the road and open these to those from other hamlets. During the annual fiesta, they go to the fair, the parade, and join the procession that are all celebrated at a site assumed to be the nexus among the barangays: the municipal plaza before the church. On the level of the barangay, Christianity offers a public space. One barangay I stayed in had no barangay fiesta. Residents belonged to different churches. However, my landlord who headed the bitterly anti-Catholic Rizalist Church, told me that he had decided to organize a fiesta to honor the barangay saint so that solidarity [*panagkaykaysa*] might prevail!

Having said all these, we should be wary of looking down on indigenous notions of community. These have a contribution to make. Moreover, we should transcend the contrast between the indigenous and the Western.

Beyond the Contrast between Indigenous and Western

Six points can be drawn, on the basis of the interpretation above, concerning the supposed contrast between indigenous and Western.

First, the transition from a largely kin-based sense of community to a more broadly based one is difficult, with diverse routes. Northern France embarked on the long road to statehood a millennium-and-a-half ago. In the 1780s, one response by French leaders to the diversity within their state was to invent nationalism whose rituals make the multitude imagine that "we are one." And yet, despite the inculcation of nationalist ideals via one of the most centralized school systems in the world, Frenchmen divided along class and factional lines in 1940–1945, in the teeth of Nazi rule, to fight each other in a disguised civil war. Moreover, in the late twentieth century, separatist resentments against imperial Paris surfaced in Brittany (Reece 1979) and Occitanie (Jeanjean 1990). Indeed the traditional French response of intensifying centralization may have aggravated separatism. Perhaps had there been more decentralization, as in Anglo countries, this local restlessness could be addressed. While centralization is needed in any state, it is good to remember that too much of it may be counterproductive. However, the challenge remains: how to strike a balance between local diversity and national unity.

Second, because of pressure from without and from within, the Philippines seeks to attain in a century what took other societies centuries to do so. We complain of the narrowness and selfishness that characterize our politics at all levels. Realize, however, that we have been forced to assimilate a broad notion of community within a relatively short process of state formation.[34] Unfortunately, debates about the Philippines' having a "damaged culture" ignore this basic fact. We should appreciate our milestones. Ilocano migrants in Hawaii form clubs on the basis of municipality, for instance, Annak ti Sarrat [Children of Sarrat] or Annak ti Batac [Children of Batac]. They are criticized for their inability to form strong organizations on the basis of their being Ilocano or Filipino. However, based on what was shown above, the fact that they do think in municipal rather than barangay terms is a step forward. Moreover, while we have every right to complain about leaders who treat political office as patrimonial booty, we should note that thousands of Filipinos now dedicate their lives to causes such as building homes for the poor or helping battered women. This breathtaking proliferation of nongovernment organizations since the 1980s indicates the spread of a broader sense of solidarity.

Third, the contrast between so-called indigenous communitarianism and Western individualism is meaningless. The Germanic peoples who destroyed the Western half of the Roman empire were divided into kindreds, each fighting for its limited interests. Just as divided were our ancestors in late-sixteenth-century Luzon and Visayas. In both Germanic Europe and Luzon-Visayas, the emergence of a broader "We" can be traced directly and indirectly to the state's advent. An institution that has fostered this broader We is the Catholic Church which was the Spanish monarchy's official religion. Both the procession and the Mass continue to be rituals where Filipinos extend a hand to people beyond their circle of familiars. At fiesta time in Tagalog and Kapampangan towns, families with vows to particular saints open their doors and feed any passing stranger who wishes to pray before their household's revered saint. During the four-day revolution against the Marcos dictatorship in 1986, the thousands of civilians who surrounded the mutineers to protect them prayed the rosary, heard Mass, linked arms to face the tanks, and shared food with Perfect Strangers. The unstated format that affirmed this "pakikipagkapwa-tao" was the traditional fiesta. Lest I be misunderstood: When I speak of the contribution of the Catholic Church, I do not claim this to be the ideal situation. I personally prefer more inclusive, secular nationalist rituals. However, for the present we must recognize that religious ritual with its evocation of the Beyond seems more effective in bringing multitudes together. Processions during Holy Week constitute the one municipal activity participated in by all social classes and all barangays. And here an even wider form of solidarity is acted out. Travelling from municipality to municipality on Good Friday and seeing similar processions at the same time, the idea of a "Philippines" becomes real.

Fourth, from a dialectical perspective, the external can become internal through assimilation and transformation. Let us be wary of reducing the "Filipino" to the indigenous and, in turn, of reducing the indigenous to what existed before 1565. The town plaza, the church, the procession, and the fiesta have been around for over four hundred years and have played pivotal roles in the unfolding of the Filipino. Surely, they can now be regarded as both "native" and "indigenous."[35] Gudeman (in Tacitus [1928] 1950, 211) notes that when the Germanic tribesmen swept through the Roman Empire, they destroyed the empire's nerve centers, the cities, for they regarded these as *munimenta servitii*, that is, hallmarks of bondage. They gloried in their freedom to roam rather than suffer confinement in an enclosed town [*oppidum*] under a lord's authority. And yet, over the course of centuries, their descendants, such as the French, so embraced urban life that we now equate the French with urbanity.

Fifth, a dialogue with pre-Western, indigenous notions of community, nonetheless, is indispensable. Despite Westernization, the indigenous past remains alive today in the city, indeed in us. It is not easy to erase established habits and mentalities. Moreover, the very syntax and vocabulary of our native languages were determined by our ancestors. Since speaking a language compels one to view the world according to its categories, we must try to understand notions of community as carried by our native languages. In this essay, I have focused on observable behavior. However, if we want to dialogue with the ordinary plow farmer and the average urbanite, we should appreciate their expressed, linguistic notions of community. Even as I have dwelt on the limitations of indigenous notions of community, I would argue for their retention—though through an *Aufhebung*, as Marx would put it.[36] Notions and words are often open-ended. Given a new context, they can generate a new constellation of meanings. *Damayan* in Tagalog refers to working together on an unpaid basis in harvesting crops or in hauling in the net. *Damay* means sharing in a friend's woes, for instance, during a time of grief. After Sen. Benigno Aquino was assassinated in 1983, while tightly guarded by Marcos's soldiers, multitudes thronged the streets that led from the church in Quezon City to the burial site in Parañaque. A funeral procession that should have taken only an hour and a half to complete took almost eleven hours. So massive was the outpouring of grief over the assassination and of anger against the dictatorship. The mourners waited for hours under the sun—and offered shade, water, and food to those who had none. For sure, one significant influence was the Good Friday procession which centers on the Bier of the Fallen Lord. But so were those words: "damay/ damayan." Perhaps if the discourse on nationalism were carried out in the vernacular, using damayan and Jacinto's *pag-ibig*, we might see drastic change.

Sixth, notions of community below the state and above it also matter. Though I have stressed the central role of the state in the emergence of a broader sense of community, I realize all too well the state's capacity for tyranny. For this reason, I suggest emphasizing the equal importance of other notions of community below the state and above it; in short, beyond it. Though the kin group's hold on the individual can tyrannize, a kin-based sense of community offers comforts that a broader sense of community does not. It is face-to-face and highly personal. In developed countries with extensive welfare benefits, the aged and the sick do indeed benefit from a medical care system that caters to all. But the sense of community can seem impersonal. Despite welfare benefits, the aged and the sick do not necessarily find someone to listen to their story. How different it is when, in addition to these welfare benefits, one is cared for by one's intimates. Perhaps one reason why Filipinos, despite their poverty, seem more optimistic than their prosperous neighbors is that they know, regardless of their failures, that they will always be accepted by one group: their kin. Other notions of community below the state involve the neighborhood, the club, the cooperative, the non-governmental organization. All of these do matter. So, too, do organizations above the nation-state.

While the state has created fora where nonkin can be recognized, states have propagated ideologies and structures that discriminate against the dissident, the heretic, the foreigner. Hence the wars over religion, territory, and national pride. The twenty-first century offers new oppportunities, such as international fora and organizations, for expressing mutual sympathies, beyond national boundaries. On the other hand a global perspective can blind us into forgetting that interests may differ on the local village level. In the end we must try to understand the limitations of each type of mutual sympathy so that together they can counterbalance each other. Human institutions have an ambivalent character: An institution that liberates in one context may oppress in another.

Notes

1. By tradition, the oil is extracted and cooked on Good Friday and kept as a protective ointment.

2. Renato Constantino exerted a profound influence on Filipino nationalism beginning in the 1970s. He claims that "Spanish colonialism accelerated this disintegration of communalism and the breakdown of the collective spirit" (Constantino 1975, 37). This is qualified by his earlier observation that the pre-Hispanic barangay's means of production was "decentralized" and "familial."

Unfortunately, many have taken on this claim without noting the context. Thus, at various conferences and workshops I have participated in, speakers blame the supposed lack of community spirit among present-day Filipinos on Western/Spanish influences. Some colleagues, not anthropologists and thus not familiar with relevant ethnographies of the twentieth century, advocated studying groups in Sulu and the Cordillera "to understand the strong community spirit of Filipinos before Western individualism came in."

3. Even in the city, this tendency to see the outside world as threatening exists to some degree. John Carroll, SJ, sociologist, told me that when he asked some of his male Ateneo students why they went out in *barkada* [small groups of loyal friends], rather than singly, their answer was, "We feel safer." The resurgence of criminality, especially kidnappings, in Manila today magnifies these fears.

4. *Bayanihan* is a Tagalog term. Ilocanos use different terms such as *tagnawa, ammuyo, betaris*, according to the task at hand.

5. Given the frequent positive references to Marx in these essays, it may seem strange that I point to the state's positive contribution. Did not Marx claim that with the seizure of power by the working class, the state, the fruit of coercion, would "wither away"? In fact, according to Avineri (1968, 203, 208), it was Engels who used the biologistic term *Absterben* [withering]. Marx used his usual dialectical term *Aufhebung* [supersession]. After the working class takes over, either through revolution or universal suffrage and pushes an agenda to benefit the majority, then will the state be transformed.

6. The classic description of the Germanic peoples of the first century A.D. is Tacitus's *De Germania*. Extensive notes have been made on this by Gudeman (in Tacitus 1950) and especially Much (1959). Since Germanic societies had changed by the time the great migrations took place, I consulted the following for the fifth century: Pfister (1913a), Vinogradoff (1913), DeVries (1956), Wallace-Hadrill (1959), Owen (1960), Thompson (1971), and Lopez (1985).

7. Did the Germanic peoples before the migrations have states? Tacitus uses *civitas*. Some, like Pfister (1913a) and Lopez (1985), translate this as "state" (in Spanish, *Estado*). Much (1959), however, translates it as *Landgemeinde*, that is, "District, or Area, Gathering." Thompson (1971, 244) uses civitas and *Stamm* interchangeably. (Note that the Latin word civitas can mean "citizenship," "society," or even "people." *Stamm*, or *Stamme*, means "tribe" or "kin group.") Thompson (1971, 245) notes that when first described by Julius Caesar in the first century B.C., the civitas was divided into *pagi*, which he translated as clans. While disputes could be resolved within a clan by the leading men, no central authority beyond the clans could issue orders. In Tacitus's time, the general assembly of warriors elected a number of the leading men to act as judges and travel through

the settlements. The judge was most likely a stranger to the disputants. However, serious disputes were settled by the kin groups themselves. This could give rise to blood feuds. Though the rudiments of the state had made an appearance by the first century A.D., Thompson nonetheless says that the monarchy did not take root among the Germanic peoples until they had entered the Roman Empire as settlers.

8. Wallace-Hadrill (1959, 70–71) comments that a man's successful exercise of war leadership should not automatically merit for him the title of "king" rather than "chieftain." Kingship supposes a sacral element wanting among the Frankish chieftians who were easily deposed when unsuccessful. This is corroborated by the observation of Pfister that the numerous tribes had no common bond. While two or more might prosecute a war in common, as soon as the war had ended they fell apart once more. Moreover, "the name Franks was given to a group of tribes, not to a single tribe" (Pfister 1913a, 295).

9. Vinogradoff (1913, 634) cites the following passage from an ancient Norwegian document lamenting that "It is known to all to what extent a perverse custom has prevailed in this country, namely, that in the case of a homicide the relatives of the slain try to pick out from the kindred him who is best (for revenge), though he may have been neither wishing, willing nor present, when they do not want to revenge the homicide on the slayer even if they have the means."

10. Much (1959, 103) qualifies this by saying that among tribes (*Stamm*) with a political unity, one can speak of lord masters (*principes*) with pedigree.

11. Anthropologists have written detailed ethnographies on the Kalinga (Dozier 1966), Bontoc (Jenks 1905), Ifugao (Barton 1938), Tinguian (Cole 1922), Ilongot (R. Rosaldo 1980) of Luzon; and on the Manuvu (Manuel 1973), Tiruray (Schlegel 1970), T'boli (Casal 1978) of Mindanao.

12. On the other hand, active nonviolence was practiced by the Kalinga women in the 1970s to drive away the soldiers sent in by the Marcos dictatorship to clear the way for a dam in the Chico Valley that would have submerged the Kalinga's ancestral lands. Their shrewd use of people power was unique and years ahead of the people power that toppled Marcos in 1986.

13. Before the 1900s, "districts" among the Ifugao were often at war with each other (Barton 1969, 70). Compare with what Alcina ([1668a] n.d., 4:149–50) reported in the seventeenth century: By the same river there would be two or three settlements not too distant from each other. Despite this, quite often they were enemies to each other. The women could not go to the river to bathe or to wash unless escorted by relatives.

14. Ilongot informants relate that death used to be inflicted even on children: either they were related to the slayer or they came from the same area of

residence. Once, a warring party chanced upon children who had come to the river to wash. Though the party hunted the adults, they assuaged their anger by killing the children for being relatives (Rosaldo 1980, 235).

15. A copperplate inscription that was found in Pila, Laguna, dates back to 900 A.D. (Postma 1992). To be sure, its authenticity is not accepted by all. An archaeologist formerly with the National Museum, who has handled it, is skeptical. Assuming it is authentic, chiefdoms existed along the rivers in what are now Tagalog provinces by 900 A.D. Written in Old Malay, the inscription recognizes the commutation of a debt by the commander [*senapati*] of Tundun (identified as Tondo) who represented the leader of Pailah. At least two levels of authority are implied by the negotiation, thus allowing us to speak of a chiefdom. Perhaps future research might even result in calling it a state, given the complexity of the negotiation and the scope of the territory. But what happened since? Early Spanish chronicles agree with each other in noting the absence of central rulers among the sixteenth-century Tagalogs, a factor that prevented large-scale armed opposition to the Spaniards. Perhaps earlier attempts at forming a more embracing polity in Luzon collapsed. Notice Soliman's difficulties in imposing his rule over the datus south of the Pasig in the sixteenth century. There are also lessons from the example of early France.

16. Loarca ([1582] 1903, 174–75) notes that "no one wanted to recognize the other as being a higher lord" [*ninguno queria reconcer a otro por mas principal*].

17. Various chronicles of the period report this: Boxer Codex of 1590 (1960, 354, 364, 376, 404, 416, 431; Loarca in 1582 [1903] 130–31, 134–37; and Chirino in 1604 [1969] 88, 327).

18. Scott (1982, 281) arrives at the figure of 10,000 for Soliman's Maynila "by reckoning five women and children to each man" but then arbitrarily lowers this to 6,000 "to exclude the environs." He bases his estimate on the eyewitness report of the 1572 anonymous author. Scott's translation reads thus, "leaving two thousand which there could have been in the said town and the other towns around, besides the children and the women, who would have been many." Reed (1978) goes by the figure of 2,000.

19. Veneración (1986, 52) suggests as much when he says that Soliman expanded his influence southward while Lakandula expanded his westward.

20. What is a "city"? What is an "urban center"? By itself, sheer size is an inadequate indicator. Structural criteria are crucial: Have the majority of the residents ceased to be agriculturists? Are they now engaged in nonagricultural occupations, such as the various fine and useful arts, commerce, and administration? Reed (1967, 25–26; 1978, 3) rightly uses structural criteria as the indicator.

He notes that the inland, sacred cities elsewhere in Southeast Asia had international linkages and permanent quarters for foreign traders, they extracted corvee labor from peasants in dependent villages, they levied taxes on agricultural lands, they were the politico-religious nerve center for administration, and they had an elaborate bureaucracy. He does not find these criteria present in either Manila or Cebu before 1565.

21. Matters may have differed had there been an inducement to settle in denser settlements along the coast because of trade. However, during the first millennium of the Christian era, there were two main trade networks in the region: (1) the trade between India and China which hugged the continental coastline and (2) the trade in spices which connected the Moluccas to Bali, Java, Sumatra, and the continent. In what came to be called the Philippines, it was Sulu that was increasingly incorporated into this trade network, resulting in a maritime state by 1450.

22. Loarca ([1583] 1903, 118–19) reports of the Visayans, who were shifting cultivators, that they considered it "an affront to have many children" (*afrentarse de tener muchos hijos*). They preferred to have just one child who could inherit their wealth. It is, after all, costly to have many children within a regime of shifting cultivation.

23. This, too, the Spaniards experienced when different groups fled to the mountains to avoid paying tribute. An example are the peoples of the Cordillera (Scott 1974, Keesing 1962).

24. Unfortunately, while the state may have diminished the notion that a culprit's kin is responsible for him, the notion that an entire ethnic group is responsible for the misdeeds of a few persists. Nationalist ideology tends to blame entire nations. Some Spanish Augustinians in the Ilocos reacted hysterically to 1896: Suspicious of all native priests, they tortured nine native clerics to extract dubious confessions (Scott 1982, 179 ff.).

25. To contextualize: Corvee labor was in force in France until 1789 (McCrea 1971). The misery of the peasantry in northwest France is graphically described by the traveller Arthur Young in 1787–1789.

26. A letter from Fray Francisco de Ortega to the viceroy ([1573] 1903, 259) and a memorandum by the Augustinians ([1573] 1903, 273–74) report that Spanish soldiers stole fowls, swine, and rice, and burned houses. In their hunger for tribute, they killed ordinary people. Corpuz (1989, 515 ff.) calculates the depopulation caused by Spanish depredations during the late sixteenth to the early seventeenth centuries.

27. Azurin (1994, 79) lists the following revolts in the Ilocos: in Dingras, 1589; of Pedro Almazan, 1660; of Diego Silang, 1762–1763; against taxation on basi [sugar wine], 1807; and in honor of Lungao, 1811.

28. Which is surprising, given the fashion for "materialist interpretations of history." Marx stresses the need to look at the economic infrastructure: not only the allocation of the social product, but likewise the technology employed. Both Constantino (1975) and Amado Guerrero (1980) use a Marxist-influenced framework but do not mention the radical transformations in the technology of seventeenth-century island agriculture.

29. Contrast this with the situation on an island in Sulu reported by Horvatich (1992). The residents were divided into factions that did not come together in common prayer at the mosque. Indeed, in addition to the original mosque, two others were built so that the three factions in conflict could avoid each other. Among Catholics, the material church belongs to the Church as an organization, and so has a public character. Private are chapels and churches belonging to institutions within the Church.

30. Loarca ([1582] 130–31) notes that the poor believed that since none of their surviving relatives could afford to offer sacrifice for them, upon their death, they would remain in the underworld and either be eaten by the god of that region or be imprisoned. Being good or bad was thus of little importance. Most fearful was to die poor.

31. Yet, when Diego Silang revolted against the Spanish authorities in 1762, he said he would retain the bureaucracy, continue levying taxes, and maintain Catholicism. For indeed, how else could he administer thousands of Ilocanos?

32. Predemocratic states (and some would say even the democratic ones) are potentially oppressive. What probably distinguishes colonial oppression is the ethnic factor. One ethnie imposes itself on another within a state, and excludes others from particular rights and privileges. Thus until the 1880s, all able-bodied native Filipinos had to render service on public works. Exempted were those who paid in monetary form, native officials and their families. Automatically exempt were the Spaniards. The latter's automatic exemption qualifies the system as colonial. In the 1880s—when a more monetized economy allowed a personal tax to be instituted for all regardless of ethnic background—a personal tax for all was introduced (Robles 1969, 72, 242). However, ethnic discrimination in hiring for high positions persisted. Thus decolonization (universal personal tax) proceeded in one sphere while colonization (discrimination in hiring) intensified in another.

33. The Nydeggers in 1966 reported scare tales told children about the *agtutuyo*: riders who catch children to sacrifice for a bridge in construction. A version of *sibrong* I heard in 1995 was, "Oh, the priests buried children in the church's foundations to make them strong." Nothing could be more ironic, given the priests' determined efforts to stamp out pagan ritual.

34. Corruption on a huge scale continues to blight older nation-states, like France. Consider the scandal surrounding Pres. Jacques Chirac and his wife. This nearly wrecked his chances for reelection. Perhaps the difference lies in the degree of commitment by politicians to social development. Despite the corruption, roads are well paved, cities are clean and orderly, and the children get their free textbooks. Here, it is a continual struggle to ensure the basics. Moreover, political dynasties on the national level are no longer common in France. Here, they have actually spread.

35. A parallelism can be drawn with how Spanish loan words have helped create a common universe of discourse. Though all Philippine languages, being relatives, share words in common, they still differ from each other in vocabulary. The widespread use of Spanish-derived words—*Kumusta* [How are you?], *pamilia* [family], *tiyo/tiya* [uncle/aunt], *nobyo/nobya* [boyfriend/girlfriend]—has multiplied bridges. Ordinary Filipinos assume these bridges to be an essential part of their world.

36. Today, indigenous institutions in some of the non-Hispanized uplands are being reinterpreted into institutions that foster local attachment while pointing toward a broader community. Villages in Bontoc continue to be made up of *ator* (Prill-Brett 1987, 20–21). This has been translated as "wards" or "precincts." The average number of people in a village used to be under a thousand. Each ator had a unique landmark: a stone enclosure with a stone platform for ceremonies. Around were large stones for sitting or leaning on, a fireplace, and a low rectangular stone-walled, formerly grass-walled, hall at the rear. The platform and the hall served as an informal clubhouse for the ator's men. Here, too, the elders sat in council to deliberate on matters affecting the ator. War ceremonies took place at this enclosure (Jenks 1905, 51). Despite the end of intervillage wars during the twentieth century, the ator continues to play a crucial role in making a man loyal to both kin and locality.

When was Paradise Lost?

> The Lord God, therefore, banished him from the garden of Eden, to till the ground.
>
> Genesis 4:23

WAS LAND OWNED PRIVATELY or communally among Filipinos before the advent of Westernization? Several authors claim that the "community" then owned rice plots and forests as a unit; individuals owned no lands in fee simple. "Each member of the village obtained the right of usufruct, but could not alienate his holdings" (Reed 1967, 22). Allegedly pre-Hispanic Philippine society had no private property in land; this came in only with colonialism (Constantino 1975, 36–37; Ofreneo 1980, 3).[1] Developmental workers, activists seeking structural change, and human rights lawyers often claim that uplanders, such as the peoples of the Cordillera, formerly did not know land as private property. To resolve social ills, they propose returning to the "communalism of our ancestors."

The question of land tenure prior to colonialism has not been raised only in the Philippines. It, too, was raised in other decolonizing nations during the second half of the twentieth century both in Asia and Africa. It gained urgency because it coincided with a worldwide surge of interest in socialism as an alternative to the abuses and failures of greedy capitalism. In this essay, I deal only with Philippine data. But the manner in which I interpret these and my reevaluation

81

of Marxist texts may prove useful to those in other nation-states faced with similar questions.

In the Philippines, twentieth-century ethnographies and six-teenth- to seventeenth-century Spanish chronicles do show that in specific contexts, people owned land privately and landlordism did exist. In conversations with activists they are surprised to find out that particular families privately own the Ifugao rice terraces. In ad-dition, when discussing the production system of Philippine societies, we should realize that some of these regarded manpower as a factor of production that was scarcer and, therefore, more valuable than land. To be complete, a picture of property relations must include perceptions of the value of manpower. In my last three long conver-sations with the authority on Philippine prehistory, William Henry Scott, shortly before his fatal operation in 1993, we often dwelt on the notion of property among non-Hispanized Filipinos.[2] For the most part we agreed with each other on the points raised here. This essay extends those conversations.

This essay reexamines primary data on property relations con-cerning land among sixteenth-century Filipinos. The data's quality is uneven. While the Visayan data by the Jesuit Ignacio Alcina ([1668a] n.d.) are detailed, the Tagalog data of the Franciscan Juan de Plasencia ([1589a] 1910) are less so. To situate both, I will exam-ine other standard primary texts; I shall also look at some twentieth-century descriptions of land tenure among upland peoples who were either not exposed or were lightly exposed to Hispanization. However, I will not claim that land tenure relations among the Ifugao of the 1900s merely replicated those of the Tagalogs of the 1590s. Though there are parallels, there are important differences.

The cultural ecological approach is helpful. It compels us to look closely at the relations among the environment, the form of technology in use, the characteristics of the population, and the social organization in place (Steward 1955; Harris 1979, 64–75). This comprehensive context helps explain why Visayan swiddeners regarded land as a free good, while Tagalog wet rice farmers bought and sold land. However, I do not regard the environmental and technological factors as absolutely determinant. Organizational factors, particularly the political, do influence this infrastructure. A dialectical relationship links polity and economy together.

Dry versus Wet Farms

Some key concepts need to be explained briefly: swidden cultivation, the state, and property.

Swidden, slash-and-burn, or shifting cultivation, is a system that aims to create temporary gardens with the help of fire, cutting tools, and sticks. After cutting, burning, and clearing a patch within a forest, the swiddener plants by punching holes on the ground with a dibble stick and dropping seeds into them. He relies on rain as the chief source of water; but he does not create either a pond or a field dedicated to a single crop. Instead he opens a dry garden that has been fertilized by the ashes of the forest, and plants and harvests various crops there throughout the year. Though productive, the swidden garden cannot be sustained for long; being unirrigated, the soil loses fertility. Ideally the garden should be allowed to lie fallow for a long period from ten to twenty years, so that the forest can take over and regenerate the soil, thus permitting the farmer to start the cycle anew on the original patch (Geertz 1963, Conklin 1957).[3]

The state is often confused with "government." As was pointed out in the previous essay, while all human societies have some form of government, not all have developed a state. A state is an organization with a formal government that claims to exercise authority over several communities. The government of a state, on behalf of the state, claims the right to levy taxes or tribute and implement laws, the right to monopolize and control the use of violence, the right to conscript manpower for war or public works. Note the emphasis on "several communities." In a stateless society, a recognized leader's authority generally does not extend beyond that of his kin group or of his village. Nor is there a bureaucracy with several levels of authority that governs on a day-to-day basis villages organized into districts, districts organized into a kingdom (Carneiro 1981, Flannery 1972).[4] The contrast between state and nonstate is important in interpreting property relations, for the presence of a state makes possible property relations that are inconceivable in a society with no state.

An example of the state is the sultanate of Sulu. But I shall not deal with any sultanate in this essay. I confine my analysis to the impact of the Spanish state on non-Moslem Filipinos.

"Property," contrary to common sense opinion, is not a thing. Rather, it is a relationship between persons in reference to a thing in virtue of which one party uses or possesses or disposes of that thing because the other party recognizes its right to do so.

There are degrees of involvement in a thing:

1. The right to use a thing without claiming sole dominion over it; this is also called usufruct;
2. The prior right to the use of a thing; while sole dominion is not claimed, this right asserts that in a conflict between two parties, party A has more weight than party B;
3. The right to the exclusive use of a thing;
4. The right to possess a thing to the exclusion of others;
5. The right to dispose of a thing whereby the possessor can either destroy a thing or pass on the right of possession to another party; this last is termed "alienation."

"Ownership" refers to the third, fourth, and fifth rights but not to the first two. Augusto Gatmaytan (1999, 11), by training both a lawyer and an anthropologist, points out that the legal system distinguishes between *res nullius*, that which belongs to no one, and *res communis*, that which belongs to a group. It is important, therefore, to specify the nature of the agent that owns. We can distinguish:

1. Individual appropriation, which is exercised by an individual person;

2. Joint appropriation employed by two or more individuals to appropriate a thing either together as a unit or separately;

3. Corporate appropriation carried out by members of a group to appropriate a thing as a single moral person.[5]

The last would constitute res communis. Though "communal ownership" is a type of corporate appropriation, the term "communal" is problematic, for its meaning is not always consistent. One connotation is that of a group of individuals whose primary links to one another are constituted not necessarily by kinship or business interests (although these could be present) but by coresidence in a locality, whether neighborhood, village, or city. Because communal seems to posit ties other than those based on kinship and business, it has become a favorite adjective of social reformers and activists who (rightly, I believe) want to promote a broad-based solidarity. At conferences, speakers extol upland, non-Hispanized peoples in the Philippines for having retained a "communalism" that contrasts with the "Western-derived individualism" of the Christianized majority.

But, the term "communal ownership" can also mean a more narrowly exercised ownership, one exercised by a kin group. Some Filipinos do speak of an estate as being communally owned, that is, owned by members of an extended family. Indeed they use the Spanish term, *comunidad*—which, like English, refers to different types of groups—for such an estate. Used in this second sense, a "return to communal ownership" cannot possibly solve the country's ills, for kin groups, such as the Marcoses, do hoard wealth communally, within their narrow circle. In some Ilocos Norte villages I have stayed in, there are woodlands that pertain to a large extended bilateral kin group. Members, largely wet rice farmers with small holdings, may cut wood for home use only at the appointed period each year and under the supervision of an elder. The term they use for this woodland is *komun*. This essay will point out that the data on non-Hispanized Filipinos of either the twentieth century or the sixteenth century indicate that the "community" owning resources is often the kin. Hence, we should be careful about using this as the anchor for an ideology that seeks social justice.

This discussion takes note of important differences between Philippine societies. Such differences are affected by various factors, namely,

1. The dominant production method;
2. The use of a piece of land;
3. The political organization of a society;
4. Population density; and
5. Pressure from other groups.

But so as not to extend this essay, I shall only glance at the last two factors.

At this point I should briefly mention the communalism of a particular type of peasant community that existed before the twentieth century in parts of Spanish-ruled Mexico and Dutch-ruled Central Java (Wolf 1967). These were true corporate organizations where land used for permanent farms, irrigated rice fields in Java, belonged to the village as a unit. Membership was on the basis not of kinship, but of residence. When a villager migrated, he lost the right to his plot; the organization took back his land and issued it to another in need. There were also pressures on members to redistribute surpluses and be content with the rewards of "shared poverty." It is probably this arrrangement which approximates the communalism extolled by local Marxists.

Because the expression "communal ownership" has been popular among those using a Marxist framework (Ofreneo 1980, 3), this essay has another objective. It will show that Marx himself does not apply the concept to tribal land tenure. A final objective of this essay is to suggest that the impact of Westernization upon property relations should be rethought. It is more complex than many imagine it to be.

Land Tenure in the Twentieth Century

We start with data concerning notions of property in twentieth-century upland Philippine societies that have been studied by anthropologists.

Until fairly recently, the Ilongot of Nueva Vizcaya, the Hanunoo of Mindoro, and the Tiruray of western Mindanao utilized swidden rather than wet rice cultivation as their basic system for transforming resources.

For them, more important than ownership of land is usufruct: a claim on the fruits of one's labor rather than on the cultivated land. For instance, speaking of Figel, a village among the Tiruray, Schlegel (1979, 21) notes:

> Thus Figel people do not conceive of themselves as formally—either individually or as a group—owning land. Individuals exercise private tenure over the land they are working, and the Figel neighborhood's "territory" consists in a general way of all land which Figel people over time use or have used for purposes of shifting cultivation. This territory, with its very imprecise boundaries, may be thought of as belonging to the neighborhood in common. People of other neighborhoods would not attempt to mark out a field within its general limits. Due, however, to the low population density of the region and to the distance between neighborhoods, such an issue seldom if ever arises. Hunting, and all other forms of appropriation of wild food resources, may occur anywhere in the forests, and neighborhood territories are not considered to be private hunting or gathering preserves of a given community.

The individual cultivator exercises "exclusive right of use" over the plot he tills, and regards himself as the owner of the productive plants cultivated on that land, for as long as they continue to be productive. Should he die, however, or leave the area, the plants "revert to the public domain" and are treated like any other wild resource of the forest (ibid.). The Tiruray swiddeners of Figel do not see land as a good that either an individual, a group of families, or a village can impose a claim upon, exclude others from, and can choose to alienate. This, too, was observed of the Ilongot (Rosaldo 1980, 277) and the Hanunoo (Conklin 1957, 147). Can we generalize that where swidden or slash-and-burn is dominant, res nullius prevails? Schlegel (1981) suggests as much when he says that plow agriculture induces private ownership. When a Tiruray farmer, who has hitherto used swidden cultivation, switches to plow agriculture, he takes away his plowed field from the public domain and has no intention of giving it back. In contrast, lands that he devotes to swidden he does not claim as his own. It seems that by requiring more investment and expenditure of energy, plow agriculture fosters an attachment to a fixed piece of land.

However, Garvan (1931, 159) claims that the Manobo swiddeners of Mindanao then regarded land for hunting, fishing, agricultural land, and other rights as pertaining to a "clan or family to the exclusion of others." They thus held land in common as a clan. Manuel (1973, 142–43) concludes similarly for the Manuvu'. Among both peoples, the res communis is kin-oriented. Gatmaytan (1999, 235–36) takes a further step. After reviewing the conflicting ethnographies on land tenure among swiddeners, he says that in the Manobo village he studied, local genealogies and oral histories reveal an "individual orientation" as early as the late nineteenth century. Landownership is linked to affiliation with a landholding family by birth or marriage. Holdings are divided eventually among the heirs. But the notion of landownership differs from that of the urbanite and the hacendero, for it is "largely nonexclusive." It does not prevent others from having access to or using the land for free.

Through permanent cultivation, with or without the plow, attachment to a piece of land takes root. Thus at the beginning of the twentieth century, areas of the Cordillera highlands with wet rice cultivation had private ownership of land. According to Jenks (1905, 160), the Bontoc regard as individually owned: "dwelling houses, granaries, camote lands about the dwellings and in the mountains, millet and maize lands in the mountains, irrigated rice lands, and mountain lands with forests." The anthropologist Roy Barton (1949, 84–85, 91–92; [1919] 1969, 32–36) points out that private ownership, depending on the land use, existed among the Kalinga, in the 1920s–1930s along with other forms of land tenure, and likewise among the Ifugao.[6] Edward Dozier (1966), who did fieldwork among the Kalinga in 1959–1960, corroborates this.

Barton lists property relations accordingly:

1. Rice paddies, among both Ifugao and southern Kalinga, are owned by a family rather than by the village as a whole, or by the entire ethnolinguistic group. The Ifugao prefer to vest ownership in the eldest son to avoid dividing the land into small parcels. Ideally a family's claim to ownership is perpetual in nature. However, emergencies do happen when family land has to be sold. Unless no other remedy exists, people take care not to dispose of inherited lands.

2. Forest lands among the Ifugao "are often the common property of a group of kinsmen and their families" (Barton [1919] 1969, 33). The same pattern was observed by Jenks (1905, 162) for the Bontoc. Among the Kalinga, according to Roy Barton (1949, 100), the owned forests are those "near the town which have been cared for for generations or which have been planted on former clearings."

3. Hill farms, that is, swidden plots, are opened by the Kalinga on slopes as a supplement to rice paddies. Their notions of property regarding this are vague. The land supposedly belongs to the first cultivator. However, should another Kalinga want to open his own farm on land previously used by someone else, all he has to do is ask permission (ibid., 97; Dozier 1966, 151).

4. The unowned are all lands not held in private ownership and waters not "held or subject to flowage rights." It is not clear whether forests fall into this category. "A powerful in-

dividual can certainly appropriate them, but a weaker one cannot" (Barton 1949, 84). The "public forests" that Jenks (1905, 162) writes about no doubt belong to this category.

Can one speak of the unowned as community ownership? Barton (1949, 85) answers negatively: "Probably there is a vague feeling on the part of the people that the lands appertain to them as a community, but it has not crystallized into a sense of community ownership." However, as lands become scarce in the future, Barton suggests that a sense of community ownership may well emerge. For now, the res communis is that which belongs to a family or group of related families.

A new sense of ownership has now appeared among the Hanunoo of Mindoro because of land scarcity. Yasushi Kikuchi (1989) observed that because of increasing migration to the uplands by plow-using lowland Christian farmers, the Alangan Hanunoo of the 1970s started to band into corporate groups. Today they have local groups, or *gado*, largely composed of kin. Each gado has a care-taker. Of course, the question we must raise revolves around the membership of these local groups: Do they admit residents who are not relatives of anyone in the group?

Not only has private ownership of land existed among non-Hispanized Filipinos; landlordism, too, has operated among those practicing sedentary agriculture. The Kalinga distinguish between an inside tenant, *tagabu,* who lives in his master's household and works a particular field for his sustenance, and the outside tenant, the *tubyao,* who lives in his own house and pays rent, consisting of one-half or one-third of the crop, the master furnishing the seed (Barton 1949, 106–7).

Land Tenure in the Sixteenth Century

We turn to Philippine societies as described by Europeans of the sixteenth and early seventeenth centuries. I purposely use the term "societies," rather than "society," to call attention to the fact that despite obvious similarities in culture, no single government nor overarching economy as yet integrated the islands together. The barangay was composed of thirty to a hundred houses, according to the Franciscan missionary Juan de Plasencia ([1589a] 1910, 471) and was ruled by a datu. In the Visayas, the term used for this polity was *haop*. A barangay, or haop, could cluster with a number of other such polities to form a settlement, but each retained its independence (Boxer Codex [1590] 1960, 359, 382; Loarca [1582] 1903, 174–75; Alcina [1668a] n.d., 4:54; Morga [1609] 1910, 191; Chirino [1604] 1969, 24). Though some datus, notably in Manila and Cebu, had emerged as paramount leaders who surpassed the other neighboring datus in authority (Reed 1978, 6), localities were nonetheless independent of one another.

Moreover, we cannot speak of a single uniform pattern of subsistence. While wet rice cultivation was practiced on lakeshores like Laguna de Bay or in swamplands, swidden cultivation was widespread in the Visayas, Mindanao, and most likely even in the countryside just outside Manila, where the inhabitants lived in scattered hamlets, or rancherias (Cushner 1976, 6; Larkin 1972, 24–25).

According to the seventeenth-century Jesuit, Francisco Alcina ([1668b] n.d., 3:88), Visayans preferred swidden even though they knew wet rice cultivation [*tubigan*]. They burned and lopped off trees and underbrush in a patch of the forest; then leveled the ground. Men punched holes on the ground with pointed stakes, women dropped seeds into them and covered them with soil. Most likely, they preferred shifting cultivation because population density was low and much forest land was available. Moreover, since the plow was unknown, preparing the ground for wet rice cultivation would have been more tedious, and its returns dubious.

Understandably, the early Visayans, being swidden cultivators, did not distinguish between "mine and yours," when referring to the land (ibid., 3:80). They had no disputes about land, for this was plentiful and fertile. What was lacking were enough cultivators.

Thus strangers were allowed to settle among them and choose as much land to farm as long as this was uncultivated. Would this constitute res nullius?

It seems not. Outsiders could not use the land without the datu's permission. According to Alcina ([1668a] n.d., 4:67–68), one of the many reasons for enslaving another took place when barangay members caught an outsider "hunting in their mountains or fishing in their waters or looking for something he needed in their land without the permission of the datu who was the master of all of these." Indeed they imposed such slavery not only on the intruder, who came from afar, but also on "neighbors themselves and who lived close to them" (ibid.). Furthermore, it is significant that members of a haop constituted a kindred. Alcina ([1668a] n.d., 4:27) uses the Spanish word *parentela*. Those who were not the datu's *oripun* were normally his relatives [*deudos*], according to the Boxer Codex ([1590] 1960, 357). Communal sharing of resources thus tended to be kin-based. In building a political ideology around "precolonial communalism," we should note this.

Moreover, we should realize that while land may have been an open resource among members of a barangay, human beings could be privately owned as slaves and could thus be bought and sold. Antonio de Morga ([1609] 1910, 193) asserts that the chief "wealth and treasure" throughout the archipelago were "slaves," for they were needed for work and for running holdings. They, rather than land, constituted the most highly valued factor of production.

There were various degrees of servitude and for various causes. For example, there was servitude connected with debts because interest rates were calculated at 100 percent compounded annually (Loarca [1582] 1903, 150–54; Boxer Codex [1590] 1960, 362). Such debts, when unpaid, passed on to sons and grandsons. A man and his family could also go into servitude as punishment for inability to pay a fine for a serious offense toward another person in the barangay, for instance, the datu. And as was pointed above, trespassing was punished with servitude.

There were thus different kinds of dependents, called oripun in the Visayas (Loarca [1582] 1903, 142–47; Boxer Codex [1590] 1960, 362–63). Scott (1992, 86–92) lists at least six kinds. An example would be that if the offender could not pay a debt, he had to render service according to the seriousness of the debt: from several days a week to working in their master's house only during a feast. Such an oripun thus retained the right to live separately in his own house with his family, while managing his own property. It was otherwise in the case of dependents at the bottom of the social ladder. Such dependents, especially if they were outsiders who had been captured in wars with another barangay, were liable to be killed, should the master die, in order to serve him in the next life (Boxer Codex [1590] 1960, 347–48, 364; Loarca [1582] 1903, 134–39). Their status resembled that of the porcelain and other moveable wealth that were buried. Or else, when the master was sick, a slave was captured from a distant village and killed in order to restore the master's health (Alcina [1668b] n.d., 3:235–36). Such dependents were true slaves; moreover their treatment signified that the master believed that, as owner, he could dispose of them as he pleased.

Though land was not an important source of wealth, it does not follow that all had easy access to resources. The aristocracy may not have competed with each other for land, but they did compete for owning slaves; they, therefore, raided not only distant communities in southern China and Ternate but each other's community as well (Scott 1991; 1992, 111–16). They always had need for slaves, for they sacrificed slaves captured in war when the master died. Moreover, such raids combined with other causes—such as perceived intrusions into the territory of a barangay, the abduction of women to serve as brides, or the desire for vengeance—to create frequent conflicts that inevitably resulted in the deaths of the high-born. This led to more wars.

While similarities in emphasizing the right to usufruct in a swidden regime link together the sixteenth-century Visayans and early-twentieth-century Tiruray, Hanunoo, and Ilongot, differences in political organization divide them from each other. Among these twentieth-century uplanders, egalitarianism was normative. If there was a leader, he was selected on the basis of seniority in a kin group, his negotiating skills, or his knowledge of customary norms. Moreover, his position was not a full-time occupation, nor did it rely on tributes and taxes from fellow villagers. He continued to lead a style of life that was the same as that of his fellows' (Schlegel 1979, 5–6; Conklin 1957, 11; Kikuchi 1989, 107–9; Rosaldo 1980, 8–9). Neither he nor his community sought to exclude outsiders from using the forest under threat of punishment.

On the other hand, the sixteenth-century Visayan datu was an aristocrat who had inherited his office. He emphasized the dignity of his person and office by compelling his followers to observe an elaborate etiquette in front of him. They squatted and covered their mouths with a fan while speaking to him (Alcina [1668b] n.d., 4:59–60). While land within the barangay's confines was open to all barangay members, he banned outsiders from using its resources without his permission. He asserted the right to exclude outsiders from the forest. In this, the Visayan leader resembles the swiddening Manobo of the nineteenth and early twentieth centuries. The Jesuit Saturnino Urios (1887, 153–54), in a letter to his Father Superior in 1883, says that the Manobos mark mountains, rivers, and large tracts of land as the property of each family or hamlet [rancheria]. Conflicts break out should outsiders intrude.

The sixteenth-century Visayan datu had added reason to be suspicious of intruders. His barangay was situated in the lowlands, at the mouth of a river or along it, and could control the exchange of goods between the uplands and coastal traders. Goods coming from the uplands, such as beeswax, gold ore, and cotton, were exchanged for the foreign silks and porcelain supplied by maritime traders. Because the datus could control the entry of prestigious goods to the uplands, they became wealthy and attracted followers (Junker 1993, 11, 14–15). On the basis of this power, they laid claim to waters and land.

Tagalogs of the sixteenth century who dwelt on the shores of Laguna de Bay practiced wet rice cultivation but without the plow. Annually the lake waters overflowed the surrounding shores (Chirino [1604] 1969, 23). According to Juan de Plasencia ([1589a] 1910, 471),

> the lands where they resided they divided [*repartieron*] among the entire barangay. Thus each person in each barangay knew his own lands, especially those with irrigation. No one from another barangay worked on them, other than after purchase or inheritance. In the *tingues* or uplands, they did not have them divided [*partidas*] except by barangay. Being therefore of that barangay, even though he might have come from another village, any person (once he had harvested rice), who has started to plant rice on a piece of land sows on it and no one can take it away from him.[7]

Two types of farmland are contrasted here. In the lowlands, paddies were divided individually. In the uplands, farmlands were most likely swiddens, and were divided by barangays. Blair and Robertson use the expression "owned in common" for lands in the uplands (Plasencia [1589b] 1903–1909, 175). But the Spanish word *partida* simply means "divided."[8]

Though land among the Tagalogs was bought and sold, nonetheless, as among the Visayans, gold, jewelry, and slaves—all forms of movable property—mattered more than real estate (Scott 1994, 229). Morga's observation that slaves were the chief wealth and treasure of the islands does not distinguish between Tagalogs and Visayans. Still the Tagalog system of servitude does differ from the Visayan and had fewer degrees of servitude, as shown by Scott (1992, 92–99; 1994, 224–28).

There were two types of *alipin:* the *aliping sa gigilid* and the *aliping namamahay.* The first type was termed *esclauos,* or slaves, by Plasencia ([1589a] 1910, 472). They served the master in his house and fields and could be bought and sold. If they were born and raised in their master's house, unlike those captured in war, they could never be sold. Presumably such slaves increased the worth of their master's assets; moreover, they would have endeared themselves to him and his kin. Captives in conflicts were more truly chattel slaves: They could be bought and sold (Rada 1577, 483–85; see Scott 1994, 227). The aliping namamahay, according to Plasencia ([1589a] 1910, 472), were *pecheros,* meaning tribute payers. Though they paid tribute, they lived in their own houses and had their own wealth and gold which they passed on to their children. They paid their master, whether datu or not, half of their field harvest [*con la mitad de su sementera*], as agreed on. They could not be bought or sold.

The alipin's masters were either freemen [*timawa*] or the datu. The former were neither rich nor poor. They enjoyed a right to land, and could harvest without paying tribute. Scott (1994, 223–24) locates a warrior aristocracy, the *maharlika,* among them. In times of war, the latter had the duty to fight with the datu and in times of peace, they, like the rest of the barangay, helped in building his house or in irrigating his fields. The datu was the lord who governed all by settling disputes, leading them in war, and protecting them against their enemies (Plasencia [1589a] 1910, [1589b] 1903; Morga [1609] 1910, 191). Proud of his noble lineage, he looked down on parvenus.

It is hard to speak of communal landownership and res communis among seventeenth-century Tagalogs in relation to paddy fields. As was pointed out above, aliping namamahay shared part of their harvest with their master. It may be that because wars were frequent, they did so for protection rather than to pay ground rent (Cushner 1976, 7). Nonetheless, the relationship easily evolves into the classic landlord-tenant relationship. In the case of the maharlika, they could become tenants of the datu. Plasencia ([1589a] 1910, 471–72) cites a case from Pila, Laguna, where the maharlika each gave their datu 100 *gantas* of rice. When they had first arrived at Pila, another datu occupied the land. Their datu thus purchased the land with gold and divided the land among them, his followers, who in exchange paid him rent [*terrazgo*]. This seems much like an hacendero of today who buys land and charges rent from followers who wish to cultivate it.

Sixteenth-century Tagalog property relations thus parallel those of early-twentieth-century Ifugao: Rice paddies were claimed privately, while lands in the hills, presumably forested and used for shifting cultivation, were claimed by a larger unit, in this case the barangay. Grasslands were most likely for common use. However, if we are to follow Scott's interpretation, there may have been a difference. Scott (1994, 229) claims that the rice paddies held by the aliping namamahay were held in usufruct, they could not be owned or alienated. I disagree; I prefer the interpretation of Reed (1971, 113), which holds that possession of wet rice fields was both fee simple and fee tail. Plasencia ([1589a] 1910, 472) clearly states that though the aliping namamahay shared part of their harvest with their master, they were "the lords of their own holdings and gold [*señores de su hazienda y oro*], and this their children inherit, and enjoy their holdings and lands [*gozan de su hazienda y tierras*]." It may be, however, that though their exercise of ownership entailed rights of possession and exclusion, this did not include the right of alienation. Or at least severe restrictions, imposed by custom and pressure from their kin, bore on their capacity to alienate their land, as was the case among the Ifugao of the 1900s.

Landlord-tenant relations thus existed among sixteenth-century Tagalogs. However, in the absence of a central, suprabarangay authority that united the various settlements and exacted compliance with its laws, it seems unlikely that this landlordism could have permitted absentee landlordism as well, certainly not on the scale Filipinos would know under Spanish rule. The Tagalog datu's authority embraced only those within his barangay. While various barangays could cluster together to form a town, there was as yet no central authority over the town or over clusters of towns. The Tagalog landowner could only have exacted either tribute or rent from people near his residence. It would have been difficult for him to exact rent from land owned in a distant barangay. Without the consent of that barangay's datu, he would have found it difficult to protect his claim. Sixteenth-century lakeside settlements were jeal-

Figure 4: Land Tenure vis-à-vis ProductionMethods, Land Use, and Political Control

Variables	Land Tenure among Swidden-Based Societies			Land Tenure among Wet Rice Based Societies			
	Visayans 1600s	Hanunoo 1950s	Tiruray 1970s	Tagalogs 1580s	Bontoc 1900s	Ifugao 1900s	Southern Kalinga 1900s–1930s
Degree of Political Control	Leadership often hereditary; demands protocol and honorifics	Leader: the eldest and most capable member of a kin group	Leader: the eldest and most capable member of a kin group	Leadership often hereditary, demands protocol and honorifics	Council of wise men regardless of class	No chiefs, no councils	Leader: a wealthy man regarded by others as brave, gives counsel on many things
Swidden Garden	Usufruct	Usufruct	Usufruct	Most likely usufruct	Usufruct	Usufruct	Usufruct
Wet Rice Field	Not applicable	Not applicable	Not applicable	Private ownership	Private ownership	Private ownership	Private ownership
Forest	Outsiders without permission excluded	Outsiders have access	Outsiders have access	(1) May be unowned, or (2) owned by either a kin group or an individual	(1) May be unowned, or (2) owned by a kin group, or (3) shared by residents of the same watershed	Owned by a group of kinspersons and their families	Owned if near the town and has been cared for by a kin group for generations

Sources: Alcina 1668, Barton 1919, 1949, Conklin 1957, 1980, Dozier 1966, Jenks 1905, Lebar 1975, Plasencia 1589, Schlegel 1979.

ous about their claim to land. Cainta fortified its territory with thick bamboo hedges and a moat (Riquel [1572] 1903, 158–62).

For that matter, large-scale absentee landlordism would have had difficulty thriving among early-twentieth-century Bontoc, Ifugao, and Kalinga. No recognized political leaders commanded the allegiance of a wide district (Jenks 1905, 167; Barton 1919, 68, 87; Barton 1949). Wealthy aristocrats did not have the political power that the sixteenth-century Tagalog datu had. Among the Kalinga, respected warrior-headhunters, who were also wealthy, held authority—but only within what the ethnography calls the "region" [*boboloy*], that is, the cluster of hamlets and their environs (Dozier 1966, 202ff.).

Figure 4 sums up the discussion above by showing how land tenure is related to production methods and degree of political control. Production methods (shifting cultivation versus wet rice) have a decisive effect on land tenure. Whether the political organization is hierarchic (seventeenth-century coastal Tagalogs) or decentralized (early-twentieth-century Ifugao), wet rice cultivation induces feelings of private ownership of riceland. In contrast shifting cultivation is associated with usufruct in all three cases analyzed. However, the presence of a hierarchic political organization among seventeenth-century coastal Visayans seems to have led to a demarcation of the barangay's boundaries and the exclusion of outsiders. This becomes more understandable—and more familiar—if we recall that the governing group in the Visayan barangay was the datu and his kin.

What then was the impact of Spain upon property relations among Tagalogs and Visayans?

Spain's Impact

Spanish influence may be sketched as follows:

First, private ownership of land became the dominant mode because of two innovations. Missionaries popularized wet rice cultivation in order to gather their parishioners "under the church bells" [*bajo las campanas*] to facilitate their instruction in the new religion.

From the point of view of lay officials, this transformation also aided the collection of taxes. To make wet rice cultivation easier, the missionaries introduced the plow [*arado*], and the use of the carabao as draft animal (Corpuz 1965, 42–44). "Often the religious was the first to plow, and sow, directing them [his parishioners] in this manner, so that they might learn" (Mozo 1763, 59). By itself this step would have compelled farmers to stake a permanent, private claim to a piece of land, as would happen among twentieth-century Tiruray. Cross-culturally, "individual ownership of land resources—including the right to use the resources and the right to sell or otherwise dispose of them—is common among intensive agriculturists" (Ember and Ember 1999, 252). All over the world the "original sin" that led to private property in land and the bitter quarrels since may have been the decision to abandon swidden for agriculture.

The other innovation was that a type of political organization formerly unknown in Luzon and the Visayas, the state, now claimed dominion over the many previously independent polities. By right of conquest, the Spanish king claimed to be the ultimate owner of all untitled land [*realengos*], thus laying the foundation for the Philippine state's claim to eminent domain; and thus, too, laying the groundwork for conflict with upland peoples who could not have known that their lands, being untitled, now belonged to a foreign monarch. At the same time, the monarchy recognized private, individual claim to land by its subjects, regardless of whether they were Spanish born or not, as long as they could prove this in court (Cushner 1976, 26).

Second, the advent of the king's domain should be reexamined. True, the notion of eminent domain can and has been used to usurp land that others have labored on. But it has also enabled the state to expropriate and open up to the public large private landholdings.

Third, Spanish laws of the late seventeenth century abolished slavery, that is, the legal right to purchase, rent, mortgage, alienate, and bequeath the body of a human being, especially if he or she was a Spanish subject (Scott 1992, 100). For those seeking wealth, ownership of land became the principal alternative. Other routes could have been through trade and manufacture. But for reasons that would take us far afield, landownership became the primary source of wealth. It should be interesting to compare attitudes toward land of Christian Filipinos where slavery was officially terminated by the close of the seventeenth century and of particular Asian neighbors where this was officially disestablished only in the nineteenth century.

Fourth, by the very fact that a state had now emerged to protect claims to land, absentee landlordism became possible. A person residing in Manila could claim lands in distant towns, if he could prove this in court, and could turn to the state for protection (Cushner 1976, 27–33, 57). Unfortunately, in practice this gave those with access to the government and with expertise in the ways of the state a distinct advantage over those who did not.

Fifth, the notion that communal land belongs to a political organization, such as the municipality, not on the basis of kinship but rather on the basis of the fact that it represents all its citizens regardless of lack of kin ties, came in with the Spaniards. The Laws of the Indies of the eighteenth century ordered that every town center in the empire, including the Philippines, should have, in addition to the plaza, an *ejido*. This was an open pastureland that belonged to the municipality and was for everybody's use (Consejo de la Hispanidad 1943, 2:20–22). Ordinance 53 of Governor-General Raon in 1768 thus provides that "in addition to the lands which the natives owned privately, each settlement or pueblo must have communal lands which are to be cultivated for the common welfare, and the products of which are to be kept in the communal fund" (Zaide 1990).

Ownership by and management of common assets by the municipality has been an important tradition in parts of Spain (Carr 1966, 7, 25, 57, 272–74). From the earnings, the municipality provided such free services as a veterinary surgeon, seeds for the crops, and a municipal credit fund (Brenan 1940; Crow 1985, 295). Spanish anarchist movements of the nineteenth and early twentieth centuries capitalized on this fact to popularize their ideas on municipal self-governance and the destruction of central government (ibid.). The Spanish Crown likewise recognized communal holdings in Mexico (Senior 1967), as was cited above. Spanish law enacted in 1567 ordained that each village had a right to a tract of common land "fixed at one square league" (Parker 1966, 91). Mexican revolutionaries of 1910–1917 revived the notion of the ejido and enshrined it in Article 27 of the 1917 Constitution to assure farmers of access to land (ibid., 361). The *ejidatario* was to own jointly with others the land on which he works, farm machinery, and equipment (Senior 1967, 48). Little has thus far been written about the communal lands attached to Philippine municipalities during the Spanish period. But they do seem to have existed even until fairly recently in parts of the country. Sidel (1999, 43) reports that in Carmona, Cavite, a Spanish Royal Decree of 1859 declared more than three hundred hectares of land as the communal possession of the residents of the municipality. Until today cultivation rights to an assortment of 180 plots have been awarded to local residents in a triennial lottery called the *sorteo*—which is a Spanish term. Unfortunately, the capital-strapped recipients offered the mayor a share of the harvest in exchange for credit and agricultural inputs.

These data raise new questions, of course: How has the practice of alloting communal lands fared vis-à-vis large landed estates that have been realities as well in Spain, Mexico, and the Philippines? What led to the demise of municipal communal lands in the Philippines?

My interpretation thus differs from the widely popular notion that ownership of land by the broad community of residents, including nonrelatives, prevailed prior to the conquest and that present inequality stems solely from the Spanish conquest. The truth is that inequality existed even before the conquest: This was based not on land, but rather on the control and ownership of manpower. Had the Spaniards not come, would absentee landlordism have developed in the islands? The experience of uncolonized societies, such as pre-nineteenth-century European monarchies and Japan, suggests that the answer is a highly probable yes (Blum 1978, 17–18; Keiji 1990). Where the traditional, predemocratic, precapitalist state, as an organization claiming jurisdiction over a wide compass of territory emerged, those who had rendered special service to the ruler could acquire and amass lands to benefit from a guaranteed rent and from impositions upon the peasantry.[9] In brief—from our developmental approach today which favors vesting ownership and management of resources in a group of nonrelatives—Spanish influence had mixed results.

I could close the essay at this point, but one reason for the popularity of the notion of "communal ownership of land" is ideological. It is seen as progressive because it seems "Marxist." So widely popular in the Philippines has Marxist thought become from the 1970s onwards that even those who would never consider themselves Marxist spontaneously use the term. We must, therefore, briefly examine what Marx did say.

Marx on Communal Ownership

Marx ([1846a] 1969, 22) speaks of communal ownership [*Gemeindeeigentum*] in early societies. But what did he mean by this? Furthermore, was he really so enthusiastic about it that he regretted its demise?

The first form of ownership, according to Marx, is "kin-centered ownership" [*Stammeigentum*].[10] Production is still undeveloped: People live by hunting and fishing, by breeding animals or, in the highest stage, by agriculture. Since the division of labor is undeveloped, the social structure merely extends the family. Above are patriarchal leaders of the kin group, below are kin members, at the bottom are the slaves who are owned. Not only does inequality occur, the communal ownership of the means of production does not even exist (Marx [1846a] 1969, 22, 29; [1846b] 1994, 142–43).

With untamed peoples [*Wilden*] every family has its own cave or hut, just as with nomads each family has a separate tent.

This separate domestic economy is made even more necessary by the increasing development of private ownership. With agricultural peoples a communal domestic economy is just as impossible as is a communal cultivation of the soil.

The second form of ownership is the "ancient communal and state ownership" that appears when several kin groups form a city either because they have come to an agreement or because one has been conquered by the other.[11] So widespread is communal ownership that even slaves are owned in common (Marx [1846a] 1969, 22). However, the individual economy, which cannot be separated from private property, cannot be abolished "for the simple reason that the material conditions were not present" (Marx [1846b] 1994, 143). A communal domestic economy presupposes the development of machinery and the common provision of services. Marx cites, as an example, the provision of services such as water, gas-lighting, and steam heating. Save water, all of these presuppose industrialization. Moreover, all of them, including water, are normally no longer obtained individually in a modern city. They require common ownership and management; in contrast to this, in a preindustrial city, each household procures its own water and firewood.

Through a dialectical process the ancient and communal form of ownership leads to another form, feudalism, which in Europe led to capitalism.

Philippine societies of the sixteenth-century lowlands and of the twentieth-century uplands would be seen by Marx as dominated by kin-centered or tribal ownership—Stammeigentum. On the other hand he probably would see the beginnings of "ancient communal and state ownership" in the municipalities founded after 1565 where particular resources, like the municipal house, the plaza, and the ejido, are regarded as belonging to the municipality as a corporate reality. Finally, it would be in contemporary cities of semi-industrialized Philippines that he would see the potential growth of common ownership and management, for here basic services, such as water and electricity, despite water pumps and generators, are generally not obtained individually by each household. The management of water in Metro Manila has shifted from government control to capitalist enterprise under the Lopezes, back to government control; while the management of electricity has been a capitalist enterprise, also under the Lopezes. For Marx, the de facto socialization of these basic services indicates that, for rationality, these should eventually be run by all the beneficiaries acting together as a corporate body.

Did Marx eulogize the tribal mode of production? Consistent with his dialectical approach, he looks at both its costs and the benefits. True, he extols the advantages of a society where little or no full-time occupational specialization occurs. It is possible to shift from one interest to the other, "to hunt in the morning, fish in the afternoon, breed cattle in the evening, criticize after dinner." In contrast, the emergence of the division of labor locks a man into a calling for the rest of his life, and intensifies the division of society into classes. Nonetheless, this has benefits. Marx ([1846b] 1994, 118, 117) says that under tribal ownership, the individual's consciousness of himself as an individual different from his group and from nature is limited. "It is the mere consciousness of being a member of a flock, and the only difference between sheep and man is that man possesses consciousness instead of instinct."

What then enables man to transcend this "sheeplike" or tribal consciousness [*Hammel-oder Stammbewusstsein*]? None other than increased productivity, increased needs, increased population, and the division of labor into mental versus manual labor. Thus the separation between mental and manual labor has no doubt divided society into nonproducers and producers and has oppressed the impoverished majority, for "the division of labor and private ownership are really identical expressions." Nonetheless, it has been the necessary basis for the emergence of "pure theory" such as philosophy, theology, ethics, all of which have increased man's understanding of himself and the world (ibid., 117, 32, 118).

Comments on Marx are needed. He takes a condescending attitude toward tribal societies. Moreover, his treatment of prefeudal modes of production has been criticized for being cursory (Harris 1968, 226). But in justice to him, we should note that the systematic study of simple societies was just beginning in Marx's lifetime. He was inspired by the anthropological observation that a society's technology and social organization are closely related (Harris 1968, 246). Only in the late nineteenth century would systematic and sympathetic studies of simple societies be undertaken on a large scale by anthropologists. Marx's observation about the ambivalent nature of the division of labor remains relevant. He says that while it intensifies class divisions and private ownership, it encourages higher productivity and more developed forms of consciousness. This is supported by contemporary anthropological research, for instance, by studies of the emergence of social classes in early societies (Adams 1966).

Thus Marx does not, in this basic text, either speak of or extol communal property in a simple society. He reviews the stages of the development of property to show that private ownership, whether of movable or immovable assets, has not been a universal phenomenon.[12] Rather than yearn for a golden past, he looks forward to the socialist future.

Rousseau, not Marx, is the true inspiration of those who idealize tribal society. Rousseau contrasts "man in his natural condition" with "civilized man." The former has few possessions, he does not own land. But he is happier than the latter who seeks to own more. Still, Rousseau ([1754] 1990, 352) does raise a conceptual fence. With the introduction of private property, agriculture emerges—

> work became indispensable and vast forests became smiling fields, which man had to water with the sweat of his brow, and where slavery and misery were soon seen to germinate and grow up with the crops.

The precolonial societies that nationalists eulogize do not qualify for Rousseau's happy garden if they had agriculture as their basis.

Drafts for a Blueprint

We cannot meaningfully speak of property relations in a society without discussing its context as well: technology, land use, and political organization.

Among swidden-dependent upland peoples of the twentieth century, such as the Tiruray, Hanunoo, and Ilongot, what has mattered most is the right to use land for cultivation purposes rather than ownership rights exercised either by an individual or a group. In contrast, among early-twentieth-century wet rice cultivating Ifugao and Kalinga, rice paddies were privately owned by particular families while the forest, depending on its location, could either be owned by a kin group or be regarded as unowned.

Similarly sixteenth-century swidden-cultivating Visayans regarded forests as an open resource. However, unlike the Tiruray, Hanunoo, and Ilongot of this century, they defined their forests' boundaries and punished strangers for intruding. For unlike those upland peoples, sixteenth-century Visayan societies were social pyramids ruled by a datu who carefully distinguished himself and his family from his followers, and asserted his authority. Sixteenth-century wet rice cultivating Tagalogs privately claimed, purchased, and alienated paddies. Owners extracted rent from the actual cultivators. This indicates landlordism. However, absentee landlordism, at least on a large scale, could not have been operative, for there was no state to defend claims by nonproducers to lands far from their accustomed residence.

Urbanized Filipinos of today look at the uplands and the sixteenth-century islands from the perspective of their own society where land is a source of wealth and prestige. This perspective can play tricks. It can hide the fact that while land may not have been as important in pre-Hispanic and non-Hispanized Filipino societies, owning and disposing of manpower was.

Spanish influence accelerated the tendency to regard rice paddies as privately owned, not only directly through its laws, but indirectly as well by promoting plow agriculture. A case may be made that by abolishing the right to own slaves, Spanish influence raised the value of land as an alternative source of wealth. In addition, by introducing a central authority with dominion over the entire archipelago, it made absentee landlordism possible. But we should not conclude that absentee landlordism, as an institution, results solely from colonialism. It has appeared in societies that have never been colonized. Absentee landlordism seems to be fostered rather by that political institution called the "state," especially in a precapitalist setting where the most prestigious resource is not owning slaves, but land.

What does this essay's reinterpretation mean for upland peoples struggling to maintain control over their ancestral domain or for landless lowland farmers?

When studying property relations among upland un-Hispanized Filipinos, scholars should examine the contextual factors mentioned above. They can then ask: Who is the agent that claims ownership over a particular resource? Is it a kin group? Or all the residents of a village regardless of whether or not they are related to one another by kinship? Or a cluster of villages? Or the entire ethnolinguistic group? These are obviously empirical questions. Having done empirical research, they could then inform the group of people affected in order to enable them to arrive at better-informed decisions.

To turn to the agrarian problem in the lowlands: advocates of structural change depict pre-Western Philippine societies as egalitarian and communal. In advocating agrarian reform, they also promote cooperatives, and blame "colonial individualism" for negative aspects in farmers' behavior. Salvation allegedly lies in returning to the Garden before the intrusion of the Western serpent. While I agree with the need for agrarian reform and cooperatives, I disagree with the idealization of the pre-Hispanic past. Though inspiring, this approach promotes a utopia that either never existed or is inapplicable today. The much praised open access to land occurred under swidden conditions. Obviously swidden cannot apply to situations with high population densities. Moreover, we should realize that the peasant's preference for thinking primarily of his family's interests cannot be attributed solely to colonialism; it may have something to do with the nature of traditional nonmechanized farm technology, as Marx sensed. In the absence, for instance, of irrigation networks that necessarily require a cooperative venture, there is little incentive for traditional peasants to work together.[13] As far as the peasant is concerned, his own piece of land gives him enough to worry about.

A return to a past Paradise cannot be the basis of an agrarian ideology. We could instead explore that very Marxist (and Hegelian) notion of "supersession" [*Aufhebung*]: New forms of social organization retain and transform what is positive from previous arrangements while rejecting what is negative. The new form "supersedes" existing elements and introduces new ones. Rather than regard arrangements from the pre-Hispanic and Spanish periods as blueprints, we should see them rather as drafts leading to a blueprint that our age has to make.

Notes

An earlier version of this essay appeared as "Land Tenure among nonhispanized Filipinos," in *Reflections on Philippine Culture and Society, Festschrift in Honor of William Henry Scott*. Edited by Jesus T. Peralta. Quezon City: Ateneo de Manila University Press, 2000.

1. A second version by Reed (1971, 113) distinguishes between property relations involving swidden and those involving wet rice fields. After rereading Plasencia ([1589b] 1903), he notes that since wet rice fields could be acquired after purchase or inheritance, possession was both fee simple and fee tail. He adds that a system of private wet rice fields had begun to develop in those parts of Luzon where wet rice cultivation was commonplace. Unfortunately this version was not published. And, in the third and formally published version (Reed 1978),

this important distinction is not discussed. Subsequent authors seem to have been influenced by his first reading (Reed 1967) of Plasencia.

Majul (1994) applies "communal" to the following: irrigated rice lands, forest lands, and grasslands adjoining the barangay. Corpuz (1989, 275) is more nuanced. While he states that the nearby woods, open spaces, and sloping uplands were communally owned, he holds that there were family- or individually owned lands.

On the basis of these interpretations, there developed a popular but mistaken notion that social inequality and many social problems began only with 1521. For instance, Salgado (1988, 11) argues that the pre-Hispanic Filipino enjoyed many rights that his present descendant does not.

2. In several conversations with colleagues and myself, Scott regretted the widespread tendency to depict all pre-Hispanic and non-Hispanized societies (particularly in the Cordillera) as egalitarian, without qualification. He said there was no ethnographic basis for the claim. He also regretted the common tendency to eliminate the discussion of slave raids and warfare among pre-Hispanic barangays. Note that Scott identified deeply with the people of the Cordillera, particularly of Sagada where he has an adopted family.

3. Valuable anthropological insights are not reaching historians. One of them is the relevance of defining the food-getting technology in order to understand other social relationships. The widespread use of swidden can help explain why urbanism appeared later in Luzon and the Visayas than in other countries of the region (Reed 1978). Swidden normally leads to dispersed low-density settlements. It can also explain why early Filipinos were seemingly "enemies of work"—from the Spanish viewpoint (Boxer Codex [1590] 1960, 361). Swidden gardens are actually highly productive. Their harvest per hectare is higher than that of plowed fields, while the number of working hours required to tend them is shorter. Thus, twentieth-century Tiruray swidden farmers have resisted becoming plow farmers (Schlegel 1979, 164ff.).

4. Barton speaks of Kalinga "regions" [*boboloy*] as "states." However, he qualifies this assignation by characterizing them as "incipient" states. The peace pact holder, who came to office through wealth, inheritance, eloquence, and victory in combat, could prevent men in his region from attacking others coming from a region with whose leader he held the pact (Barton 1949, 147, 195). Political anthropologists since the 1960s, such as those cited in this essay, would characterize Kalinga "regions" as nonstates though with an emerging control over violence.

5. "Corporate" today connotes business interests because of the expression "business corporation." I am using it in the original sense, meaning a "single body." Corporate is from the Latin word for body: *corpus*.

6. Conklin (1980, 7–8), who did fieldwork in Ifugao within recent decades, classifies property relations according to the cultigen and land use, thus:

a. Forests are public for residents of the same watershed region.

b. Woodlots (timber, fruit trees, climbing rattans, some bamboos) are privately owned and managed.

c. Swiddens have discrete temporary boundaries for a cultivation period of several years.

d. Drained fields are privately owned.

e. Pond fields are privately owned.

June Prill-Brett (1992, 7), an anthropologist who grew up as a native Cordilleran, points to a similar pattern for irrigated rice fields among the Ibaloy, and notes that cultivators tradionally owned not the forests, but the crops within them. Moreover the concept of "corporate property," that is, property held in common by a descent group, used to be absent.

In our last conversation, W. H. Scott said that when the Episcopalian Church officials sought land in Sagada, Bontoc, they were encouraged to settle out in the forest, in a no-man's-land between the Sagadans and their quasi enemies. They were to act as a buffer! The Sagadans did not claim the forest as theirs. It was simply there.

7. "Las tierras donde poblaron las repartieron en todo el Barangay, y assí, conocía cada uno de cada Barangay las suias, en particular la que es de regadio, y ninguno de otro Barangay labraua en ellas, sino se les compraua, o heredándolas. En los tingues o serranías no las tienen partidas, sino solo por Barangays, y assí, como sea de aquel Barangay, aunque aia benido de otro pueblo qualquiera, como aia cogido el arroz, quien comiença a arrozar una tierra, la siembra, y no se la pueden quitar" (Plasencia [1589a] 1910).

8. At times the Blair and Robertson translation is tendentious. "Eran estos principales de poca gente, asta de cien cassas . . . y esto llaman en tagalo un Barangay" is rendered thus: "These chiefs ruled over but few people; sometimes as many as a hundred houses. . . . This tribal gathering is called in Tagalog a barangay" (Plasencia [1589b] 1903, 173–74). Nowhere does the original speak of "tribal gathering." It is unlikely that a sixteenth-century author would use such a post-nineteenth-century expression.

9. This needs qualification. Absentee landlordism on a wide scale will appear in a precapitalist, predemocratic state if land is deemed a prime source of wealth. However, if owning manpower that can be bought and sold is regarded as more important, then absentee landlordism will not be as important. This seems to have been the case in the sultanate of Sulu where, until this century, the primary source of wealth was slaves, captured through raiding (Warren 1985).

10. *Stamme* is the cognate of the English word, stem. Its derived meanings are "clan" and "tribe." Lawrence Simon's translation of *Stammeigentum* as "tribal ownership" is perfectly valid, except that *tribal* in English does not necessarily connote a system centered almost exclusively on the kin.

11. The French word, *commune,* from which *communisme* and the English communism were derived, continues to refer to a township, thus to an urban center, however small. Marx was fluent in French, and disdained rural life as inferior to the urban. It is thus surprising that Marxists of a particular line should advocate agrarian communes as the key to socialism.

12. In his notebooks of 1857–1858, he analyzes in more detail the difference between the German tribes and the Roman state regarding property. Though communal, or people's, land, as distinct from individual property, also occurs among the German tribes in the form of hunting land, grazing land, and timberland, it does not appear among them as a determinate piece of land differentiated from private property. For "the economic totality (among the German tribes) is, at bottom, contained in each individual household" (Marx [1857–58] 1973, 483–84). German tribesmen form a community only when they assemble together. Otherwise each is independent of the other. In contrast among the Romans, "the city with its territory is the economic totality" (ibid., 484). For, in contrast to the German tribes, a state as a continuous political organization, exists and expresses its presence in the city through land it owns as the state (ibid., 483–84). Taking our cue from Marx, it is among Hispanized Filipinos that communal land as a determinate piece of land differentiated from private property emerged, first on the level of the municipality, second on the level of the state as a continuous political organization. Among non-Hispanized shifting cultivators and wet rice cultivators, communal land is present only in association with a lineage.

13. Industrialization in the countryside may encourage a more socialized form of production, as Marx clearly saw for the city. Mechanization requires more capital; it also demands highly technical, specialized skills. Both encourage farmers to be more interdependent. It could be that mechanization might finally make cooperatives more feasible among farmers. Meanwhile, we should note that the corporate organizations seen by Wolf (1967, 236–37) in Mexico came about because the Spanish state gave rights to land to Indian communities on the basis, not of kinship, but of residence in a locality. In Java, Dutch policy led to the concentration of villages. Other than these, plus examples from Japan and Russia, loosely organized, noncorporate peasant communities, such as those in the lowland Philippines, seem to be quite common in nonmechanized contexts all over the world.

Bourgeois yet Revolutionary in 1896–1898

Marx and I are partly to blame for the fact that the younger people sometimes lay more stress on the economic side than is due to it.

—Friedrich Engels 1890, *Letter to Bloch*

MIGUEL MALVAR COULD NEVER have been a revolutionary hero, were we to use a perspective that has dominated Philippine history writing since the 1960s. According to this perspective, since he came from the economic elite, he could not have committed himself to a revolution that was proletarian. Yet he sacrificed much to help the Revolution and then the war against the Americans. He rallied to the revolutionary cause in 1896, fought against the Spaniards and, later on, against the Americans until he was captured in 1902. At that moment his wife was running a high fever and had not eaten for several days. He came from a family with logging operations on Mount Makiling; he had personally become rich from his orange farm on the slopes of the same mountain (May 1993, 42–43). Also prominent in that Revolution were Arcadio Laurel of Talisay's political elite, Santiago Rillo de Leon, formerly the gobernadorcillo and the justice of the peace at Tuy, and Ananias Diokno of Taal (ibid., 50). The latter's substantial ancestral house in Taal indicates wealth. May (1993, 50) concludes that, as in Cavite, those individuals who normally dominated political life in their communities "were among the first to commit themselves to the cause." A distant uncle of my father was Agapito Zialcita of Bataan. His family's extensive landholdings enabled them to send him to London for his studies in industrial engineering. When the Revolution broke out, he rallied to Aguinaldo's cause and became a colonel. He likewise fought the Americans until he was captured by them (*Sunday Times Magazine* 1951, The *Evening News* 1955). Although he spoke English, he refused to utter a word of it as a protest. Only when the Commonwealth of the Philippines was proclaimed in 1935, as a preparation for independence, did he relent. In Tarlac, a major figure was Servillano Aquino, direct grandfather of Ninoy Aquino, the martyred senator. Educated briefly at the University of Santo Tomas, he came from a landed sugar family that had contributed members to the local mayoralty. In January 1897, he became a major in Makabulos's army, and would fight for the Republic until 1900, when tuberculosis contracted in the mountains compelled him to surrender (Joaquin 1986, 66).

The case of Gliceria Marella of Taal is likewise significant. By raising and trading in tobacco, rice, and sugar, she and her husband Eulalio Villavicencio became very wealthy. To the exiled Jose Rizal in Hong Kong, Eulalio personally brought P18,000 and came back with manifestos, appeals, and copies of Rizal's two novels. These he and his wife distributed. When the August Revolution blew up in 1896, in their storehouses they met Miguel Malvar, Ananias Diokno, and Mariano Trias to draw up war strategies. Eulalio was arrested and imprisoned in Bilibid. Though released a year later, the hardships had broken him. He died in 1898. Gliceria fought back. When in February 1897, the Spanish generals seized her house and used it as the headquarters of their counteroffensive against the revolutionaries in Cavite, she spied on them and relayed information (along with food, clothing, and arms) to the rebels hiding in the nearby mountains. After Aguinaldo proclaimed the Republic in 1898, she donated the steamship *Bulusan*, the Republic's first and only warship. In February 1899, the American troops entered Batangas. By chance, a letter she sent Gen. Mariano Trias and the rebels, promising aid, fell into enemy hands. She was placed under house arrest, confined to her room with twelve soldiers at the doors, and cross-examined everyday for eight hours at the point of a gun. Only when all resistance had been crushed in Batangas in 1900 was she released (Zaragoza 1954). Glenn May (1997) assures me that though he does not mention her in his study of the Revolution in Batangas (1993), the accounts on her are authentic.

Teodoro Agoncillo (1956, 282–83; 1960, 622–23) argued that the "middle class" had opposed and then betrayed the Philippine Revolution. Renato Constantino was more nuanced. He claimed that in addition to workers and peasants, the Katipunan attracted "soldiers, government employees, merchants, teachers and priests" (Constantino 1975, 168). It thus drew the "lower-middle class." But the Manila elite held back, while the provincial elite seized its leadership in Cavite with disastrous results. Eventually only "the people . . . confronted the Americans" (ibid., 250). During the 1970s and 1980s Marxism, in its Leninist-Maoist variant, finally became popular in the Philippines. It provided useful tools for dissecting social reality in the islands. The Americans had their military bases in the islands, and despite evidence of the human rights abuses of the Marcos dictatorship, continued to support him. Poverty had increased. Land and capital were concentrated in a few families. Led by a Maoist communist party, guerrilla warfare had spread from Luzon to Mindanao. It sought to shatter the oligarchy's hold, it vowed to expel the Americans. The thesis that the economic and political elite had been both exploitative and antirevolutionary during the First Philippine Revolution was eagerly adopted by the Extreme Left. In *Philippine Society and Revolution* (Guerrero 1980, 27), a book that lays out the basic position of the reconstituted Communist Party of the Philippines, Amado Guerrero (reportedly Jose Ma. Sison) states that the ideology of the 1896 Revolution was liberal democratic, for it continued the ideals of the French Revolution (of 1789). However, its leadership and following were proletarian. The thesis of a collaborationist elite has become widely popular among the educated public, even among the many that are suspicious of the Communists.

In 1977, the Agoncillo thesis was critiqued by Nick Joaquin, whose own father had been a colonel under Emilio Aguinaldo and who presumably was privy to oral histories about people in the Revolution. He stated that while the membership of the Katipunan in Manila was proletarian, that of the Katipunan in Cavite was "petty bourgeois." Attracted to it were not the very wealthy, but rather "engineers, lawyers, schoolmasters, poets, town mayors, businessmen, and small landowners" (Joaquin 1977, 114). Shortly after, Jonathan Fast and Jim Richardson (1979, 70–71), who were familiar with Marxist categories, questioned whether even the Manila Katipunan was proletarian in membership. Deodato Arellano was a clerk in the arsenal of the Spanish artillery corps; Roman Basa was a clerk in the Spanish naval headquarters; Pio Valenzuela was of the economic elite of Bulacan and was a medical student; Emilio Jacinto, the son of a well-known Tondo merchant, was enrolled at Santo Tomas. Even Andres Bonifacio may not have been of the "lowest class." Although a tailor, his father had served in his district as teniente mayor. His parents had sent him to a private tutor for a sound elementary education. His occupational status in two foreign firms, Fleming and Company and Fressel and Company has not yet been determined with precision.

Whatever Bonifacio's exact duties may have been, Fast and Richardson (1979, 69) cite the observation of John Foreman (1906, 258), a Britisher who resided in Manila, that it was common for those of Manila's high society to begin their careers as "messengers, warehouse-keepers, clerks, etc. of the foreign houses." It has also been pointed out in open fora in 1996–1997 that in those days to be a Freemason, which Bonifacio was, a candidate had to be a man of means. The ideology of the Katipunan was certainly not socialist. Other than expelling the friar Orders, nowhere does it speak of redistributing the wealth of the rich (Fast and Richardson 1979, 83–84). Glenn May's (1993, 65) study of the revolution in Batangas questions whether it was a "revolt of the masses." He sees it rather as "the continuation and culmination of at least a decade of political agitation by elite residents of the province." They felt frustrated by Spanish interference in local government, and had been repressed for their militancy. May (1993, 51–52) also questions whether the masses as a whole were enthusiastic about the Revolution. While some joined because of Spanish abuses, others thought military life would be glamorous. Others had been compelled to join by their upper-class patrons.

Despite this alternative tradition, the thesis persists that 1896 was proletarian in aim and composition. Because of this, that noble word *ilustrado* has become widely used and—as a catchall for the petty bourgeoisie, bourgeoisie, lower-middle class, middle class, and aristocracy—has acquired a derogatory ring. But *ilustración* in Spanish has a progressive meaning. It means, at one level, education and intellectual cultivation; on another, it refers to that great movement of the eighteenth century called the Enlightenment which, by subjecting every institution to rational critique, prepared the way for the 1789 French Revolution and other revolutions since. Using this definition, Mabini, Jacinto, and Bonifacio were all ilustrados. Terming them such would have flattered them. This essay, therefore, will use instead the term "political elite" or "economic elite."

I suspect there are other reasons for the persistent belief that the elite uniformly rejected the Revolution. People misunderstand how and why revolutions take place. The notion that *only* the masses at all times and at all places have led revolutions has become an indubitable of the same order as "the earth revolves around the sun." Shoring it up are the obvious injustices committed by the Philippine elite today in government, in the farms, and in the factories. Nationalists and activists today find it incredible that the elite's ancestors could have manned a revolution. Moreover, Marxism became a fashion, and it seemed "Marxist" to state that the bourgeoisie in a society are antirevolutionary at all times and at all places because they fear losing their privileges. But is this really what Marx wrote? I propose going back to a reading of Marx's texts on revolution. We should not passively accept the widely popular Maoist and Leninist commentaries; they simplify Marxist dialectic. The Catechism is not the Bible. Meanwhile the study of Western history has been deemphasized in many schools. The student chooses between "Western history" or "Asian history." Awareness of the difference between the several French Revolutions has disappeared. With it has evaporated a sense of context and the insight that the class background of a revolution's leaders can vary according to its goals.

The lack of historical context has led to another popular (if comic) misinterpretation. The menu of the inaugural banquet of the Republic at Malolos was in French. Nationalist friends take this as proof that the Filipino elite was totally out of touch with the population. My question is: In what language should it have been written? Not in Tagalog, for at that time this would have alienated the non-Tagalog speaking majority. Nor in Spanish either even if Spanish was the preferred language of the Republic. Spanish may have been spoken in the former colonies of Spain in America. But it was not a world language then. Only a world language would do. And that language in the 1890s and indeed down to World War II was French. It reigned supreme in diplomacy, in the arts and sciences, in world congresses and, above all, at the table. Indeed, among the elite in Russia, French was the preferred everyday medium in polite circles. Although Tolstoi's *Anna Karenina* is in Russian, nonetheless he lets his characters converse with each other in page after page of French. Significantly, English translations of Tolstoi until fairly recently did not translate these long French passages. The educated English-speaking reader was expected to know French. In Spanish America, French used to be the first language after Spanish. Despite invasion by French troops in the nineteenth century, French culture exerted a strong fascination on educated Mexicans long after (Lemperiere 1998, Novo 1998). Only around the 1960s did this hegemony end because of the emergence of the U.S. as a superpower. In the Philippines, French, too, was widely popular among Spanish-speaking Filipinos during the 1890s to the 1910s. We have only to recall Rizal's enthusiasm for that language. For Spanish language speakers, French is relatively easy to learn because it is a sister language.

Misconceptions about the role of the elite in 1896–1898 have both (1) a racial dimension and (2) an educational dimension. In the 1950s–1980s, mestizos, whether Chinese or Spanish, formed a significant percentage of the island elite. Members of the elite continued to speak Spanish among themselves even as it disappeared from the public sphere. There is also an educational dimension to this misconception. As Nick Joaquin has pointed out repeatedly, the Americanization of the educational system that began in the 1920s–1930s alienated succeeding generations of Filipinos from both their Spanish heritage and their fellow Spanish-speaking Filipinos. Educated Filipinos of non-Spanish ancestry simply assumed that Filipinos with Spanish blood could not possibly have joined any movement for self-determination. In contrast Filipinos exposed to Spanish culture and language, either at home, at school or both, saw no contradiction in fighting against Spanish colonialism yet loving its literature and language at the same time. For them, vivid examples were their own ancestors who had fought against Spain in 1896–1898. Or authors like Fernando Ma. Guerrero and Cecilio Apostol who had witnessed the Revolution, if not participated in it, had written burning poetry celebrating it, but at the same time celebrated the Spanish heritage. Spanish-speaking Filipinos also valued their ties with Spanish America. They knew that the Wars of Independence from Mexico down to Chile were led by the creoles who occupied middle positions in the Church and the state. But Filipinos, who were educated wholly in English and had little or no interest in Spanish and Spanish American history and culture, seemed to find it impossible to believe that Spanish-speaking Filipinos could have been serious about fighting Spain whom they admired. English-educated Filipinos saw it as an "either/or" situation whereas for Spanish-exposed Filipinos it was rather a "both . . . and."

Not surprisingly, Marilou Diaz-Abaya's 1998 film *Rizal* shows Padre Burgos as *indio* whereas historically his father was a Spanish lieutenant and his mother a mestiza from Vigan (Villaroel 1971, 1–2). In Intramuros's Light and Sound Museum of 2003, the narrator says that while Spaniards clustered within the walls of Intramuros, "Filipinos" (understood as indio) and Chinese lived outside and formed "the paradigm of a new race." The implication is that Spaniards did not live outside the walls and so were isolated from the mainstream. They did in fact live outside the walls—in Binondo, Sta. Cruz, Quiapo—and intermarried with non-Spaniards, as family trees, for instance of the Aranetas and the Legardas, attest. We should be concerned about the reduction of culture to race, of nationalistic feelings to biology. This was the very argument used by the Nazis in exterminating the Jews! They argued that the Jews could not feel German because of their "race."

Although by training an anthropologist rather than a historian, I have always been interested in the role of the socioeconomic elite in the Revolution against Spain. First, because some of my ancestors wholeheartedly participated in the Revolution. They were not proletarian. Mention was made of Agapito Zialcita. My mother's father was Julio Nakpil whom Bonifacio appointed as deputy presiding Supremo of the Katipunan before leaving for Cavite (Alvarez [1927–1928] 1992, 405). Yet he was a musician and a piano teacher, and his family were owners of a popular jewelry shop. They were petty bourgeois. Second, the late nineteenth century was an era when Filipino culture reached new heights in the arts and humanities. Since much of this was due to the patronage of the supposedly traitorous island elite, many Leftists hesitate to claim this refined culture as part of their patrimony. At the root of Nick Joaquin's perennial theme, that the bourgeoisie did risk their lives for the Revolution, is his concern that the many achievements of nineteenth-century Filipinos, for instance, in the fine arts and the arts of living, are in danger of not being transmitted to future generations of Filipinos because of the widespread prejudice against the ilustrados and anything influenced by Spain. [1] I share his concern.

In this essay, I concentrate on the questions: Did sectors of the island elite welcome the Philippine Revolution? If so, why? To answer the second, I draw on my background as an anthropologist.

First, I distinguish between "etic" and "emic" ways of interpreting data. An etic perspective looks at the data from the point of view of the detached observer who wishes to analyze, classify, and interpret them according to supposedly universal, scientific categories. An emic perspective, on the other hand, looks at the data from the point of view of the actor; it seeks to understand in their own terms the reasons advanced by the actor for his thinking and acting. There are different ways of conducting etic and emic studies: Marxism and phenomenology are options among several. I would like to do two things: Reread Marx and show how by so doing the island elite's participation in the 1896 Revolution becomes understandable. Then I would like to go beyond Marx by showing how using a phenomenological approach clarifies the elite's reasons for making common cause with the Revolution. Second, I emphasize the need to look at society as a system in motion whose components, like social classes, change positions vis-à-vis each other in response to new factors. Marxist dialectics enables one to look at society in precisely this manner. Third, because of my anthropological background, I would like to take a comparative perspective; comparing the Philippine Revolution with preceding revolutions, the French and the Mexican, helps articulate underlying patterns.

With Marx

For Marx, a dominant class's nature and its relations with other classes do not remain the same forever. These change in response to what he calls the "mode of production." The meaning of this famous key concept has been the subject of much debate. I do not intend to pronounce the final word. For purposes of this essay, the following points can be made about Marx. At the risk of boring the readers, some of whom are familiar with the general outlines of Marx's thought, I shall discuss them in summary form.

For Marx, all human activities are influenced by the manner in which a particular society earns its sustenance. The system by which materials are extracted from the environment in order to create sustenance is a "mode of production." This has several components: (1) the resources accessible to a society at a given time, (2) the technology available in a society for exploiting the environment, and (3) the manner in which the product of labor is divided in a society. Together these three components influence what property is valuable in a society, who own property and who do not, and ultimately, therefore, what kinds of class exist in a society.

There are several modes of production (MOP) that Marx sketches. Relevant to our discussion are his sketches of the feudal and capitalist modes of production.

The feudal MOP is characterized by a contrast between town and country. In the latter, the direct producers are the peasants who use basic farm tools like the plow for "simple, small-scale and primitive cultivation of the land" (Marx and Engels [1845–1846] 1972, 117). But the owners are the town-dwelling nobility who use their retainers to control the peasants. In the towns, what is considered valuable property is "the labor of each individual person" (ibid.). Industry is at a craft level, capitalization is low. Workers thus are organized into guilds where the top position is occupied by a journeyman, the lowest by the apprentice. Neither in the town nor in the countryside is there free movement of labor: The craftsman is tied to his trade guild, the peasant to the landowner. Consequently neither does capital exist as a dynamic entity.

The contrast between town and country is heightened in the capitalist mode. As an industrial center, the town attracts labor from everywhere, for labor has now been freed to sell itself to the highest bidder. Meanwhile the trader and then the manufacturer introduces highly mobile capital. Aided by the invention of machines, capitalist enterprises produce goods on a massive scale, thus bringing their cost down. The vastly expanded market generates enormous wealth for the capitalist who then reinvests part of his profits to create more wealth (ibid., 146 ff.; Marx [1867] 1972, 239).

Within each mode of production, there are contradictions which lead to the emergence of a new one. In feudalism, the appearance of the bourgeois with his mobile capital subverts the landed estates and the guilds, for he attracts labor away from them, while applying machinery that destroys the crafts. His power in society increases with his wealth; at the same time, by eroding feudal, personalistic relationships, the increasing use of money extends his influence. The nobleman, who disdains trade and manufacture as bourgeois, becomes poor (Marx and Engels [1845–1846] 1972, 144 ff.). The French Revolution of 1789 demolishes the feudal order and sets in motion a chain of revolutions that continue to shake society in Marx's own era.[2]

On the eve of the First French Revolution, the dominant economic elite were the nobility and the clergy.[3] Though they constituted only 2 percent of the population, together they owned and controlled much of the land in France. And yet they were exempt from taxation. The burden fell on the bourgeoisie, the workers, and the peasants. Though the last was the most disadvantaged and the most exploited, it was the bourgeoisie that was most articulate in critiquing the existing order. Marat, Danton, and Robespierre came from its ranks. For though they were educated and economically powerful, they were looked down upon by the nobility. In the Estates-General, which was the Parliament, the three classes were represented: clergy, nobility, and commoners. The last embraced the rest of society: merchant, artisan, and peasant, whether rich or poor. But the first two estates often voted together to defeat measures by the third. The Revolution of 1789 destroyed the privileges of the first two estates by introducing individual votation into the newly constituted National Assembly and by instituting suffrage. However, the right to vote was extended only to property holders. In effect the bourgeoisie who, by definition, were property-holders and at the same time more numerous than the clergy and the nobility, emerged triumphant.

Marx ([1848b] 1986) reads the 1789 Revolution as bourgeois both in leadership and ideology. It brought in a new social system and replaced feudal notions of property with capitalist notions. Its emphasis on freedom was indeed a breakthrough, but its concept of freedom was abstract, for it dwelt exclusively on the bourgeois's desire to act as he pleases. It said nothing of the necessity of providing a man's basic economic needs. However, even if the proletariat and the other common classes opposed the bourgeoisie during this revolution, they fought to advance the latter's interests, for, as commoners, their enemies were the absolutist king and the feudal Church and nobility who demanded much from them.[4]

But the bourgeoisie's triumph set the stage for another conflict, this time with the ascendant proletariat. By the 1830s, capitalism had become the dominant mode of production in France, and the bourgeoisie, the dominant class. However, according to Marx ([1848a] 1972, 342; 1867, 283, 318), the capitalist MOP creates its own contradictions on two levels. More than in previous MOPs, the organization of work in capitalism is social in character, for large numbers of people with different skills are brought together under the supervision of the capitalist. But the production process is contradicted by the system of appropriation. The capitalist, as individual owner, appropriates the profits. Another contradiction, too, is that as the capitalist's profits increase, the worker, whose labor is counted as part of the cost of production, becomes increasingly poor. However, the workers do not remain passive. For as more and more of them enter the factories, they form associations that begin to challenge the owners.

For Marx ([1852] 1972, 510–11), the February Revolution of 1848 in Paris, which deposed the constitutional monarchy to set up the Second Republic, had proletarian goals. Suffrage was extended to all regardless of whether one was propertied or not. In addition the workers demanded that they be granted work through national workshops that would be set up. However, frightened by talk of socialism and by the critique of private property, the bourgeoisie and the peasantry banded together against the workers. A workers' revolt in June was mercilessly suppressed. This time, therefore, the oppressor was no longer the nobility but the former ally of the workers: the bourgeoisie.

The Second Republic, however, was itself aborted by the coup of Louis Napoleon who proclaimed the Second Empire which lasted until 1870 when it was defeated by the armies of Bismarck. In the ensuing chaos in besieged Paris, the common people seized arms and organized a system of government where they could govern themselves directly without need for intermediaries. The Commune of 1871 was, in Marx's ([1871] 1972, 554) reading, proletarian both in aims and in membership. The members were working men; and it was "to be a working, not a parliamentary, body, executive and legislative at the same time." Here again the nature of the enemy was sharply drawn. The bourgeoisie put it down and butchered thousands of participants.

For Marx ([1871] 1972, 389), therefore, the revolutionary or, for that matter, the reactionary character of a class is always in relation to other classes. In relation to the proletariat, whose advance it impedes, the bourgeoisie is reactionary. However, in relation to the feudal lord, the bourgeoisie is revolutionary.

A Frustrated Bourgeoisie. With this rereading of Marx we can now look briefly at revolutionary Mexico before turning back to the Philippines to reexamine the 1896 Revolution. Mexico's 1810 Revolution is significant for Filipinos because it was anticolonial, it had an ethnic dimension, and it influenced Spanish policy. During the second half of the eighteenth century, a crisis had emerged in Spanish-ruled Mexico over the issue of free trade. The creoles wanted to trade freely, but the peninsulars wanted to limit this to the Peninsula (Florescano and Sanchez 1976, 225). Businesses that the creoles wanted to open were prohibited by the Crown if these competed either with those in the Peninsula or with a Royal Monopoly. Other creoles became priests, lawyers, low-level administrators but they could not rise higher because the highest positions were given to Peninsulars. "More than any other class, this middle class was conscious that it could not fulfill in society the role its formation and calling had prepared for it" (Villoro 1976, 313). However, it had a powerful weapon: its *ilustracion*. They could articulate the issues and could rouse the other social classes, particularly the marginalized (Villoro 1976, 314). In 1810 Miguel Hidalgo, a creole priest, called the people to arms.

To claim that the bourgeoisie has been "revolutionary" at a particular juncture is thus not a contradiction in terms. The Marxist-influenced Fast and Richardson analyze the forces in contention then by claiming that throughout the nineteenth century, the capitalist system had increasingly penetrated the Philippine economy with the willing consent of the landed elite that sought greater participation in the international capitalist economy.[5] They wanted to import machinery to improve the processing of products like sugar; they were eager to export their products at a competitive price in the world market. Both they and ordinary Filipino consumers wanted to buy cheaply manufactured (and therefore imported) goods. But despite initial protestations of adherence to free trade, the Spanish government after 1869 turned protectionist by raising customs duties on all imported goods, including agricultural machinery. Imported rice and cotton textiles became more expensive, especially for the poor. Conversely, it imposed excise taxes on all leading exports. In the absence of free trade, Philippine products became less competitive on the world market. Madrid was jealous of the British and the Americans who bought Philippine sugar and other products and in exchange supplied the bourgeoisie with credit and sold superior but cheaply priced textiles (Lopez Jaena [1887] 1951, 110–11; n.d., 128–29; Legarda 1999, 199 ff.; Fast and Richardson 1979, 58). Madrid's response was to impose a monopoly—admittedly unsuccessfully—on Philippine trade. Colonialism shackled the expansion of capitalism.

Meanwhile there was another contradiction at work, this time in the political sphere. Though the local elite had become wealthier, more educated, and more aware of the world beyond the town, the available positions of power in government were not commensurate. They could only become municipal mayors. Higher positions were closed. At the same time, the Spanish government demanded more efficiency in taxation. However, "every year the cabeza de barangay would pay with his own money big amounts to make up for deficits" (Aguinaldo 1967, 4). Failure to do so was punished with seizure and public auction of the cabeza's properties or with fines. Antonia Santos (1999) documents the sufferings this caused the cabezas in, for instance, Tondo whose residents were active in the Katipunan. In the Church, the local clergy could not aspire to an equivalent position by becoming parish priest. Out of fear that the native priests might lead a revolt, as in Mexico, the curacies were often given to religious from the Peninsula (Schumacher 1991, 26–27). There were no avenues for expressing grievances. The press was censored; the islands were not represented in the Spanish parliament.

Inspired by the French Revolution of 1789, Emilio Jacinto and Andres Bonifacio wrote of liberty [*kalayaan*] and equality [*pagkakapantay-pantay*]. But they spoke of these in an ethical sense, they had no program for redistributing wealth other than expelling the landed friars (Santos 1935; Agoncillo 1956, 83 ff., 91 ff.; Guerrero 1977, 431). To solve the problems of the Philippines, they advocated separation and rule by Filipinos themselves. One can understand, therefore, why sugar planters like the Villavicencios of Batangas and the Aquinos of Tarlac would have been attracted to this vision. It promised liberation from the economic shackles of Spanish colonialism without threatening their position in local society. For the political elite, the possibility of assuming higher positions of power would have been an added incentive. Some sectors of the Filipino elite thus played a "revolutionary" role in 1896: They rejected encumbrances that kept capitalism from developing fully. Ironically, within our own century, encumbrances, imposed this time by Filipinos, continue to hinder the expansion of capitalism. For instance, until fairly recently the Philippine government imposed substantial taxes on the importation of components necessary for the production of goods. Philippine textiles and processed foods have thus been uncompetitive both locally and abroad. Moreover, capitalism generates its own contradictions: The gap between capitalist and worker continues to widen in our days and is creating a host of social and economic problems. Nonetheless, the more visionary members of the Filipino elite of 1896 should be credited for attempting to inaugurate a new era where ultimately *only* Filipino leaders would be responsible for the country.

While the Marxist approach clarifies, it also raises questions which future research could look into. Fast and Richardson's portrait of the Filipino bourgeoisie reveals a division within it: some factions (the Manila Katipuneros and the Caviteños under Aguinaldo) actively promoting the Revolution; other factions (the Manila upper crust and the Negros planters) opposing it. Each had its own economic interest to follow. The Negros planters feared disorder and the possibility that their lands might be seized by the workers. This fear seems to have overridden any dream that they could control the economic policies of the emergent republic (Fast and Richardson 1979, 103–5). However, data from other parts of the islands show sugar planters, like the Aquinos and the Villavicencios, actively risking their lives for the republic. Why the difference? What economic interests were at work in one and absent in the other?

A Marxist approach discloses economic interests at work. Unfortunately, if one follows the logic of economic determinism, other motivations for acting are unexplained. One ends up with a caricature. Can one say that Marella, Malvar, and Aquino accepted physical and emotional torment in order to gain a high position under a triumphant republic?

The bourgeoisie now dominates Philippine society, yet some of its members did join the Huks in the 1940s when they fought first against the Japanese, then against the landlords of Central Luzon. Casto Alejandrino came from a family of landowners but became convinced of the rights of the poor. He had been a picket leader for striking workers in 1938. Later on he became the vice commander of the Huks (Taruc 1953, 66, 84). On the eve of World War II, the treasurer of the KPMP, the National Peasants' Union of the Philippines, was Mateo del Castillo, son of a landowner of means from Batangas. He became the political director of the Military Committee of the Huks. It is fashionable to assume that mestizos have been incapable of taking arms against the established order because of their privileges. And yet both Alejandrino and Del Castillo came from Spanish-speaking mestizo families. Alejandrino was a descendant of Levantine Jews from Alexandria, Egypt. Hence the family name, according to a relative Juan Eulogio Alejandrino Medina (1997, p.c.). Del Castillo's father was a liberal who had come from Spain in the nineteenth century and became a justice of the peace (Taruc 1953, 88–89). Scions of the economic elite again joined the Communist underground in the 1970s and 1980s and suffered hunger, thirst, torture, and imprisonment. There was the martyred Ed Jopson, "the son of a shopkeeper," as Marcos sneered. Or the thinkers and leaders of the movement: Jose Ma. Sison, the son of a landowning family in the Ilocos, and Luis Jalandoni whose family name alone conjures old sugar wealth in Negros Occidental. Was Sison's courageous acceptance of solitary confinement in chains under the Marcos government inspired by his wanting to control the movement? The question is absurd.

Beyond Marx

Marx and Engels themselves were aware of the limitations of economic determinism. They had proposed materialism as a corrective to the German tendency of their day to explain behavior solely in terms of abstract ideas. Nonetheless Engels ([1890] 1972, 642) says that they cautioned against attempts "to lay more stress on the economic side than is due to it . . . we had not always the time, the place or the opportunity to allow other elements involved in their interaction to come into their rights."

Another important motivation is the quest for total meaning, and, likewise, things like the desire for honor, for respect, for sharing, for compassion. These can become powerful reasons.

An "emic," or an insider perspective, offers another lens on reality. One method is phenomenology which studies how a self faces and is faced by things as they appear in consciousness. The self is seen not merely as something determined by the external world, but also as a subject reaching out toward the external and, in the process, organizing things (Tiryakian 1973, 194–95). The self's way of constituting meaning is accepted as a given and is not judged, for the phenomenologist's purpose is to gain insight into how that self sees the world differently as an individual. Etic and emic perspectives thus complement each other: Marxism uncovers hidden economic factors that influence an individual while phenomenology reveals how he sees and understands the world.

Data for phenomenological analysis are interviews, autobiographies, letters, conversations, poems by actual participants. So can inferences from actuations by the participants, risky though such inferences can be.

In his autobiography, Manuel Luis Quezon, a Spanish mestizo, reports a confrontation with the Spanish parish priest in Baler, his hometown. After finishing his B.A. with a summa cum laude at the Dominican college in Manila, he and his father called on the Franciscan priest. When they entered, the priest was lounging in his easy chair: the right leg was up resting over one of the chair's long arms. He did not change position when the Quezons entered. Manuel's father bent over and kissed the hand which the Franciscan extended to him. Manuel merely took the hand and shook it. The priest ignored him. Later on the Spaniard told his father that his son's studies in Manila had spoiled Manuel: If the priest were the father, he would keep Manuel on the farm, whip him, and make him work. Comments Quezon (1946, 13–14): "I realized that we Filipinos were treated as inferiors and my racial pride was deeply hurt." A similar experience was reported by Agapito Zialcita, another Spanish mestizo, to his son Bernardo (Zialcita 1997). Educated in Hong Kong and in England, familiar with France, and exposed to the liberal currents of his time, he refused to kiss the hand of the parish priest in Bataan. The result was that every Sunday he and his brother would be criticized by the parish priest in the sermon: "Some people become conceited just because they have studied abroad." But the parish priest could not do much against them, for they owned much land in Bataan.

Quezon recounts another incident. The corporal of the civil guards had a taste for young girls. He would compel their relatives to deliver innocent creatures to him. Otherwise they would be flogged. "I began to understand the why of the Katipunan" says Quezon (1946, 15). The corporal soon noticed Quezon's cousin; he ordered him to bring her over under threat of whipping. Manuel avoided him; however, Manuel finally hit him with a club. Soon Manuel was falsely accused of joining the Katipunan and detained for fifteen days. His father approached the Spanish authorities to assert his son's innocence. Manuel was released on condition that he would leave, continue his studies in Manila and not join any subversive society. But his brother, Teodorico, who was not bound by any such promise, did join the Revolution and later on led the attack on the Guardia Civil at Baler and arrested the lascivious corporal (ibid., 31).

Manuel Quezon enjoyed privileges. His father had served in the infantry as sergeant and, like his mother, had become a school teacher. With their earnings, they bought rice land and became the number one family in Baler. They were close to the parish priest. Yet neither their ethnicity, education, wealth, social status nor military connections won them the respect of the representatives of the pope and the king. Quezon admired the liberalism of his Dominican teacher, appreciated Spanish culture, and when the Spanish flag would be taken down in 1898, felt sadness. Nonetheless he and his brother were resentful. Similarly Agapito Zialcita may have been the grandson of the Spanish naval commander at Cavite (B. Zialcita 1997), but he experienced how readily their Spanish parish priest would attack him from the pulpit for not kissing his hand.

The case of Emilio Aguinaldo, leader of the victorious Filipino forces in Cavite, is illuminating. His father had been the *gobernadorcillo* of the important town of Kawit. When his father died, the burial ceremonies had been carefully organized by the parish priest who was close to the father: The bier was three tiers high, the cortege was accompanied by eight priests. At nineteen, Emilio became the *cabeza de barangay;* in 1895 at twenty-six, he became the *capitan municipal*—the new title of the gobernadorcillo after the Maura Law. He was on friendly terms with some of the priests; indeed during the Revolution he spared the life of prisoner-priests and forbade their torture. In his old age, Aguinaldo, who was no Spanish mestizo, wrote an introduction to the biography of Gliceria Marella. There were two Spains, he claimed: one a Noble Spain, another a Dark Spain (Zaragoza 1954). It was against the latter that he and others that he fought even though clearly he was prosperous: He ran a ranch, had a little molasses factory, and traded in the Visayas. What was the Dark Spain against whom he fought? In his autobiography, he complains that in collecting personal taxes from people sixteen to sixty years of age, the cabeza had to use his own money to cover the deficits in collection for fear of punishment by the authorities. He also reports that the friars were relentless in persecuting, torturing, banishing, and even murdering their enemies which included people who were not masons (Aguinaldo 1967, 24). His elevated position did not win him respect either from the authorities. When, in May 1896, the town officials paid their respects to the parish priest before going to the tribunal, the Spanish commandant of the civil guards in Kawit accosted Emilio, as capitan municipal, and ordered him to prepare a calesa for him there and then. He did not accept Aguinaldo's explanation that all the calesas had been taken. "I felt humiliated and embarassed," writes Aguinaldo (1967, 30–31) in anger. He had been demeaned before his subordinates by a fellow who, though lower in rank, happened to be a Spaniard. To make matters worse, acting on the commandant's complaint, the military governor summoned

Aguinaldo to appear before a council of war to answer charges of discourtesy to a military authority (Aguinaldo 1967, 31).

A Marxist approach looks at external behavior and stresses the conflict between classes: Quezon, A. Zialcita, and Aguinaldo belonged to an educated, landholding class, familiar with local governance, whose ascent was barred by the existing colonial barriers. Looked at phenomenologically, another dimension opens up. All three wanted to behave according to what they had learned in school and according to their high status. But they were blocked from so doing by the whims of people who were either their equal or their subordinate in experience and skills. Because this was a colonial order, an individual with inferior education could become powerful by merely reminding others of his ethnicity. Thus the anger of Quezon and others despite their sympathy for Spanish culture or for particular Spaniards.

Doubtless, members of the island elite, like Aguinaldo, expected potential material benefits from the Revolution. When he had encircled Manila in July–August 1898, Aguinaldo promised his followers lands and titles of nobility (M. Guerrero 1977, 138–39). Yet it would be simplistic to conclude that the hope of material gain was what prodded him to risk his life. Human beings can choose to act simultaneously for two differing goals: for *other fellow human beings* and for *themselves*. Moreover, acting for one's self can mean pursuing both a material goal, like wealth, and a symbolic one like self-esteem. As capitan municipal, Aguinaldo witnessed the sufferings of fellow *capitanes;* at the same time his own self-respect had been wounded.

One important reason not connected with political or economic status was the desire to avenge a beloved. This has not received enough attention because of the current preoccupation with Marxist explanations. Gen. Jose Alejandrino came from an hacienda-owning family of Arayat, Pampanga, and had studied in Belgium. He joined Emilio Aguinaldo in 1896 and fought for the Republic until 1901. In his autobiography, he relates that his father had been exiled to Kiangan in the Cordillera at the instance of the Spanish parish priest of their town (Alejandrino 1933; 1949, 218). While Gliceria Marella has not left us a memoir we can infer from her circumstances and her letters that she was responding to a chain of interconnected events: each leading to the next. The execution of the three Filipino priests had shaken both her and her husband. They joined the educational campaign that was the Propaganda. The brutal treatment of her husband during the Terror in 1896 strengthened her resolve. He was tied, lifted with a crane like an animal and dumped onto a ship deck, resulting in severe contusions that, together with his imprisonment, led to his early death. This marked the point of no return in her relations with the colonial authorities. "After my husband's death, my love for the Motherland intensified" (Zaragoza 1954, 219). Moreover, her religiosity and her patriotism merged to convince her of the justice of her cause: "We are born and are in this world, first to serve God, second in order to serve the Motherland and afterwards the family . . . Fight on, fight on therefore, until death" (ibid.). It may be that Julio Nakpil finally decided to join the Revolution for a similar reason: A beloved had been tortured. He seems not to have been a Katipunero. But his elder brother, Francisco, was. Francisco was arrested during the Terror and tortured. From a cultural perspective, Alejandrino, Marella, and Nakpil's behavior recall earlier patterns. A theme in epics like *Labaw Dongon* and *Lam-ang* is precisely the desire to vindicate family honor. The sons fight for their fathers who have been humiliated. For that matter this, too, is a theme of Rizal's *Noli me tangere.*

Another possible reason may have been admiration for a leader. Even today, Filipino politics is personality-oriented. Alejandrino deeply admired Rizal, his one-time roommate. Years later he declares that Rizal was "my mentor and his spirit continues to this day to be my guide and inspiration" (Alejandrino 1949). Agapito Zialcita had prepared his bags to flee to Singapore. But a chance conversation with Andres Bonifacio in Tondo changed his mind. The *supremo* asked him, "What country in Europe won liberty without bloodshed?" He immediately returned to his Bataan hacienda to gather arms for the revolution (B. Zialcita 1997).

Given their diverse motivations, are they worthy of esteem?

A Hero for Whom?

Our perceptions and decisions as human beings are all contextually situated. There are concrete circumstances that enfold us in relation to which we react and reflect on the world. The configuration of circumstances may not be the same as those for other individuals. We thus view the world from an angle: Try as we wish to view the world from another angle or to imagine other angles, unsuspected angles escape us. Our social class, our education, our personality, our life history and even the language we use combine to create for us a particular window on the world. What may be obvious to a later generation may escape our attention, not necessarily because of ill will on our part, but because our perspective on the world, or any perspective for that matter, necessarily highlights certain features while leaving others in the shadow. Inevitably, the individuals whom we admire are seen by us from our perspective. We imagine that they share our concerns.

For the key organizers of the Revolution against Spain, the overriding concern was political emancipation. They did not mention redistributing locally owned factors of production. They seemed to believe that once Filipinos could decide for themselves, then social problems would be resolved.

But, since World War II, mainstream political discourse in the Philippines has emphasized not only full political emancipation from the U.S. and its military bases, but the redistribution as well of locally owned land and capital. On the basis of this preoccupation, nationalists, especially of the Left, want to read Bonifacio and company as proletarians with a proletarian agenda. And because the descendants of the late-nineteenth-century elite own urban estates and rural farms, the Left paints the elite as having consistently betrayed the People's Cause whether in 1896 or in 1980. The articulated aspirations of the leaders of 1896 do not match the concerns of the nationalists of the 1970s–1990s.

Marx read the paradigmatic revolution, the French, as moving in stages: bourgeois in 1789, proletarian in sympathy in 1848, and proletarian in leadership and agenda in 1871. The triumph of one class over the other created the stage for new conflicts with an erstwhile ally, the class below it. The heroes of one phase of the struggle become the villains in the next. Implicit is the notion that knowledge is contextual. People act in virtue of their class interests and the opportunities present at a historic juncture. There is no need, therefore, to proletarianize all the predecessors of a contemporary movement such as the Philippine Revolution of our days, of the 1970s–1980s, whose agenda was indeed proletarian.

However, I propose going beyond Marx by highlighting the subject-centeredness of knowledge. A perspective on the world that transcends time and space is reserved only for the Omniscient. But we are not Omniscient. Therefore, despite our good intentions, aspects of our neighbor's needs may escape our attention. Moreover, we as humans do act for simultaneous ends: for self-interest and for altruism. Thus I assume that the elite participants of 1896 acted on the basis of what they thought was good, not only for themselves, but for the country as a whole—and were willing to suffer for their ideals. Alejandrino writes that fraternity "between social classes" existed in areas held by the revolutionary forces. Cockpits had been abolished, no crimes committed, few offenses committed against property even though no police force has been organized (Alejandrino 1949, 210–10). For him this was sufficient proof that political liberty by itself would have sufficed to solve the enduring social problems of the Filipino. Yet we know from the study of Milagros Guerrero (1977, 137–38) that crimes against property were taking place: The ascendant Filipino elite in the liberated areas were appropriating lands for themselves or for their familiars. Alejandrino was not insincere. He merely acted on the basis of assumptions he had inherited from youth. He probably did not anticipate that his own first cousin, Casto Alejandrino, would play a major role in the socialist-inspired revolution of the 1940s which unmasked the lack of fraternity between classes in Central Luzon.

Were the elite participants of the First Philippine Revolution heroes or villains? A larger question is involved here: a question involving the reading of history. One position reads the past exclusively in terms of present concerns and thus criticizes predecessors for not sharing these. It also demands that a hero be beyond fault. Logically worked out, this position may not give us any heroes. I believe it is better to assume that our heroes, being human like us, interpreted the world from an accustomed viewpoint and, on the basis of this, made fateful decisions. They could not, however, have anticipated other subsequent viewpoints. Neither can we.

Notes

This essay is a rewritten version of "Hero or Villain? Notes on the Filipino Elite in 1896–1898," which appeared in Bernardita Reyes-Churchill and Francis A. Gealogo, editors, 1999, *Centennial Papers on the Katipunan and the Revolution,* pp. 14–30. Quezon City: Manila Studies Association; Manila: National Commission on Culture and the Arts Committee on Historical Research.

1. The principal figure of Joaquin's first and most famous play, *Portrait of the Artist as Filipino* (1952), is Don Lorenzo Marasigan. A soldier in the Revolution, a painter, a lover of Latin and Spanish poetry, he is a magnificent Renaissance man. (His many talents remind me of real-life figures like Gen. Antonio Luna.) But both his adult children and the Manila public cannot understand his commitment to his craft and to the Revolution, nor his classical allusions either. The play suggests that those of the 1896–1898 generation have no spiritual heirs.

2. As is well known, the 1789 Revolution is one of the most thoroughly studied events in history. For this essay, I relied on the overview of De Bertier-Sauvigny and Pinkney (1983) in their history of France. For an in-depth study, I consulted the well-esteemed work of Furet and Richet (1973).

3. François Furet, a specialist on the French Revolution, dedicated an entire book to Marx's views on the French Revolution. Though sympathetic to Marx, he criticizes him for being too rigid and deductive in his study of that event. He

reduces everything to the struggle between social classes. As a result "the autonomy of political history" is denied (Furet 1986, 79).

4. Thus, according to Marx ([1848b] 1986, 227), the Terror launched by Robespierre may not have accorded with the usual bourgeois way of doing things; it was plebeian in method. But it did eliminate the enemies of the bourgeoisie.

5. Because land has been the major source of wealth in the nineteenth- and twentieth-century Philippines, the Left has characterized it as "feudal" and would thus not agree that the nineteenth-century elite was "bourgeois." What they fail to see is that in the classic feudalism of Western Europe, the landed aristocracy disdained anything relating to manufacture and commerce. In nineteenth-century Philippines, the landed elite had no such scruples. However, they seem not to have been fully capitalist. A common criticism made about them is that because of the easy accessibility of land and their quasi monopoly, they did not reinvest their profits in improving their production; for instance, their irrigation systems and their sugar mills. I would characterize them as "rentier bourgeois."

PART II

A New Civil Culture Emerges

The Costs and Benefits
of Civil Culture

> The greatest division of mental and manual labor is the sepa-
> ration of town and country. The antagonism runs through the
> whole history of civilization to the present day.
> —Karl Marx and Friedrich Engels 1846, *The German Ideology*

When Islam came to Sunda on the western part of Java in the sixteenth century, many fled to the forests together with their chief,
Siliwangi, and there became tigers. The factual basis for this popular
tale is that not all Sundanese accepted the new religion. Those refus-
ing to convert chose to live in the many forests that until this century
covered the hills of southern Sunda. Over the course of five centuries, however, the Islamic tide eventually entered the remote hamlets,
except those of a small society, the Badui, also known as the Kanekes.
This people have rejected not only Islam, but also new forms of
social organization and technology: plow agriculture, machines, electricity, the sultanate, the republican nation-state. Numbering 4,587
in 1984, the Kanekes live in two types of community: (1) an "outside" one in contact with the larger society and (2) an "inside" one
that refuses to allow just anybody into their hamlets. The latter
number 476 individuals. They practice swidden. Each of their three
hamlets is headed by a male adult (*puun*) who holds office for life
but does not differ from the rest in clothing, food, housing, and
occupation. He, too, cultivates his own garden.[1]

Two things are notable about the Kanekes. First, there has
been a plus side to their withdrawal. True, they have not partici-

141

pated in the momentous transformations that Java has undergone over the centuries. However, they have escaped the poverty and the inequality that afflict many villages in Java even as farming techniques become more sophisticated and hours of work lengthen. Secondly, the ambivalent attitude of the Sundanese majority toward forest people is significant, for it recurs in many societies, including ours, though in different guises. True, the Kanekes are regarded as less than human for rejecting the accustomed norms of the majority. Indeed it is said that the Kanekes avoid baths, drink the fluids of animals, and know the secrets of the tigers. "They do not walk, they run as fast as the tiger" (Ekadjati 1995, 51). Yet, they are also esteemed as more than human, for statues of Siliwangi as tiger dignify public places in Sunda. Moreover, Moslem Sundanese have the custom of trekking to the isolated non-Moslem Kanekes to ask for their prayers. In brief, as an aboriginal people living outside the pale of civil culture, they are regarded as the classic Other.

Rejecting a more complex and a more developed way of life for the sake of a simple one has been a common alternative in many societies, for instance, in Indonesia (Keyfitz 1961, 349). This has been easy to realize in Southeast Asia because of the mountainous terrain, the once extensive forest cover, and the many islands. Stateless societies living in small, isolated, independent villages have managed to retain, until recently, their traditional way of life. In Thailand, the Karen, the Meo, and the Yeo in the uplands contrast with the sophisticated Siamese of the central flood plains. In Sumatra, the Bataks of the mountains were described in 1783 as "divided into numberless petty chiefships" prone to war with each other on "the slightest pretext" (Marsden [1811] 1966, 374–75). And yet the Buddhist empire of Sri-Vijaya had appeared on the nearby lowlands by the sixth century A.D., to be followed by other states since. On Mindanao, the Tiruray and T'boli have alternated between trading with the Moslems of the lowlands and fleeing into the interior (Schlegel 1970, 4, 8; Casal 1978, 29).

This rejection is often prompted by the exactions of the state. Simon de la Loubère, a French envoy at the court of Siam during the late seventeenth century, reports that those who chose to resist the king's will sought asylum in the forest (Reed 1971, 348). The Manobo epic, *Agyu*, explains how the Manobos came to reside where they are now, in Central and Eastern Mindanao. In response to a sultan's demand for tribute, Agyu speared him and fled eastward with his kin. Avoidance of Spanish demands may have goaded the Ifugao, Tinguian, and Ibaloi to leave the lowlands for the safety of the Cordillera (Keesing 1962, 324–25, 328, 338). In the case of the Kanekes, they may be resisting not only taxes, but also the attachment to privately owned land that emerges when wet rice cultivation supplants slash-and-burn cultivation.

The culture that most Filipinos, like most Southeast Asians, are familiar with is a culture we can call "civil" in contrast to the "primal" culture of nonstate societies. While there are obvious benefits, there are also costs. When speaking of pre-Western kingdoms and empires and their culture, we tend to dwell only on the benefits and ignore the costs. For this reason, many Filipinos insist against all evidence that the Philippines was part of both the Sri-Vijaya and Madjapahit empires.[2] Dazzled by the prestige of cultures with an ancient courtly tradition, they overlook the costs. They do not realize, for instance, that to this day the Sundanese refuse to name streets in their region in honor of anyone connected with Madjapahit, an empire founded on the same island of Java, for the empire overcame their resistance through deception and force. On the other hand, when discussing Spanish rule, many concentrate only on the costs, without weighing possible benefits. We must thus understand the characteristics of primal and civil cultures, together with their costs and benefits.

What is civil culture? How does it differ from primal culture? The discussion seems academic, yet this is important for four reasons.

First, these concepts affect ways of looking at the Philippines' past and present. Many assume that to defend the national honor, they must affirm that there existed in Luzon and the Visayas, during the sixteenth century, a highly developed civil culture—like those which flourished in Japan, Siam, or Java. I propose that this need not be a point of honor for two reasons. All cultures, whether complex or not, have their own contributions to make to humankind's fund of knowledge. Moreover, the type of culture at issue, which I prefer to call "civil culture," has its own shortcomings. For this reason, many societies both here and elsewhere have preferred to hold on to their "primal culture," as shown by the phenomenon of flight into the wilderness. Indeed one of the continuing problems in civil cultures today is how to equalize opportunities for all their members.

Second, we live in a neighborhood where countries vie with each other in showing off the antiquity of their civil cultures. The oldest is that of Mesopotamia [now Iraq] which dates back over five thousand years, followed by India (four thousand and a half years ago) and China (four thousand years). From their vantage point, the Chinese tend to grade others, even today, on the antiquity and quality of their civil culture. Facing truths about our past and taking pride even in modest achievements will help us in relating with our neighbors as equals. Fantasies will not.

Third, as will be discussed in the last two essays in this book, "civil culture"/"civilization" refers to a community of cultures that transcends a narrow locality and is based on shared, unquestioned indubitables about the nature of reality. Important vehicles are a shared religion, philosophy, and art.

Fourth, by examining predemocratic civil culture, both in pre-twentieth-century Philippines and in other societies, as a three-dimensional object with highlights and shadows, we might look at the civil culture that arose in the Philippines under Spain with a kindlier eye. For this civil culture was a product of its period; similar shadows were present even in societies that were sovereign. By looking only at the shortcomings, we make it more difficult for ourselves to take pride in the civil culture that has become our own despite the change in language and, without which, there would be no modern Philippines.

Having said the above, I must admit writing this essay has been the most difficult and the most challenging in this book. Imperialists have used "to civilize" as a pretext for colonizing others. Thus in the 1890s–1920s, French imperialists justified expansion on the basis of their *mission civilisatrice*; while President McKinley asserted that the U.S. had the right to annex the Philippines in order "to Christianize and civilize" the inhabitants. Moreover, I will wound sensitivities, be accused of being unpatriotic, and be read out of context. However, I decided to take the risk because the concept of civil culture is important both for self-understanding and for understanding ourselves vis-à-vis our neighbors.

Primal, Chiefdom, and Civil Cultures

My position is that the cultures that flourished in the uplands during the sixteenth century and that remained fairly isolated until the middle of the twentieth century were of the primal type. However, in selected areas in the non-Moslem lowlands of Luzon and Visayas, notably along the coast and the river valleys, some sixteenth-century societies were "chiefdom cultures."

Primal versus Civil Culture. But first, let us draw the difference between primal and civil cultures. The contrast drawn between the two has a long tradition among British and American anthropologists, particularly among those specializing in archaeology, ecological anthropology, and political anthropology.[3] Unfortunately, their insights, formulated since the 1950s, have not become a component of scholarly discourse in the Philippines. And yet they clarify basic issues.

The usual terms are "civilization" versus "primitive culture." I prefer not to use those terms to avoid persistent confusions. Outside Anglo-American anthropology, civilization and culture often are used interchangeably. The confusion began with Edward Tylor's ([1871] 1958, 1) famous definition of culture:

> Culture, or civilization, taken in its wide ethnographic sense, is that complex whole which includes knowledge, belief, art, morals, law, custom and any other capabilities and habits acquired by man as a member of society.

Figure 5: A Comparison of Three Cultures

	Primal Culture	Chiefdom Culture	Civil Culture
Type of polity associated with	"Autonomous locality"	Chiefdom	State
Features: Nature of science	Observation of the material environment	Observation of the material environment	Observation together with increasing use of mathematical calculation
Interpretations of ultimate reality	Reflections on the ultimate meaning of Life and Death	Reflections on the ultimate meaning of Life and Death	Systematization: Interpretations are grounded on first principles; commentaries and debates on basic, founding texts for further elaboration
Moral system	Particular to a particular locality	Develops a cult around the paramount chief who stands beyond kinship	In nondemocratic states: A cult around the ruler. Universalistic: Assumes that its vision is true for all either within a society or for all societies; may proselytize
Material construction	Impermanent to semi-permanent constructions	Large, permanent constructions to show the power of the paramount	Constructions in permanent materials (stone, timber) to show the power of particular individuals and groups
Nature of art	Largely utilitarian, functional art	Appearance of luxury art: the product of many man-hours	Appearance of high art, likewise the product of many man-hours. Justifies its existence by inviting contemplation and analysis
Storage of information	Oral information	Oral with the beginning of notation	Written information; stored in centers of learning
Diversity of tradition	Single tradition	Emergence of an economic and political elite with its own exclusive practices	Elite tradition (Great Tradition) vs. popular tradition (Little Tradition)

Sources: Armillas 1968, Earle 1989, Hally 1996, Redfield 1953, Sahlins 1958, 1968, Sjoberg 1960, Service 1966.

Anglo-American anthropologists today would distinguish between the two. Culture, as the all-embracing concept, refers to all knowledge and skills that are learned by human beings, via symbols, as members of a society. Civilization is a particular type of culture not found in all societies.[4] Another confusion: Civilization, in contrast to primitive culture, connotes moral and esthetic superiority. It is difficult to square this, however, with the deliberate genocide effected by highly civilized countries of our century such as Nazi Germany and Soviet Russia; or with the kitsch spewed out by factories today. To avoid these confusions, I propose alternative terms. "Civil" is ultimately derived from the Latin *civitas* which can mean both state and city. As will be shown below, civil culture is a form of culture closely associated with the two. "Primal," on the other hand, comes from the Latin *primus,* meaning "first." Primal culture is an earlier and more basic culture than civil culture. I will use it interchangeably with "aboriginal" [*ab origine*, from the beginning]. "Primitive" used to mean the same, namely, as that which is "original." Over time, however, it has acquired negative connotations among the general public unused to anthropological distinctions. In response to this, a new museum in Paris dedicates itself to *Arts prémiers* [First Arts].

In American archaeology, civilization is regarded as a culture associated with the state,[5] and thus requires a configuration of economic, political, and social factors as a context. Such likewise is my understanding of civil culture.

Civil culture develops within a state society.[6] It develops as a response to full-time occupational specialization, particularly to the separation between mental and manual labor and to the concentration of power in a group of individuals who claim to oversee the interests of their society as a whole. The locus of the former is generally the city where dwell people who do not live as food producers, and indeed depend upon food producers. (Some authors claim that in a few civil cultures genuine urban centers are not present. But this is controversial.) Though there are differences between (1) preindustrial civil culture and (2) industrial/postindustrial civil culture, I will stress the overall continuities so as to focus the attention on the contrast between primal and civil cultures. Civil cultures can be discussed in terms of (1) indicators and (2) mode of transmission.

Indicators. The indicators of civilization (which I call civil culture) have been discussed by other anthropologists. I do not propose to add anything radically new to this discussion. Instead I shall simply articulate the connections with the city, the state, occupational specialization, and class stratification. The indicators all mutually imply each other in constituting civil culture, and cannot be discussed singly without the others.

1. *Exact and Predictive Sciences.* All human societies observe the world around them to look for patterns. They classify these and develop new knowledge from them. Thus, primal societies developed their own botanical systems that made it possible to domesticate plants and to develop cures for diseases (Lévi-Strauss 1966). Civil cultures built on this unacknowledged heritage and developed sciences that increasingly used more complex mathematics. This was facilitated by the invention of writing. Thus, among societies as widely different as ancient China, India, Babylon, and the Maya, astronomy arose and scanned the configurations in the starry sky in order to determine the beginning and end of an agricultural season. Engineering sprang in response to the need to construct irrigation networks, fortifications, palaces, and large places of worship. Mathematics developed because large sums of data in business transactions had to be tabulated and analyzed. Geometry's calculations of distance, mass, and volume became relevant when monumental architecture appeared (Armillas 1968). The tendency to mathematize observations reached a climax in the development of modern science under Galileo.

2. *Systematic Thought.* Questions about the meaning of existence are raised in all cultures, whether aboriginal or civil. A peculiarity of civil cultures is that there are individuals who devote much of their time—and earn a living—from raising and answering such

questions. The answers that they produce thus tend to be carefully worked out; often they attempt to draw specific principles from basic, indubitable principles. There is a sense of wholeness imparted by world views such as Confucianism, Buddhism, or Christianity even if the original ideas of the founders consisted of anecdotes and sayings. For, over the centuries, disciples wrote books and commentaries that drew out implications in the original texts. These, in turn, attracted other books and commentaries.

At the same time a skeptical, secular attitude appears. The world ceases to be accepted as a given. Redfield cites an ancient Mesopotamian document that finds love, charity, and piety empty; it admonishes that good and evil alike will be forgotten and so will be indistinguishable. The literate elite experiences "a new freedom of mind to criticize and to record" (Redfield 1953, 119). Thus, according to him, the Book of Job raises questions about why the good must suffer and wonders if there is a God; both Plato and Buddha regard the world as appearance, and subtly criticize belief in the ancient gods.

3. *All-inclusive Moral Systems*. The moral systems of primal societies are particularistic. They direct behavior within a small society and make no pretensions about being applicable to all of humankind. Reflecting on ethnographic data, Sahlins says that the badness or goodness of an action in a tribal society is never absolute, for such criteria are regarded as dependent upon a situation. For instance, while stealing from a fellow member will be condemned, done to an outsider it might not be condemned.[7] As was pointed out in the previous chapter, the political boundaries of a person's world coincide with those of his kin group in a nonstate society. Understandably, therefore, those outside the kin group either do not matter or are suspect. In contrast, in a state a person's world expands, because the state embraces villages and cities, the poor and the rich, the manual workers and their administrators. This requires moral systems applicable to all the members. Thus all-inclusive moral systems, such as Confucianism, Buddhism, Christianity, Islam. They all arose in states.

Some moral systems go further. They reach out to other societies and preach conversion and moral regeneration. Thus, the phenomenon of the missionary and the moral prophet (Redfield 1953, 55). These are not found in "precivilized folk societies." Redfield (1953, 55) notes that though the Tewa Indians have lived among the Hopi for two and a half centuries, no missionaries were sent to each other. Nor indeed does one hear of pre-Christian T'boli and Tiruray proselytizing among other peoples in Mindanao whereas Moslem preachers reached out to them. The construction of universal moral and ethical systems characterizes civil cultures. However, this can and has led to authoritarian systems of thought that look at any dissenting morality as a dangerous particularity to be crushed lest it overthrow the universal whole. Thus, in the name of Confucian norms, Chinese Confucian scholars forcibly uprooted the indigenous belief systems of the Vietnamese (Taylor 1983, 34) while Christianity and Islam persecuted heretics and nonbelievers. Thus, too, the fascism of the twentieth century. These attempts at mind control are impossible in primal villages because neither the proselytizing impulse nor the means for ensuring ideological purity exists.

4. *Substantial Architecture.* Large constructions, particularly of stone, are difficult to realize in an aboriginal culture because they require a variety of specialized skills and a high level of planning and coordination that go beyond the resources of small village-centered societies. Besides, they may not serve any useful purpose. Such skills become available in a state in response to new needs. Any state seeks to emphasize its power and authority in order to command respect from ordinary citizens; wealthy and powerful families display their wealth and stress their high status; cities defend their restricted perimeter and at the same time worry about fires. Monumental architecture, in the form of battlements, palaces, imposing places of worship, therefore, appears in a civil culture (Childe 1955). Problems in hauling materials from vast distances and in bringing them together into a harmonious whole are made possible by the presence

of full-time masons, sculptors, and architects. The development of geometry leads to precise measurements.

5. *Nonutilitarian Art.* In primal cultures, art serves to transform ordinary, everyday objects into objects of pleasure. Thus pottery, weavings, weapons, boats, and houses are given finer forms or are ornamented. Art also fosters community solidarity, for the epics, chants, and dances create a sense of togetherness while transmitting valuable lore from the past. In civil cultures, art does all these things; at the same time it multiplies objects whose connection with both practical use and community solidarity is not evident. For the emergence of a wealthy, educated social class that is not obliged to farm everyday summons the "fine arts": forms whose main purpose is to please by offering well-shaped yet imaginative products. A landscape painting, a novel, or a lyric poem has no immediate practical use. I use the word "multiply," for though lyric poems may exist in primal cultures, other forms of such nonutilitarian art forms proliferate in civil cultures. The fortunate in civil cultures can afford to pay others to invest more labor on refining particular goods and services. A good example of the "estheticization" of ordinary objects and activities is the cult that surrounds food and drink in cultures such as the French and the Japanese. Aside from the immediate gustatory and olfactory qualities of a particular recipe, its colors, texture, and manner of presentation are analyzed and contemplated. This estheticization can permeate even popular culture. At a public market at Hue, Vietnam's imperial capital, I ordered the Vietnamese version of *balut*, the unhatched but cooked duck embryo. I was pleasantly surprised to see it served in style on a tray: a metal saucer for the egg, another for the mint and fish sauce, and a small spoon.

6. *Information Storage Systems.* In primal societies, information is transmitted in oral form. There is an advantage to this: It develops an acute ear and a good memory, both of which have been lost in our society that depends heavily on the printed word. But there are also disadvantages: Despite precautions, the bearer's memory can fail; there may be no heirs to relay the information; the information may

get confined to a small, local group. It is otherwise in a civil culture. Because of the increasing commercial transactions, the stores of wealth to be inventoried, the need to record the ruler's achievements, and the state's need to monitor its members' activities (Giddens 1982, 169–70), a system of notation develops. In its most abstract form, this becomes writing. While most civil cultures have developed a script, a few, like the Incas, relied instead on a system of notation that was not a script. They knotted ropes. Through writing, information is stored and is transmitted from one generation to the next, and from one culture to another culture willing to learn the language. Information accumulates, not only in written documents, taken singly, but also in archives and libraries such as those which appeared in Imperial China, the Roman Empire, and in medieval monasteries. Today information is kept in computer disks and can be relayed over vast distances. Such stores of information become indispensable in the management of large, centralized organizations. Expanding information storages lead to greater complexity and subtlety in mathematics, the sciences, and the humanities, for one can dialogue with and critique predecessors. Meanwhile the sense of time expands into the remote past since documents of several thousand years ago are available; and it advances into the distant future, for on the basis of past trends, speculation about years ahead is possible.

Some of the material artifacts that become abundant in a civil culture, like painting, sculpture, and architecture, should also be considered information channels. Buildings, bas-reliefs, and paintings transmit easily accessible information.

All these six indicators—exact and predictive sciences, systematic thought, all-inclusive moral systems, substantial architecture, nonutilitarian art, information storage system—suggest a differentiation between mental and manual labor. Bureaucrats, teachers, scientists, and philosophers have arisen to devote their waking hours to plotting exact calendars, developing new mathematics, speculating about the nature of matter, articulating a universal morality, working out the dimensions and symbolism of material structures, critiquing paintings and music, or writing down their ideas. Marx (rather condescend-ingly) characterizes the consciousness of tribal societies as "sheeplike," for the ego is hardly differentiated from other egos. With the divi-sion of labor into the mental and the manual, abstract learning in the form of philosophy and theology becomes possible. Though he is sensitive to the inequities in this division, he nonetheless sees abstract thinking as an important stage in humankind's development. Indeed he regards the division of labor as necessary before the advent of "com-munism" in the future (Marx and Engels [1846b] 1994, 117–19).

Elite versus Popular Tradition. Another important difference be-tween primal and civil cultures lies in the mode of transmission. In primal cultures, there is a single tradition that all members share in. However, in those where differences have appeared because of owner-ship of land, the elite may emphasize the uniqueness of their knowledge.

The state both results from and intensifies class stratification. It is also the result of increasing efforts by an elite to consolidate their power over the rest of society. The locus of these efforts is the city—the state's "power-container" (Giddens 1982, 6). The state and the city, therefore, have an ambivalent nature that haunts tradi-tional civil cultures all over the world. For instance, schools have tended to cluster in the cities along with the seat of government and the major places of worship. Literacy has been, in most states, the preserve of a small, powerful elite generally residing in the cities. Until the spread of industrialization and liberal democracy in the nineteenth century, it was not considered important to organize for-mal education for the majority (Sjoberg 1960, 23, 299–300).

Thus in a civil culture, tradition divides into what Robert Redfield (1956, 41–42) calls, the "Great Tradition" and the "Little Tradition."

> In a civilization there is a great tradition of the reflective few, and there is a little tradition of the largely unreflective many. The great tradition is cultivated in schools or temples; the little tradition works itself out and keeps itself going in the

village communities. The tradition of the philosopher, theologian and literary man is a tradition consciously cultivated and handed down; that of the little people is for the most part taken for granted and not submitted to much scrutiny or considered refinement and improvement.

Though Sjoberg does not use these categories, he contrasts the lifestyle of those in higher ranks of the political, military, and economic hierarchy with that of urban workers, ordinary merchants, and peasants. The former engages in "mental, non-manual work" (Sjoberg 1960, 123–24). Culture, in the restricted sense of a cultivated intellect and senses, can be interpreted as referring to those who are familiar with their Great Tradition.[8]

The Great and Little Traditions can also be contrasted with each other in terms of their scope. The relevance of this will be discussed in a later chapter. The Great Tradition of a society tends to be part of a broader Great Tradition which covers different state societies. For instance, the Great Tradition of China is defined by practices such as Confucianism, Taoism, Mahayana Buddhism, calligraphy, and a monumental architecture where corner roof eaves curve upwards. Because these practices were exported to Vietnam, Korea, and Japan, the Great Traditions of the latter three cannot be understood without referring to the Chinese. Understandably, their educated elites have sympathized with Chinese ideas and customs because of this shared universe of symbols. At the same time, there are traditions that are particular to villages or regions within all four societies which serve to differentiate one locality from the other. For instance, though the Japanese elite imported Confucian notions that only the father's relatives matter and passed laws inspired by these, in actual fact the Japanese peasants continued recognizing the importance of both sets of grandparents (Nakane 1967, 29 ff.).

The six characteristics of a civil culture create the environment for a new consciousness. First, the individual ego begins to stand out and its interior space explored. It is worthwhile comparing medieval

Gothic sculptures, Japanese Buddhas, Borobudur reliefs, and seventeenth-century saints on the high altars of our churches such as in Cavite. They all attempt to represent, in a more naturalistic way, particular human figures, and, through the medium of their eyes and their face, to disclose the world within. Though modern art of the twentieth century seems to negate the individualizing tendency of civil culture, it in fact affirms it. For, in a Picasso or in a Dubuffet, the sensibility and the inner tensions of the painter become the paintings' theme. When both painters allude to aboriginal art, they refashion it into a channel for their anguished expressions. This preoccupation with the inner world is inevitable. After all, systems of thought, such as Brahmanism, Buddhism, Platonism, Christianity, Islam, or Existentialism, lay the burden of seeking salvation not on the kin group, but on the individual. Secondly, there is a broader "We" that takes form in a civil culture. Theologies and philosophies recognize as fellows those outside the circle of family and friends if they share the same beliefs or citizenship, or simply the same human nature. Thus, the wide variety of subjects that appear in the literature, paintings, and sculptures of civil culture: saints, goddesses, monks, kings, beggars, sailors, potters, merchants, and farmers.

Pluses and Minuses. Each type of culture has its pluses and minuses. Primal cultures classify data in a concrete manner far different from our abstract categories; yet they generate valuable information (Lévi-Strauss 1966, 15 ff.) Thus, the Agta of Mount Pinatubo in Zambales may have had a simple material culture in the 1950s; they did not have the hospitals, laboratories, libraries, and schools of lowland Christian Filipinos. However, they developed a profound knowledge of the plants and animals around them, a knowledge that they transmitted orally rather than in writing. Most Agta men easily described at least "450 plants, 75 birds, most of the snakes, fish, insects, and animals, and of even 20 species of ants" (Fox 1952, 188). There are benefits to primal culture, just as there are costs to civil culture. One benefit of primal culture is a sensitivity to the natural environment, a sensitivity that fades when a society adopts a more complex technology. Another benefit is that the individual's world is intimate and reassuring, even though enemies lurk beyond the confines of his village and its adjoining villages. In this little world, he personally knows everyone that he must be responsible to and responsible for. Moreover, precisely because full-time occupational specialization does not exist, he participates in the varied activities of his group be this in hunting, gathering, and planting; in governance; in celebrations; in healing; and in war. The several aspects of his personality are thus developed. Thus, while he may not be "individualized," he is "individuated" (Service 1966, 83–84) unlike the peasant or the average urban dweller in a civil culture. Unsettling change is controlled by collective decision in which he participates as decision maker. Contrary to our usual stereotypes, societies dependent on either foraging or on swidden cultivation are better able to meet the food requirements of all their members than those with peasants and industrial workers. Working hours are shorter because there is no need to build dikes nor irrigate fields. Foragers and swiddeners thus have more time for rest and sleep (Sahlins 1972, 11 ff.).[9]

In a civil culture, the individual's world is indeed wider and there are opportunities to hone particular skills. But these often benefit better those who are educated, have access to resources, and live in the city. The peasant, precisely as peasant, contracts obligations toward power holders residing in the town and city. He ceases to be the independent farmer that the tribesman is. "When tribute is regularized into taxation, a tribal people is on the way to becoming peasantry" (Redfield 1953, 32). In a parallel manner, full-time occupational specialization benefits those in the more mental occupations but not necessarily those in manual work. The owner of a store enjoys the experience of planning and expanding his operations, but his employees have little opportunity to develop the other aspects of their personality. Everyday they must pass through the same boring routine. Though many advances are made in the city, the full enjoyment of these has tended to be confined to a small elite with the resources. The twentieth century is unique in its efforts to open these achievements to all through universal education, public museums, and radio-television programs. Nonetheless, even in highly developed countries, it is evident that today there are many who are imprisoned in overly specialized, repetitive, and often poorly paid jobs.

For instance, to go back just a century ago: Between the 1880s and the 1910s, brilliant innovations appeared in Paris that had an impact all over the world. In painting, the Impressionists and Cezanne; in poetry, the Symbolists; in music, Debussy; in architecture, Eiffel and Guimard. French haute cuisine and haute couture pioneered in developing new, exquisite flavors and new styles of dressing. Meanwhile Henri Bergson taught at the Sorbonne; and the Curies discovered radiation. La Belle Epoque is summed up by Renoir's pink, plump, and cheerful bourgeoisie.

But many Frenchmen in the countryside were far from being pink with health. In Eugen Weber's (1976) synthesis of regional and local data on the late-nineteenth-century French peasantry, the prevailing picture is one of misery. For lack of clothes, many peasants rarely changed clothes. To keep warm during winter, whole families snuggled in with the farm animals in the barns and tried to conserve their meager food supplies by stretching their sleep. Meals consisted of gruel and soups to make up for bulk, and only occassionally of expensive wheat bread. For lack of alternatives, brackish water was drunk; wine was a rare luxury to be dreamt of. In many places, the stench of uncollected manure enveloped farmhouses and schoolhouses. Teachers were often poorly trained and had few materials with which to train the schoolchildren. Illiteracy was widespread. Only at the beginning of the twentieth century did the lot of the French peasant improve when the state began to invest in building roads, schools, and health facilities. As Robert Redfield (1953, 36) observed of peasant society in general, "the precivilized hunter or villager is preliterate, the peasant is illiterate."

Accounts of other peasant societies of the same period, for example, Japan, reveal a similar wide gulf between an oppressed peasantry and a brilliant urban elite. During the late Tokugawa period, woodblock printing and the Kabuki reached a zenith. However, the peasants were compelled to turn over as much as 60 percent of their produce to the lords. The latter needed more income to support their increasingly luxurious lifestyle. In response, the peasants sold their lands, fled to the cities to become landless artisans, or killed their infants (Nakane 1967, 50–51). Closer home, the lords of Sulu excelled in statecraft and developed a fine tradition in weaving and gong music. However, they despised the landless and destitute Bajau who risked their lives diving for pearls for them (Warren 1985, 68). They also relied on a large pool of slaves that annual raids all over Southeast Asia caught for them (ibid., 151 ff.).

Not surprisingly, though civil culture may seem eminently desirable to those like us who benefit from it, it has been rejected by those who refuse to relinquish control over their personal affairs or to pay taxes to the state. As shown above, a favorite response in many parts of the world has been flight into another country or into the wilderness.[10] In the West, joining communes, where members share the fruits of their labor together, forego attachment to an occupation and live simply—either as monks, Hutterites, socialists, or hippies—has been another recurring pattern down through the centuries. Moreover, a yearning for the simplicity and egalitarianism of "primitive" culture recurs in complex cultures (Sontag 1971). An outstanding example is Rousseau ([1754] 1990) who regarded civilization as corruptive. Resistance against incorporation into civil culture has also characterized some of the peoples of Indonesia, as suggested by the case of the Kanekes and the Batak. In China, Taoism's insistence on flight to the wilderness, on simple living, and on mutual sharing of resources can be intrepreted as another such antiurban and anticivil critique (Needham 1954, 2:104–5). Seen in this light, we can understand the ambivalent attitude of civil cultures toward primal cultures. While civil cultures look down on primal cultures as less than human, they also look up to them as more than human.[11] Like the Moslem Sundanese who asks for prayers from the animist Kanakes, the lowland Christian Luzon peasant buys Igorot or Hanunoo beads soaked in coconut oil, on the supposition that they must be powerful amulets since they come from people who live beyond his known world.

Chiefdom Culture

We turn to a third type of culture which I call "chiefdom culture." Admittedly, the term is awkward. However, I find it to be accurate, for it is associated with a specific type of society, the chiefdom, in the same way that civil culture is associated with the state. A chiefdom is a type of polity where attempts to consolidate power and centralize authority under one paramount leader result in two layers of authority: Above the local headman is an acknowledged paramount. There may even be three layers of authority, but not more. Moreover, in contrast to state-level societies, chiefdoms are characterized by "highly generalized and functionally undifferentiated leadership roles, in which chiefly administrators occupying different levels in the political hierarchy (i.e., 'paramount' and 'district chiefs') have similar obligations and duties, though operating at different levels of integration" (Junker 2000, 66; Earle 1989; Sahlins 1958). I propose that all these features result from a chiefdom's inherent limitation. Lacking sufficient power, it has no consistent system for collecting taxes. It cannot thus multiply levels of authority nor encourage administrative specialization. While a paramount chief will pay for expert weavers, carpenters, goldsmiths, and metalsmiths, he might not be as eager to do the same for high-level administrative personnel, often priests, who specialize in such abstract quests as astronomy, mathematical study, or record keeping. The usefulness of such nonmanual quests may not be that obvious to him. And yet such quests open the door for more achievements in the realm of thought. Record keeping creates a need for writing and becomes the basis for history writing, the natural sciences, and higher mathematics. Regular mathematical inquiry leads to advances in a wide variety of fields, such as astronomy and engineering.

Nonetheless, the beginning of the separation between manual and mental labor is evident in the rituals surrounding the person of the paramount chief. An example is the famous complex of taboos that resulted from contact with the body of the paramount Hawaiian chief. Any object that he touched became charged with power, and thus taboo [*kapu*] to the commoner. This included the ground he touched (Sahlins 1958, 20–21). While these enhanced his aura, these also distanced him from everyday affairs. Moreover, the emergence of a cult around the paramount needed justification before his subjects. This justification was worked out by himself and his retinue of priests. While the paramount's dwelling might be of light materials like the rest of the population, the ceremonial center might be larger and use heavier material because this enhanced the paramount's prestige. Thus the platform-mound constructions in the southeast of the U.S. enshrined the bones of the paramount's ancestors, while some of his duties as chief were performed on the mound (Hally 1996). Through this need for ideological justification, an elite tradition springs up, separately from the commoners' tradition. The increasing resources available to the paramount will encourage him to commission artifacts whose cost and esthetic spectacle outweigh its immediate practical use. An example from Hawaii are the paramount's capes that were made from hundreds of yellow and red bird feathers sewn together.

The Advent of Civil Culture

When did civil culture begin in the Philippines? Understandably, the question of origins has been a touchy one. In Jose Rizal's time, discussions of "civilization" had racist overtones. In that heyday of imperialism, it was claimed that Western Europe was more advanced than the rest of the world because the whites had bigger and more developed brains (Harris 1979, 80). Rizal ([1890] 1961) thus annotated the *Sucesos* of Antonio de Morga to show that pre-Hispanic Filipinos had a highly developed culture that colonialism would corrupt. But Rizal's contemporary, the Ilocano Isabelo de los Reyes, took a different tack. He immersed himself in folklore, in prehistory, and in the ethnographies of the primal peoples of his day, particularly the neighboring non-Hispanized uplanders of the Cordillera. This cofounder of the nationalist Iglesia Independiente de Filipinas and promoter of labor unions believed in describing Filipino societies three-dimensionally. De los Reyes (1890, 235) reported, for instance, that the ancient custom of slaying strangers upon the death of a wealthy man, was still being practiced in some Ilocos villages. His pride of country was based not on an idealized, Edenic past but on an acceptance of the Filipino with all his shadows and highlights.[12]

Against Racist Theories. Two things should be noted about the question concerning the origins of civil culture: (1) age and achievement have nothing to do with civility; (2) race has nothing to do with it either.

The indigenous cultures of the Philippines are ancient and well-adapted to particular niches in the environment. The Tabon Caves were inhabited around 40,000 B.C. (Casiño 1982, 57). It appears that their residents are related to the present-day Agtas who have, over millennia, developed a profound understanding of the forest. However, most Filipinos belong to the Mongoloid race which came in from southern China via Austronesian speakers. The Philippine "stock" of languages branched out from the Austronesian about 1300 B.C. (Thomas and Healey 1962). Contrary to the popular misconception today, the Philippines was not peopled by "waves of migration" composed of "Malays" and "Indonesians" coming from the south. During the period of the empires, migrants did sail to the shores of Manila Bay from Sumatra, as suggested by oral tradition and a Bulacan barrio called "Palimbang" (Veneracion 1986, 53, 59). They may have escaped from tribute (Casiño 1982, 64, 169). But for sure, they found Luzon and the Visayas already populated, however sparsely, with fellow Austronesian speakers.

One niche that our ancestors mastered was the sea. Even without the compass, they could find their way across the sea by observing wave patterns, marine flora, and fauna. They constructed boats that were swift but well-balanced because of an innovation: the outrigger. The houses they built, being on stilts, could stand in the water, as well as on land. Unlike in French peasant houses where, up until the nineteenth century, the residents shared quarters with their animals (Weber 1976, 162), our ancestors neatly segregated themselves from their animals by staying upstairs in the elevated rooms. The taste of the sea suffused their cooking with its fine aroma, for they flavored food with fermented shrimp paste and fish sauce. (Indeed this affinity for the sea continues to give many other aspects of our culture today a particular tang.) They created epics whose nuanced interpretations of human emotions continue to move us today. The Ifugao's communal epic is listed by the UNESCO as a masterpiece of intangible heritage that belongs to all of humankind. They wove textiles, like the T'boli *tinalak*, whose many complex designs are based on memory, rather than on written patterns, and thus are more challenging to execute.

Nonetheless, though we should be proud of all these, we should be wary of using terms like "civil"—or for that matter "urban"—without careful analysis.

The second point to consider about civil culture is that this has nothing to do with "innate intelligence," still less with race. Twentieth-century anthropologists point out that societies differ in their achievements, not because of biological inheritance, but because of culture which, by definition, is learned by anyone who grows up within a particular society. Culture, in turn, according to cultural ecologists and Marxists, is influenced by other variables. For the former, technology, economy, and demography influence people's behavior (Harris 1979); for the latter, economic relations determine culture (Kahn and Llobera 1981). Thus the Visayan and the Javanese do not differ at all in race, moreover both come from the same family of languages. Yet by the sixteenth century, they had differed greatly from each other in level of development. By then the Javanese had behind him over a thousand years of kingdom and empire, expertise in rearing mountainlike stone temples, and a sophisticated understanding of the theologies of Brahmanism and Buddhism. The Visayan had none of these. But, for that matter, neither did the Dyak of Borneo nor the Batak of Highland Sumatra. Why then the difference in achievement? Clearly race as an explanatory variable is irrelevant. Anthropologists thus prefer to look for variables like the means of production, proximity to major trade routes, the natural environment then, size and density of population, the political controls and organization in place. Some of these variables, like location, are the product of chance.

The question concerning the origins of civil culture is closely connected with the origins of the state which, in turn, is a response to variables listed in the preceding paragraph. Political complexity in pre-sixteenth-century Philippines varied according to region. A chiefdom, possibly even a state, was in place in the Butuan that sent red parrots and tortoiseshell to the Chinese emperor as its tribute in 1003 (Scott 1989, 3). However, in Chinese eyes, Butuan ranked lower than Champa (now Southern Vietnam) with which Butuan had close relations (Patanñe 1996, 106). In Luzon and the Visayas, some coastal settlements, like Tondo, were old chiefdoms by the sixteenth century, whereas inland, mountain settlements tended to remain small and independent of each other—indeed down to our days.[13] Doeppers and Xenos (1998, 1) estimate the total population of Filipinos under Spanish control in 1591 to have been only 668,000 and that the colony's population "grew at a low rate of only 0.41 percent per annum to reach 1.6 million by 1800—producing an entire archipelago with only one-fifth the population of Java." The low population density and the thick forests made it relatively easy to escape incorporation into urban centers and demands for taxes by ambitious overlords. Not surprisingly, only the sixteenth-century port of Tondo produced fine, silky *husi* (Scott 1992, 77) whereas other lowland communities made cotton weaves.

Coastal settlements that were already under Islam and those that were not likewise differed from each other. Expectedly, not only would the former be more statelike than the latter, they would have a civil culture. For Islam opened the doors to the knowledge and skills of long-established Islamic states in Southeast Asia, whether in statecraft, theology, or the arts.

Civil Genesis

Seven indicators of civil culture were listed. Let us focus on four of them. In general, a separation between mental and manual labor, together with a division into social classes, was operative in the coastal chiefdoms. A complex etiquette surrounded the datu's person. Commoners were obliged to squat while addressing him and speak in lowered tones (Chirino [1604] 1969; Scott 1994, 136). He endowed serving plates and cups with a sacred power that made commoners ill should they touch them, according to the missionary Lisboa (Junker 2000, 124). His women were kept (*binokot*) in an inner room of his longhouse. His wives were carried on the shoulders of his slaves when they left the compound (Bobadilla [1640] 1990, 337; Alcina [1668b] n.d., 3:65). Among Tagalogs, different kinds of religious specialists had appeared (Plasencia [1589b] 1903), suggesting various specializations in the mental domain. As mentioned in the earlier essays, both Visayan and Tagalog aristocrats had many retainers to attend to their various needs.

A Morality Beyond the Kin. As mentioned previously, the moral system of non-Christian, non-Moslem Filipinos in the past was particularistic. It centered almost exclusively on obligations to the kin who was often a fellow villager as well. Though trade flourished between barangays, when people wanted slaves, sacrificial victims, or heads, they raided other barangays. It is thus hard to imagine that there existed a moral system in place that preached obligations to care for even the fellow who was anonymous, not a neighbor, and not a relative. Still, the beginnings of a morality transcending the kin were in place in the chiefdoms with the datu as a bridgehead. A cult had sprung up around the datu and his body. This was carried on after death, for his mummified corpse was kept in the innermost chamber of his longhouse (Alcina [1668b] n.d., 3:261). If we grant that, in a chiefdom, even nonkin were obliged to respect him as the paramount among all chiefs, then clearly a morality beyond the kin had appeared.

A More Substantial Architecture. As would be expected, more substantial buildings appeared where particular families exercised coercive, extractive powers, for instance, in the coastal lowlands.

Though the Visayan barangay relied on swidden cultivation, its datu drew on a varied source of revenues. He exacted tribute from particular sectors of his followers; he had a retinue of captives of war to work for him; he traded and raided. Thus we find that he had a longhouse that stood on eleven rows of thick wooden pillars and had wooden walls decorated with carvings. No other house in the settlement could be as tall or as big as his (Alcina [1668b] n.d., 4: 36, 41). On the other hand among the Tagalogs, fortifications had appeared in particular places possibly because of economic competition between settlements. Soliman's fort, located by the bay and river, had a wooden palisade and earthenware. Farther up the river, on the shores of the lake was Cainta which was protected by an enclosure of bamboo hedges and a wooden tower (De San Agustin [1698], 341; Conquest of the Island of Luzon [1572] 1903, 158).

Again it is in coastal settlements, particularly in Luzon, that some site planning appears. Early Spanish travellers mention that settlements in Luzon and the Visayas had irregular streets; houses were haphazardly situated; coconut trees grew on the roads (Boxer Codex [1590] 1960, 391). For indeed, whether in Renaissance Spain, Aztec Mexico, or Imperial China, the main roads of the major towns and cities were laid along an axis. (The Spaniards did not consider that in small settlements with a low population density, it was easier to attract wind from all sides if the houses were irregularly laid out.) Nonetheless, the author of the Boxer Codex ([1590] 1960, 370) noted that settlements in the Tagalog areas were more orderly than those in the Visayas. Possibly this indicates a tighter control by the local leader over the activities of his subjects; it could also be a response to increasing levels of population density.

The trading coastal towns of Luzon and the Visayas probably differed little in appearance from their counterparts throughout Southeast Asia which, including their rulers' palaces, were built of light materials such as bamboo, wood, and thatch (Reed 1971, 70). What Luzon, Visayas, and, for that matter, Mindanao lacked were the equivalents of the sacred cities of Java, Cambodia, Siam, and Burma. Built inland and of stone, the temples, walls, avenues, and moats of these sacred cities were laid out to represent Hindu-Buddhist models of the universe (ibid., 26). In addition to the simple political structure, both wheeled vehicles and the use of draft animals were absent from Luzon and the Visayas prior to the late sixteenth century (Scott 1992, 10). This hindered the development of a more substantial architecture.

In a class by itself are the awesome Ifugao stone terraces which boldly climb mountainsides. Roger Keesing argues that they were built after the sixteenth century by Ifugaos who had migrated upland to avoid Spanish demands for tribute. Not a thousand years were needed to carve them. For instance, in two years' time, terraces were built in the Loo Valley (Keesing 1962, 322–23). The terraces represent the beginnings of a more complex form of engineering. True, the terraces themselves may be the work of particular individual families sculpting their part of the hillside rather than of a team coordinating hundreds of such efforts. Regardless of how long it took to build the terraces or when they were built, I believe that the coordination involved in drawing water from mountain springs is in itself impressive.

Luxury Art. Full-time specialists in goldsmithery, silversmithing, jewelry, ironsmith works, and carpentry appeared in the lowlands because the Tagalog elite became wealthy through trade both in the islands and abroad in Malacca (Scott 1992, 30–31, 77 ff.). A glimpse of the high level of sophistication of their prowess in goldsmithery is given us by extant examples where hundreds of tiny gold wires loop together to form a dazzling mesh. Equally expensive in terms of man-hours is a liquor that was so exquisite that the Spanish author of a Tagalog-Spanish dictionary defined it as "Dalisay—a liquor 24-carat strong, which burns without fire" (Scott 1992, 82).

The Storage of Information. Vital information was beginning to be stored, though in limited form. Native scripts were in use, for instance, among the Tagalogs (Chirino [1604] 1969, 46). However, contrary to common belief, these were not that diffused all over Luzon and the Visayas. In his overview, Scott (1994) makes no mention of them as existing in the Cordillera or Cagayan Valley. The script used by the Visayans was derived from the Tagalog and may have entered the Visayas only in the 1660s (ibid., 94). Moreover, even among Tagalogs (as among Hanunoo and Tagbanua today), the script seems to have been used to record love poems and letters rather than to record business transactions and the chronicles of rulers. It is well known that in Mesopotamia, writing had developed millennia earlier and had flourished in conjunction with those two latter factors (Goody 1986, 49ff). Transmission of information among sixteenth-century non-Islamized Filipinos was thus still largely oral. Moreover, the indigenous script was syllabic; the vowel endings were not always clear. While these ambiguities may not have mattered in poetry, they could cause problems in prose communication where exactitude is important (Lumbera 1986, 25). Perhaps this ambiguity would have been eventually corrected, but the native script was supplanted by the Latin script which recorded and fixed sounds with more accuracy.

It may be that a civil culture had appeared in Butuan by the tenth century A.D. Future research will throw more light. In the case of coastal settlements in sixteenth-century Luzon and the Visayas, instead of an extensive civil culture, a chiefdom culture was in flower. Thus, after surveying Southeast Asia, particularly Java, the geographer Robert Reed (1971, 1978) observed that the uniqueness of the Philippines in the region lay in that full-blown urbanism in Luzon and the Visayas emerged under Western influence. In contrast great cities like Hue, Angkor, Ayutthaya, and Pagan were already centuries old when Western colonizers came. To my mind, the spread of Islam in coastal Tagalog settlements would have transplanted a mature civil culture: the Islamic.

The Spanish period is often dismissed today as "the colonial period." In fact it was more than that. During this period, civil culture, in this case the Western, finally plunged deep roots in the lowland, coastal settlements of Luzon and Visayas. The Spanish period thus plays a role in Filipino culture far different from that of the Dutch period in Java or the French period in Vietnam. In the latter two, pre-Western civil cultures were already large, ancient trees at Western contact in the sixteenth century; in pre-1565 coastal Luzon and Visayas on the other hand, elements of civil culture were more like saplings attempting to grow. Noteworthy, too, is that, like Java and Vietnam, pre-Hispanic Mesoamerica had civil cultures that produced a Mexico-Tenochtitlan that surpassed Western cities in size and wealth, towering stone pyramids, an advanced calendar, and a mathematics that knew the zero. Questions can be raised about how urban pre-1571 Manila and Tondo were, but not about Intramuros de Manila.

Chiaroscuro

Under Spain, an all-inclusive moral system, Catholic Christianity, spread. This was accompanied by an abstract, speculative system of thought, Scholasticism that was transmitted via an exact script, stored in libraries, and taught by professional thinkers. Starting in the nineteenth century, a skeptical Rationalism deriving from the Enlightenment gained ground.

A comparison between Ilocanos and Tinguians of the late nineteenth century illustrates the achievements and shortcomings of both primal and civil cultures. The two peoples are closely related linguistically, for their languages separated from each other only in the twelfth century (Fox 1965, 109). Op-artlike concentric circles are a recurring motif in the blankets of both. Tinguians may have fled to the Cordillera only during the Spanish period in order to escape the exactions of the state.

Late-nineteenth-century Tinguians lived in clusters of small villages that were independent of each other. The headman was elderly who differed little from the rest in food, clothing, and housing. He, too, farmed. Though households may have differed in wealth, each had access to land (Cole 1922, 360). In contrast the Ilocanos lived in villages, towns, and cities linked to each other and to the rest of the Philippines. Differences in wealth and status were marked. The cabezas de barangay came from families with high status and elected the mayor or gobernadorcillo. A Spanish government report of the nineteenth century laments that poor *indios* were losing their lands to the Chinese mestizos, and that the parish priests should report on the matter (BRAM Real Cedula de 2 Febrero 1818).

Tinguians of the interior still engaged in headhunting expeditions against neighboring Tinguian villages down the road or over the mountain to proclaim male valor or to end a mourning ritual (Cole 1922, 372). While these were no longer done by the Ilocanos, divisions of another sort existed among them: divisions by class and, vis-à-vis the Spaniards, by ethnicity. Despite these divisions and petty jealousies between families, however, the Ilocanos were able to form large armies to revolt against the Spaniards in 1762, under Diego Silang (Routledge 1979, 20ff.), and to mobilize the region against the Americans in 1900–1901 (Scott 1986, 67). Diego's Tinguian allies were unable "to coordinate among themselves" (Routledge 1979, 21, 38).

The average Tinguian and Ilocano both lived in cogon-thatched bamboo houses where the sidings were made of vertically halved bamboos (De los Reyes 1888, 8). But a more substantial architecture had appeared in Ilocano towns: two-story houses of stuccoed brick with sliding shell windows and imposing churches with curving buttresses. Within was a variety of ornately carved statues, furniture, and paintings by local masters. One son of the Ilocos, Juan Luna, gained fame in Madrid as a painter. Among both the Tinguian and the Ilocanos, traditional lore was transmitted orally. However, writing in Latin script had appeared among the Ilocanos, while formal schools were opened on the elementary level. Those seeking a career in the Church went to Vigan's seminary for higher learning; others with ambitions in law and medicine went to Manila's colleges. Another Ilocano, Isabelo de los Reyes, mastered Western learning and could critique its claims concerning racial superiority. The Ilocanos had thus entered into new fields of endeavor not open among the Tinguian. Still, this high culture was not accessible to the average Ilocano peasant, unless he went to school or became wealthy.

The Spaniards emphasized the division of labor, and made this possible through a state that guaranteed the extraction of surpluses from the countryside to the city. Thus, the ordinary Ilocano had to pay the *tributo,* a tax laid on each family unit; to yield the *comun,* an annual contribution to community purposes; to render personal services on public works; to provide guard duty; and to garden for priests and officials. These taxes compelled the ordinary man to share part of his earnings to support government officials and weighed on the poor (Routledge 1979, 9). In contrast, among the Tinguian where the older, primal tradition of no taxes prevailed, specialization in occupations was minimal, and each settlement self-sufficient. And yet, despite the vertical divisions among the Ilocanos, a broader sense of community, transcending kin and locality, appeared among them rather than among the Tinguians. Precisely because Tinguians were independent even of each other, suspicions between kin and locality were commonplace.

Had not the Spaniards come in, would a more complex society combining both egalitarianism and occupational specialization have developed? Many in the Philippines today would say "yes." I disagree. William Henry Scott characterizes sixteenth-century Tagalog culture as having two contrasting qualities. On the one hand it seems "simple, even primitive." For, except for boatbuilding, it resembles the present culture of "interior tribes"—which Scott, the adopted son of a Sagada family, knew well. Thus, the use of G-strings or keeping a corpse fully clothed in the house until it putrefied. On the other hand it "was sophisticated and rich to the point of luxury." It had red nail polish, eyeshades for falling asleep, and exquisite liqueur that took many man-hours to produce. How then was this elegance possible with such simple technology? (Let us note that the plow and the wheel found in neighboring kingdoms were not present locally.) Scott (1992, 83) finds the answer in "techniques for exploiting human populations," specifically (1) in raids and (2) in usurious practices which sought to reduce the debtor into a slave. (Under Spain, these sporadic practices were superseded by institutionalized techniques for extracting a percentage of an ordinary man's earnings, for instance, through taxation from a wide number of subjects.) Moreover, consider the Ifugaos who were not Hispanized. Ethnographies of the early part of the twentieth century reveal sharp divisions in wealth: the rich, who had more rice fields, lived in big houses under which stretched out like a snake, the long, expensive wooden seat called *hagabi*. The landless were despised; landless men had little chances of getting married (Goldman [1937] 1961, 171).

Many of the criticisms leveled against the Spanish system that prevailed in the sixteenth to nineteenth-century Philippines are justified from our present perspective which values democracy and human rights. On the other hand, the inequities were not peculiar either to colonialism in general or to the Spanish version of it. They were common to many pre-twentieth societies that had no democracy, and no concept of a redistributive welfare state. For instance, much of the resentment of the French peasant toward the nobility centered on the issue of taxes which were many and pressed on him, but spared the nobility (Furet and Richet 1973, 41). Discussions of the costs of Spanish/Western tradition thus need to be examined within the context of the period.

Since the Americanization of the Philippines, the Spanish civil tradition has become a virtual dark continent to many Filipinos. Surely, however, a civil tradition that gave Rome, Western Christendom, Judaism, and Islam dazzling thinkers such as Seneca, Ignacio de Loyola, Moises Maimonides, and Ibn Rushd (Averroes) must be more than shadows. By the sixteenth century, the Spaniards had behind them over two thousand years of urban tradition.

They had been apprentices of the Phoenicians, the Greeks, and the Romans, and had developed their own version. Bad government and lack of popular participation plagued the monarchy, but not necessarily the municipalities. According to the American anthropologist Nutini (1972), Spain led the rest of Europe in urbanization until the rise of the Italian city-states during the early Renaissance. During the early Middle Ages, cities governed themselves for ordinary citizens could vote, but gradually lost their autonomy to the jealous Crown from the thirteenth to the fourteenth centuries onwards (O'Callaghan 1975, 269 ff., 447 ff.). Today Spanish municipalities are self-governing and actively promote their projects before outsiders. What elements of this tradition are still relevant to us today? Two come to mind.

First is the vivid sense of community on the level of the municipality. Many Spanish municipalities have a tradition from the Middle Ages of owning communal land which have helped the poor and have paid for public services (Carr 1966, 203, 273–74). There is a strong civic pride that expresses itself in the care lavished on urban planning, on public buildings, and on public spaces. "The medieval Spanish town was above everything else a work of unity, a work of art. The town was constructed of a piece with harmony, with beauty, and with devotion. Everyone lent a hand for the labor . . . Use was seldom conceived as separate from beauty" (Crow 1985, 128–29). This enthusiasm for civic art and public spaces continues to enliven modern cities in Spain and Spanish America. For the Spaniard, the ideal life was one led, not in isolated farms or in the confines of the kin, but rather one lived in common within a broader community, precisely within the civitas, understood as the city.

The Laws of the Indies, which was the basic legal framework for the Americas and the Philippines, thus lays out detailed regulations concerning the plan and layout of the new cities with an eye to practicality, comfort, and beauty.[14] According to Book 4, Section 7, Law 9, the size of the main plaza "should be in proportion to the number of the people (*vezinos*)" (Consejo de la Hispanidad 1943, vol. 2). Being a public space, the plaza was made attractive by raising dignified buildings around it. Care was also taken to ensure that new buildings should harmonize with existing, older ones without having to copy their style. Though buildings in traditional Hispanic towns were built at different periods and in different styles, they form a visual unity.[15] Thus, the dignity exuded by Vigan, Taal, and Silay.[16] Moreover, each town was to have a commons for the use of all, whether rich or poor.[17] A history of the rise and decline of municipal commons in the Philippines has yet to be made. Still, they did form part of the framework of government during the Spanish period. It is fashionable today to criticize Western "individualism," all the while ignoring that Latin urbanism builds up the community on the municipal level.

Second is the respect given by the Hispanic tradition to abstract speculation and to learning. True, because of severe Church censorship, the development of modern science in seventeenth- to nineteenth-century Spain was arrested. Nonetheless, it is worth noting that wherever Spaniards have raised cities, they would, within a matter of decades, open schools both for Spaniards and the locals. This was the case in the Americas. This likewise was the case here. The University of Santo Tomas was opened in 1611. At the start this catered largely to the creoles. But by the late eighteenth century, in a paper read by Fidel Villarroel, OP, at the March 2004 conference in Manila on Legazpi's legacy, university records indicate that most students were of mestizo and *indio* ancestry. Meanwhile, the Jesuits opened schools for the sons of native leaders (De la Costa 1961, 188–89, 358–59). Of course, the schools tended to cater to a small elite. But this emphasis typified other civil cultures as well prior to the nineteenth century (Cipolla 1969, 65 ff.). With the advent of democracy and industrialism, attention was given to the ordinary citizen and to the worker who needed specialized skills. Universal public education thus became an urgent issue. In 1825 and in 1857, the Spanish government passed laws making formal, public education on the primary level compulsory in Spain (*EUIEA* 1925, 1738). Shortly after, in 1863, they passed the same for the Philippines. In his overview of education in nineteenth-century Asia, the Swedish economist Gunnar Myrdal (1968,

3:1632–34) singles out the governments of Japan and Spanish Philippines for their commitment to public education. Unfortunately, many continue to believe that public education began only with the Americans! That the quality of schools in nineteenth-century Philippines was uneven is true. But so was it in a major world leader like nineteenth-century France (Weber 1976, 303). Still, through the better schools passed such poor boys like Emilio Jacinto and Apolinario Mabini who absorbed the Spanish civil tradition and used its key concepts in envisioning a new nation and a new republic.

Democratic and Nationalist Ideals in Conflict

The claims of democracy and nationalism do not always coincide with each other. Looking back to the past, the democrat seeks an order where all individuals are truly equal to each other in opportunities. On the other hand a particular type of nationalist wants a splendid past with a rich material culture: court ceremonials and temples. It is difficult, however, to imagine a society of the past that was radically egalitarian yet, at the same time, had a dazzling material culture. Someone had to shoulder the cost. In the recent past, some of the most radically egalitarian cultures were the Agtas, Ilongots, and Hanunoo. But this came at a cost: Their material culture is much simpler than that of the hierarchic societies of coastal Visayas and Luzon in the sixteenth century or of Ifugao in the 1900s.

There is, of course, a way out of this dilemma and that is by fostering a more modest and more realistic nationalism that takes pride in the less spectacular but still solid achievements of our indigenous ancestors: their mythology, epics, botany, jewelry, carpentry, shipbuilding, and navigational skills. Such was Isabelo de los Reyes's position; such is mine as well.

Where then does this situate Spanish influence? My approach to this is pragmatic. The costs of having a civil culture are enormous. Yet in the world today, or over the past two hundred years as nation-states have expanded all over the world and become the dominant political organization, developing a civil culture has become an inescapable necessity. The Spanish contribution has then this significance. Elements of civil culture had taken root in particular coastal towns of Luzon and the Visayas, particularly those that were converting to Islam. (Among the Taosugs who had originally migrated from Butuan it was, of course, in bloom even before Islamization.) Spanish influence enabled this tree to mature; elsewhere in other areas of Luzon and the Visayas, particularly in the hinterlands and uplands, it introduced civil culture. In other Asian countries, ancient civil cultures met the British, Dutch, and French when they came. Here, our earliest examples of stone public buildings, portrait and landscape paintings, written chronicles, and libraries do not go back beyond the seventeenth century.

Because civil culture has thus far implied occupational specialization and the separation between mental and manual labor, we should not be surprised to realize that the civil culture introduced by Spain has been elitist. Indeed one response to it has been flight into the wilderness. But this elitism has characterized other civil cultures as well in Southeast Asia and elsewhere, under their own rulers, before the advent of democracy. Hence a similar response: flight.

Undoubtedly, we should critique Hispanized Filipino civil culture from our present democratic perspective. However, we should be equally open to the possibility that it may have some positive features, and that such features may help us in constructing a more egalitarian culture. For instance, Filipinos today criticize the fact that in Spanish-designed towns, the houses of the wealthy and the powerful cluster around the focal point: the plaza. The critique is indeed justified and we should work to change the situation. At the same time, however, let us remember that the plaza and the rapidly vanishing municipal communal lands represent public space that was meant to be accessible to all residents, rich or poor, old or young, men or women. This sense of public we can enjoy in Vigan and other Hispanic towns in Luzon and the Visayas, where residents, rich and poor, congregate at the plaza, in the afternoons. But we miss this sense of public in fenced-in subdivisions built since 1945, or in post-1980s shopping malls which belong to private individuals. In working for a future society where the division between mental and manual labor will have lessened, shared public areas like plazas, parks, municipal libraries, and state schools are crucial. This Latin legacy enables different groups with conflicting interests to communicate with each other.

Notes

1. Sources for this are Ekadjati (1995) and Garna (1987). Various theories have been advanced concerning the origins of the Kanekes. One is that when the kingdom of Pajajaran fell before the armies of Moslem Banten, many of its citizens fled into the hills. Another is that the Kanekes were originally Hindus who refused to accept triumphant Islam. Still another is that the Kanekes may have originally constituted a mandala, "an unpolluted place for realizing religious ardor," where they voluntarily imposed extraordinary taboos on their behavior (Ekadjati 1995, 62–63). Old Javanese manuscripts speak of such types of mandala. The Kanekes may not be an example of a primal people resisting the state. Nonetheless, their previous way of life had been extremely simple and was on the level of simple, primal societies. They, thus, are a good example of a people who reject the social and technological complexity of the larger society.

2. Lourdes Rausa Gomez (1967) came to these conclusions after reviewing the literature on Sri-Vijaya and Madjapahit. There certainly is no indication in the classic works of Wolters and Hall on Sri-Vijaya that Luzon, Visayas, and Mindanao were part of that empire. Why indeed should the kings of that empire have bothered with those northern islands? They had enough problems controlling the lords, under them or near them, who sought to break their monopoly on the trade with China. And in the mountains were the unconquered Batak.

3. For instance, Childe (1955), White (1949), Steward (1955), Adams (1966), Armillas (1968), Sahlins (1968), and Baer (1986). It would be too easy to accuse them of racism and discrimination. In fact their definition of "civilization" excludes their Germanic ancestors of the first century B.C. but would definitely include the Maya and the Chinese of that period. Moreover, some of them, like Childe and White, admired Marxist theory on the emergence of stratification. Others, like Sahlins and Baer, point out the problematic aspects of civilization. Though Baer accepts that it has been an "inevitable phase in cultural evolution," it has created a host of problems like poverty, racism, and pollution. Our only hope for survival is "to work toward an authentically progressive stage" (Baer 1986, 9).

4. However, in the rest of the Anglo-American world, for instance, among historians, "culture" and "civilization" are sometimes not distinguished from each other. The one outstanding exception is Arnold Toynbee (1972) who listed all known civilizations and attempted to explain how they arose in response to challenges from the environment. In French anthropology and history, *civilisation* is used interchangeably with *culture* à la Tylor. The problem is that by not distinguishing between the two concepts, it becomes difficult to identify the differentiating features of complexly organized societies (e.g., Shang China or Moslem Maguindanao) vis-à-vis more simply organized societies that preceded them (e.g., pre-Shang cultures or pre-Moslem Mindanao cultures) or other such societies.

5. A good example of this is the definition of "civilization" given by Clifford Jolly and Fred Plog (1978) in their introductory textbook on physical anthropology and archaeology.

6. This point is emphasized by Leslie White (1949, 373) who sympathized with Marxist approaches to social analysis. Though White uses the term "civilization," he also uses another, "civil society." Unfortunately this second term has a tradition behind it that cannot be ignored. It is used to denote the vast majority of citizens in a state society who are not working for the government, especially those citizens who wish to actively participate by organizing themselves into associations. For this reason, I prefer to use "civil culture."

7. Sahlins uses data concerning the Siuai of the Pacific and the Navajo of the U.S. Southwest. He quotes this example from Clyde Kluckholn's ethnography on the Navajo. "The rules vary with the situation. To deceive when trading with foreign tribes is a morally accepted practice. . . There is an almost complete absence of abstract ideals" (in Sahlins 1968, 20). Kluckhohn notes that the only conduct that is condemned without qualification is incest.

8. In a similar vein, the Javanese distinguish between *alus* and *kasar*. According to Geertz (1960, 232): "Alus means pure, refined, polished, polite, exquisite, ethereal, subtle, civilized, smooth. A man who speaks flawless high-Javanese is alus, as is the high-Javanese himself. A piece of cloth with intricate, subtle designs painted onto it is alus. An exquisitely played piece of music or a beautifully controlled dance step is alus. . . Kasar is merely the opposite: impolite, rough, uncivilized: a badly played piece of music, a stupid joke, a cheap piece of cloth."

9. Sahlins (1972) thus calls primal societies the "Original Affluent Society."

10. There is another irony in this insistence that the Philippines was part of Madjapahit and Sri-Vijaya. Casiño (1982, 63–64, 169) raises the possibility that some of the subjects of those two empires may have fled northwards toward Mindanao, Visayas, and Luzon precisely in order to escape the taxation and tribute imposed by those states.

11. Because inland villages in forested areas often relied on swidden cultivation as their primary subsistence base, they inevitably tended to be smaller in size.

12. De los Reyes thus calls himself "brother of the wild Aetas, Igorots, and Tinguians" (Scott 1982) and asserts that "There are Aetas who are more intelligent than the Tagalogs. And people know that Tagalogs are on the same intellectual level as the European" (Retana 1890, 43). William H. Scott appreciated De los Reyes both as a scholar and as a nationalist. Scott (1982) says that if Rizal was the First Filipino, then De los Reyes was the First Filipino Nationalist.

13. Patanñe dates Tondo back to the tenth century because of a convergence between data in Chinese chronicles and in the excavated copper plate. If he is correct, we may surmise that it must have been a chiefdom and that there may have been constraints that kept it from developing into a state or from developing a more civil culture. One was the low population density and the thick forests. It was relatively easy for entire families to escape the exactions of an ambitious ruler. However, such conditions would not have dampened the desire to trade. Thus, enterprising traders from Luzon engaged in commerce in Malacca and elsewhere in the region (Pires 1971). Some became wealthy and influential in Malacca (Scott 1992, 30–31). This, of course, enabled them to participate in the civil culture of the Malays.

14. The Laws of the Indies, Book 4, Section 7, Law 10 (Consejo de la Hispanidad 1943, vol. 2) stipulates that "the streets should be wide in cold countries, and narrow in warm countries." Wide, to allow more sun; narrow, to create shade.

15. James Michener, whose sharp eye cannot be doubted, says that an important Spanish value is the desire for *ambiente*. The Spaniard will travel miles to find a spot with ambiente, with graciousness and charm, be this a restaurant, a vacation spot, or a city (1968, 53). Thus, the care for a town's appearance.

16. These town centers were not only for Spaniards. The most prosperous and most beautiful quarter in Vigan is called Mestizo, sometimes Kasanglayan after the Chinese mestizos who were the offspring of Chinese (Sanglay) and native unions. Malolos's historic quarter is called either Kamestisuhan, or Pariancillo, indicating its Chinese mestizo origin. Taal had only a few Spanish-blooded families among the elite. The case of Silay is unique among provincial towns and cities. It has a substantial number of families of European descent because of the sugar plantations.

17. Communal lands (*ejidos*), according to the Laws of the Indies, Book 4, Laws 13 and 14 (Consejo de la Hispanidad 1943, vol. 2), should be in "sufficient quantity," to be used for recreation and for grazing both work and meat animals. A popular term for communal lands in the Ilocos, that is, common to a kin group, is the Spanish-derived term: *comun.*

More Original than We Think

Las filipinas no saben aun desmayarse.
Filipino women still do not know how to faint.

—Jose Rizal 1887, *Noli me tangere*

SOCIETIES THAT HAVE NOT LOST their political independence can behave nonetheless like cultural colonies. Consider the German states before unification in 1871. From the sixteenth to the nineteenth century, France fought to keep the many German states independent of each other, for fear that they might form one powerful state. The French crown contracted alliances with some, notably in the Catholic West and South, and warred with others, especially Prussia. Yet the elite of many German states, including Prussia, looked up to France as a model. (Note the German expression: "Happiness is to be like God in France.") Complained a writer (Ergang 1966, 25) in 1680:

> For us Germans hardly a piece of clothing is proper unless it was made in France; nay even the French razors cut our German beards better than any others, the French scissors manicure the nails better, and French tweezers pull out the hairs better than ours. The clocks run better if they were made by the Germans in Paris.

The eighteenth-century German aristocracy derided German and German literature. They spoke with each other in French. As a result, French words abound in German, often in their original spelling. Though Frederick the Great of Prussia warred against the French king in 1757, he was a Francophile in his readings and in his speech. He confessed that "since the days of my youth I have not read a German book and I speak German no better than a coachman" (Ergang 1966, 26). He made of his court a center of French culture (Tenbrock 1968, 147–48; Gebhardt 1955, 2:278–79). From 1802 onward, Napoleon drew chunks and pieces of the German states into his empire. However, in alliance with other European monarchies, the Germans waged a successful War of Liberation in 1813. German nationalism was kindled. Educated Germans rediscovered their language, began to study their past, and investigated their folklore past and present. Indeed folkloric studies all over the world have been inspired by the German example, notably by the works of Herder.

To turn to our part of the world: Java has looked up to India as a model in many things from statecraft to sculpture. This seems natural to us because of the similarities in culture between the two. But these "similarities" are really the result of over a thousand years of interaction. In fact there are incongruities between Javanese and Indian cultures. Both the Javanese and the Balinese adopted in modified form the Indian caste system which divides society into priest, warrior, merchant, and manual laborer. Below all are the untouchables. In India members of the priestly and warrior castes are descendants of white-skinned Aryan-speaking cowherds, which include the Europeans; while members of the merchant and laboring castes are dark-skinned Dravidians, the original peoples of the subcontinent. By Indian standards, both the Javanese and the Balinese are dark-skinned peoples. Moreover, it is rather surprising that in W. Stutterheim's 1935 report on castes in Bali, the three upper castes of priest, warrior, and merchant constitute only 7 percent of the population while the manual workers, called *kaula,* or *sudra,* constitute the vast majority (Coedes 1964, 56). Another instance of incongruity: Before contact with India, the Javanese, like other Austronesian-speaking peoples, recognized women's right to equal inheritance. Women thus had a status they did not enjoy in India. While in India, the gods and goddesses are clearly differentiated from each other, in Hindu Javanese bas-reliefs, they, including Shiva, may wear unisex clothes (Suleiman 1986, 172–73). And yet, both in India and Java, Shiva so burns with wild energy that his symbol is the phallus.

The Filipino's openness to Western ways of thinking and doing is often attributed solely to colonialism. Moreover, even Filipinos characterize their culture as "imitative" or "derivative." How well-founded are these allegations?

Civility's Prestige

I would like to show that there is another side to this story. The introduced culture, first of the Spaniards, then of the Americans, was one that had developed within the context of the state and the city. In contrast, the culture of most sixteenth-century Philippine societies, outside the sultanates of Sulu and Maguindanao, had thus far been that of small, self-contained, and sovereign villages. No civil culture had spread throughout Luzon and the Visayas to challenge the invading culture as an equal. In contrast, when Westerners entered the lowlands of other Southeast Asian societies outside the interior of Borneo and Eastern Indonesia, they met societies with several centuries behind them of civil culture, and with their own ways of dealing with the more complex context of a state and a city. Such societies could thus more easily distance themselves from the new culture. This was not the case in the Philippines. Yet Filipinos have not been merely passive recipients. They, too, transformed influences to conform to their own needs in the Philippines where, as we saw, a chiefdom culture, rather than a civil one, was in place.

The following points should be made:

1. The qualitative difference between primal and civil culture matters, for it affects all spheres of activity: from kin relations to the economy to the arts and learning. All over the world civil culture enjoys more prestige than primal culture because of its developed technology, its association with powerful urban centers, and its highly varied material products.

2. Few societies have negotiated the transition from primal to civil culture without an outside model. Ancient Mesopotamia, Egypt, the Indus Valley, Northern China, the Valley of Mexico, and the Andes in Peru are examples of states that arose using wholly indigenous models. The civil cultures that developed without an outside model can be called "primary." Those of other states that were inspired by them can be called "secondary." There are two ways by which a secondary civil culture forms: (a) the elite of an emerging independent state may borrow from the civil culture of another or (b) members of a society that is the colony of a state may either borrow or be forced to borrow elements of their ruler's civil culture. Northern Germany and the Scandinavian countries were not colonized either by Rome or by France. But they have looked southward to these. Similarly Japan was not colonized by China; nor Java, Sumatra, Cambodia, Siam, Burma by Indian states; nor Sulu by other Islamic states. Nonetheless the imprint upon them of outside societies is deep. Examples of societies whose civil culture was either begun or at least stimulated by outside forces during colonization are Britain, France (then Gaul), Spain, and Portugal under Rome; Vietnam and Korea under China; Luzon and Visayas under Spain.

Let us first examine the reasons behind the admiration of the Germans and the Javanese for outside cultures.

The Germans. They looked up to Rome and the other Italian cities, despite memories of the Roman invasions or wars between the Germanic peoples and Rome, because "Rome" connoted a great empire that excelled in almost everything: architecture, shipbuilding, animal husbandry, warfare, commerce, statecraft.

When the Germanic peoples entered the Roman Empire in the fifth century seeking refuge from the invading Huns, they had been living in small scattered settlements. The immediate family was the unit of organization. Beyond it, the *Sippe* was crucial during the frequent feuds. Etymologically related to the English "sib," this was a kindred, and it could be organized into an assembly of kin groups. However, except in the case of the Franks, it did not attain territorial unity (Guichard and Cuvillier 1996, 342–43). Each kindred was independent of the others (DeVries 1956, 173; Vinogradoff 1913, 631–33). Fond of war, the Germans originally were capable only of raids. They bypassed fortified cities because to attack them would have required organizing themselves into groups larger than the kindred.[1] Needed were "patience and discipline, and the temper of the Germanic warriors was not always equal to the task" (Owen 1960, 126).[2] Their material culture was comparatively simple. For instance, many lived in frame houses of rectangular construction whose walls of leaves and twigs were smeared with clay and whose roofs were thatched with grass or straw (ibid., 139 ff.). Likewise of frame construction were the assembly halls where chieftains congregated with their followers. These were large halls with tables along the halls and a high seat for the leader. Cut stone was not used extensively. As for their lore, this was transmitted orally. By the fourth century, the Germanic peoples had invented the runic script. This was used to record, not the epics, chants, and proverbs, but only "to denote ownership, or to give the name of the runic engraver, for magical purposes and for grave inscriptions" (ibid., 209).

In contrast the Romanized peoples lived in towns and large cities, some of which were fortified with stone walls. The empire was protected by armies whose leaders plotted battle strategies with complex maneuvers. The armies were capable of long drawn-out campaigns because they had auxiliary baggage trains. Within the urban centers, community life centered on huge public baths, marketplaces, libraries, amphitheaters of cut stone, concrete and marble built by the state. Ordinary people in the urban centers lived in houses of stuccoed bricks, with roofs of tiles. By the fifth century, the Romans had developed a vast store of knowledge ranging from dramas to lyric poetry, from essays to treatises. They recorded this knowledge with their efficient script and stored books in libraries and private homes (Grant 1960).

As was mentioned earlier, the migration of the Germanic peoples into the Roman Empire during the fifth century aggravated the tensions within an empire divided by conflict over the imperial office, and demoralized by increasing taxes. Using battle tactics they had learned observing the Romans at war, some Germanic chiefs and their followers conquered fortified cities and vast portions of the western Roman Empire and founded their own kingdoms on its ruins.[3] While the Frankish lord, Charlemagne, tried to revive the Roman Empire, his empire, after his death, fell apart into three kingdoms: West Francia, Lotharingia, and East Francia. East Francia, which extended from the Rhine to the Elbe River and from the Baltic Sea to the Alps, was the nucleus around which Germany formed. Though the southern part of this territory had known direct Roman rule, along the Rhine and on the foothills of the Alps, the northern part had never known it. Still, the new empire that emerged looked southward to Rome for its legitimation, as its very name implied: the Holy Roman Empire. Because the emperor was both Caesar's heir and a Christian, he had to be crowned by the bishop of Rome (Heer 1968, 11 ff.).

Despite the collapse of the empire, Roman civil institutions survived in Italy. So did Roman stone buildings, Roman law, and Latin. Constructions with arches that spanned wide distances provided models for the Germans who had previously built only wooden halls using post-and-lintels. Thus, those two expressions of royal majesty, the tower-churches of the Frankish kings and the Romanesque three-aisled churches, had wide spans made possible by the rounded arch. Similarly Roman law was an imperial system whose broad, conceptual scope linked diverse communities with conflicting interests together under a central ruler. Latin unlocked the accumulated learning and literature of the Romans and their predecessors. When in the twelfth and thirteenth centuries, the study of Roman law revived in the newly prosperous Italian cities, the Germans, like other Western Christians, took note (Holmes 1992, 134; Bloch 1961, 117). They, too, looked southward again in the fourteenth to the sixteenth centuries when the Italians created a more naturalistic art and a science that reinterpreted sensory data using mathematical reasoning. Meanwhile in France and in French-speaking Burgundy, another synthesis between Germanic culture, Roman civil culture, and Christianity was forming. This synthesis was likewise crucial to the formation of what came to be called "Western" civil culture. Medieval France developed feudalism that regulated the relations between lord and follower; chivalry that tamed the warriors' hunger for violence with a code that demanded respect for women; scholastic philosophy which proposed a systematic rational explanation for the existence of all beings; and Gothic architecture. Medieval Burgundy, a vassal of France, spawned monastic Orders such as the Cluniacs who reformed and strengthened the papacy. It created a widely imitated court ceremonial that, by exalting the sovereign's glory, helped him defend his claims against lesser lords (Heer 1968, 130–31). From the seventeenth to the nineteenth centuries, while they undermined German attempts at unification, the French pioneered in new ways of thinking and doing. Their enthusiasm for pursuing rationality resulted in dynamic forms of mathematics; Cartesian philosophy; a more efficient army, bureaucracy, and diplomatic corps; and an advanced technology. They also cultivated new forms of urbanity: the café, the restaurant, the salon, the haute cuisine. Like other Westerners, the Germans adopted these as emblems of civility.

Significantly enough, while the Germans may have been on the "defensive" toward influences coming from France, they were aggressive toward their neighbors to the east, the Slavs (ibid., 35). There German culture was looked up to and imitated, not only because Germans had migrated eastward as settlers, but also because civil culture had developed earlier among the Germans than among the Poles and Bohemians.

The Javanese and the Sumatrans. When the first century A.D. opened, the Javanese and the South Sumatrans, like other Austronesian speakers in the surrounding islands, had most likely been living in small scattered villages that were independent of each other. Sumatra, like the Batak, who, until the beginning of the twentieth century, had managed to fend off domination by outsiders. [4] Marsden ([1811] 1966, 374–75) observes that the Batak of the 1800s were divided into many "petty chiefships." Relations were brittle. "They are at the same time extremely jealous of any increase of their relative power, and on the slightest pretext a war breaks out between them" (ibid.). On coastal Sumatra, however, some chiefs during the first century A.D. began to exert dominion over others. Over time, their exercise of power gave rise to monarchical states. Components of Indian kingship were imported because they helped shore up the claims to superiority of the emerging kings over other local rulers (Hall 1976). With Indian notions of statecraft came other components of Indian civil culture.

The origins of Indian influence on Java, Sumatra, and Mainland Southeast Asia have been debated. Writers in the past spoke of conquests by Indian colonizers. Others saw Indian merchants as the transmitters of Indian culture (Coedès 1964, 50–52). More recent views hold otherwise. The Austronesians were not passive recipients waiting for Indians to come to their shores. Chinese records show that during the first centuries of the Christian era, Austronesian ships and seamen based in Southeast Asia had opened the sea route between India and China (Wolters 1967, 65; Hall 1985, 42).

The Indonesian islands produced aromatics and spices which were exchanged for exotic foreign goods. The lucrative maritime trade enabled chiefs of coastal settlements to exert dominion over others. If the leader headed a settlement at the mouth of the river, he could dictate his terms to settlements upstream or in the mountains. The highly valued foreign goods could not reach the latter without first passing through the entry village. Eventually taxes could be imposed. With growing wealth, he could exact tribute from surrounding and upstream villages in recognition of his preeminence; he could demand manpower for his constructions and for his army (Hall 1976, 64). However, these demands plus claims to superior authority would have been questioned. There was no fully articulated indigenous ideology that offered justification. But notions from Indian statecraft gave support (Wolters 1982, 10–11).

For instance, the cult of the god Shiva could legitimize his claim. Shiva was the lord of the universe and patron of asceticism. By practicing Hindu asceticism, the ambitious chief could claim special affinity with Shiva and be recognized as his authority on Earth. Indeed he could claim to partake of the god's divinity. Thanks to this, his followers could enter into a relationship with the god (ibid., 9–12). Even if he was not regarded as divine, he was regarded as manifesting the gods' spiritual energy (De Casparis and Mabbett 1992, 326). Mahayana Buddhism was another possible source of legitimacy—if the ruled were Buddhists. An inscription honors a Sri-Vijayan ruler who led a *siddhayatra* to a rival riverine port to compel it to submission. Kenneth Hall (1985, 83–84) interprets this event as two interrelated activities. It was an ordeal that the enlightened Buddhist ruler was expected to experience when seeking supernatural prowess. At the same time, it was an expedition that enabled him to fulfill traditional, indigenous expectations that the ruler should be a war chief. Rather than weakening desire, this Buddhist path quickened it instead.

The building of monumental sacred structures no doubt helped awe the population into submission. At the same time they taught the general population, in a vivid manner, the Hindu-Buddhist world views and the place of the elite in it. The technology and the accompanying ideology for such constructions came from India. Imported likewise from India was an advanced mathematical astronomy (ibid., 6). Doubtless, this gave the elite crucial information for managing the irrigation system on which the planting of rice depended. In the event of a prosperous harvest, this enhanced their image in the eyes of the peasantry and helped justify their claims to special privileges. Indian epics, such as the Ramayana, when chanted and danced, entertained all classes but, at the same time, celebrated the dignity of royalty, for their heroes and heroines were of royal stock.

In both the German and Javanese cases, foreign influences thus facilitated the transition from a simple type of polity to a large complex state by new, creating sources of legitimacy. With politico-religious ideology, came in sophisticated literature, architecture, poetry, music, dance, costume, and social etiquette to shore up the pretensions of the ambitious, local leader. Through him and his followers new fashions spread to the general population and became part of their culture. Because of this, a foreign civil culture became for centuries a model in both societies. A similar situation took place in other societies that were trying to form their own civil culture. As is well known, Rome conquered the Greeks but succumbed to their art, literature, philosophy, and language. The English, like other Northern Europeans, looked up to France and the Italian city-states for inspiration in many fields. Eventually, as English culture became highly sophisticated, it in turn became a norm for others. Chinese civil culture exerted a strong influence upon the civil cultures of Korea, Japan, and Vietnam, starting in the first five centuries of our era. At times this led to incongruities. A Japanese acquaintance once lamented that he and others have difficulties reading sections of Yukio Mishima's novels because of the esoteric Chinese characters. As a quick solution, they read translations into English and then go back to the Japanese! Like Japanese, Vietnamese is polysyllabic. In contrast the Chinese language is monosyllabic. While the Vietnamese originally tried to develop their own script, eventually they abandoned even this for a Romanized script brought in by a French missionary. They use this script to this day. There were other incongruities in the realm of architecture, personal adornment, gender relations, and politics (Zialcita 1995).[5]

Since the Christian Filipino elite were subjects of the Spanish king, they would have found it expedient to adopt Spanish customs and institutions. Initially, this gave them legitimacy in the eyes of the Spaniards who controlled the direction of the emerging state. Eventually, when the general mass of followers had become Catholic, this would have given them legitimacy as well in the latter's eyes. There must have been another reason for their acquiescence:

sixteenth- to seventeenth-century Spain had behind it over two thousand years of experience running a state and cities and showed expertise in diverse endeavors such as cuisine, stone architecture, courtly poetry, or philosophy.

We cannot, however, simply assume that this elite merely blindly idolized and imitated all that was Spanish. Nor can we assume that the ordinary people merely followed the fashions and whims of their social superiors. Most likely, they would have still retained some autonomy, especially if they were far from the centers of power. The mere fact of residing far from the town center would have allowed a farmer, then as now, to behave as he pleased. The question of imitation and originality should be settled, not in the abstract, as many do today, but by comparing Filipino artifacts with Spanish counterparts, item by item.

Local Genius

How have the Javanese and Germans transformed influences from their admired countries? The process by which they have done so helps clarify the process by which Filipinos have transformed influences from the West.

The study of the diffusion of cultural traits and their transformation by the host culture is an old theme in anthropology. It goes back to the anthropologist Franz Boas, a German national and university graduate who became an American. He observed that every culture has traditional forms and thought which act as a barrier and a filter to modify new ideas from the outside (Voget 1975, 322). He saw the diffusion of new ideas across cultural boundaries as a common phenomenon. Boas was most likely influenced by Herder who had earlier criticized the Frenchifiers by asserting that every people has a *Volksgeist* that is the wellspring of its originality. Though Boas's notion has been picked up by some Filipino scholars, many thinkers and the general public continue to assert that the lowland Christian Filipino has merely copied from others. I hear expressions like "derivative," "imitative"—even from anthropologists. This is worsened by the fact that well-intentioned American scholars tend to brand as "Spanish" anything in the Philippines that has some Spanish influence. In contrast, Spanish and Mexican scholars, who are familiar with the different variations on a particular style within the Hispanic World, would use either "Hispano-Filipino" or simply "Filipino." Thus Spain's top expert on the baroque, Antonio Bonet, remarked after sampling Filipino food and art-forms that "your culture is original." While admiring the façade of Paete Church in 2002, he observed that "Filipino baroque has a fleshiness (*carnosidad*)."

We Filipinos envy the Indonesians, particularly the Javanese and the Balinese, for developing a cultural tradition that is original and "free" from outside influences. This picture is not accurate. Though Javanese and Balinese civil cultures have a worldwide prestige, until recently the extent of their originality vis-à-vis India was not appreciated enough. There used to be a tendency among foreign art historians to regard their stone masterpieces as "Indian" and to overlook local innovations. It didn't help either that Indonesia like the rest of Indianized Southeast Asia was called "Farther India" by Western scholars. Mindful of this tendency, Indonesian scholars in a collaborative book (Ayatrohaedi 1986) stress the importance of "local genius" (the English term is used). It is a reality that transforms outside influences.

Thus Koentjaraningrat (1986, 89) has conceptualized a model where the intellectuals, religious officials, architects, court litterateurs, popular litterateurs, and artists of Indonesia are the channels through which Indian elements came in: language, technology, social organization, religion, knowledge systems, art. Various factors acted on these specialists: (1) on the one hand Indian consultants to the local courts, Indian traders in Indonesia, and the experience of Indonesian students in India; (2) on the other the existing social organization, the natural environment, and the island economy of Indonesia. The influence upon local specialists of these various factors gave rise to a "local genius," which in turn stimulated these specialists to create an Indianized-Indonesian culture.

The art of building towering sacred stone buildings came to Java and Mainland Southeast Asian countries from India. Buddhist stupas rose over mounds and carried a sacred relic; Hindu temples housed, as a central symbol, a representation of the god. The local genius, however, of the rulers, the priests, and the artisans altered the configuration of these constructions. We can look at the process from another perspective. Seeking to establish their legitimacy by building stone monuments in the Indian fashion, the rulers found themselves compelled to incorporate local tradition into these monuments. The pre-Hindu Javanese raised pyramidlike stone platforms in honor of the ancestors (Suleiman 1986, 168). This indigenous tradition persists in Borobudur, a stupa that honors both the Buddha and its builders. The pilgrim who ascended the sacred mount meditated on the stages of Gautama's journey from sensual pleasure to self-control to the attainment of enlightenment, while looking at narrative bas-reliefs on the galleries of the formerly nine terraces. At the summit are Buddhas seated in meditation inside domes that ring a central stupa pointing to the sky. Undoubtedly the monument was built to gain merit for its patron. However, the pile had an additional purpose: to proclaim that its builder, a member of the Sailendra dynasty, had attained enlightenment and, therefore, enjoyed a special authority that ought to be respected. Also honored by the stages are the nine Sailendra princes who preceded him. Significantly enough, Sailendra means "Lord of the Mountain" (De Casparis and Mabbett 1992, 319; Hall 1976). There is another difference: In Java, more than in India, the temples were sites of instruction and initiation into religion. Hence the many bas-reliefs depicting scenes from Buddha's life (Suleiman 1986, 168–69).

With modifications, Koentjaraningrat's model can be used for other parallel situations elsewhere, including Germany and the Philippines. I would like to stress that in all these situations power relations have surely been at work. The various players accept, reject, or modify foreign elements according to their own perceptions.

Thus the Germans welcomed Latin influences but modified them to suit their own needs. An example is the transformation of Gothic. As is well known, the French invented Gothic architecture. They made the rounded arch pointed, reduced wall space to admit more light, elevated the stone vaults on ribs to create a soaring feeling, and kept the resulting skeletal structure in place with flying buttresses. French Gothic, therefore, has a pronounced upward thrust. However, this is counterbalanced by strong horizontal patterns. Since the side aisles on both sides of the nave are half its height, their continuous roofline parallels that of the nave's roof. The triforium, or middle row of arches, which separates the painted windows of the uppermost story from those of the arches of the aisles and naves, also deliberately interrupts the eye's vertical ascent. On the facades hang huge rose windows whose circularity—a feminine shape—contrasts with the insistent, strongly vertical, masculine rhythms. Even more than the French, the Germans emphasized skyward yearning. They invented the "hall church" [*Hallenkirche*] where the side aisles are as tall as the central nave and where consequently the eye climbs, unimpeded, to the vaults above. Whereas in France there are three roofs seen from the outside: those of the nave and of the two side aisles, in German hall churches, there is only one roof to cover the entire structure. It thus peaks steeply. On the facade, instead of a rose window at the center, a large pointed window lifts upwards.

Several factors led the churchmen, burghers, and artisans to conceive of hall churches. In winter, it is easier to shed off the snow from a single roof (Mondadori 1988, 302–3). Within, the pulpit and altar could be seen from all parts of the church. The distinction between clergy and laity was thus minimized in these churches funded by an increasingly assertive merchant class (Tenbrock 1968, 88). The hall church prefigures Luther's Reform. In addition, I sense in these churches a recurring theme in German culture: deeply felt emotions and a yearning to break past the limits. I find this in other German masterpieces, for instance, the tortured paintings of Schoengauer and Gruenewald; Romantic landscapes of the nineteenth century with their infinite horizons; and Expressionist paintings of the early twentieth century.

Filipino Genius

"Local genius," too, asserted itself in the encounter between Spanish and indigenous culture, and resulted in what we now call "Filipino culture," more accurately the culture of lowland Christian Filipinos. The creators of this new culture came from the different ethnic groups of the islands: the indigenous peoples of the lowlands; the mestizos, whether Chinese or Spanish; and the creoles, or island-born European settlers. The "we" I discuss is thus broader and more inclusive than the "we" of doctrinaire, reductionist nationalism which would confine the "we" to the native and the indigenous which supposedly are "not tainted" by outside influences. My model for nationalism is the French which revolves around sentiment rather than blood, and which regards as "French" anything excellent created on French soil even if by foreigners. Thus Scholasticism, which was created in Paris by Abelard (French), Aquinas (Italian), and Albert the Great (German) is French. So is Modern Art: Matisse, Braque (French); Picasso, Gris, (Spaniards); Modigliani (Italian); and Chagall (Russian). My other model is the Mexican which, in spite of reaction against colonialism, resembles the French in its generous definition of the "national." This I discuss in the next essay.

I propose seeing these different ethnic groups in the Philippines as taking into account, consciously or unconsciously, the natural environment, the existing social structure, and the local economy in their response. In brief they made use of available local knowledge. Another factor should be considered: There were Peninsular Spaniards, like the priests, who came over to stay. When, for instance, they had to commission a building or to organize rituals, they had to take into account not only Spanish conditions, but the Philippine as well. Meanwhile the Filipino also received influences from China, India, and Islam. But this was not a matter of blind acceptance. In real life, many Filipinos have not been like Rizal's Doña

Victorina who aped foreign ways. Brumfiel (1992) has shown how the cultural ecological approach can be enriched if we look at the relationships between people as a continuous negotiation where social class, gender, and membership in a faction exert influence. What we regard as the culture of a society is really the outcome of this negotiation. I would like to look at the relations involving Filipinos and Spaniards from the same angle. In this case, I would use gender, social class, and ethnicity as influential factors. The text below is an outline that, I hope, opens doors for future resrach in cooking, costume, architecture, and religion.

Local cooking styles at the advent of the Spanish centered on boiling, steaming, broiling, roasting meats, fish, and vegetables, or on steeping raw fish in souring agents. Flavoring was with salt, *patis,* bagoong, and souring agents like green tamarinds. It is not clear whether pepper was used, despite our proximity to the Spice Islands. The local term is Spanish in origin: *paminta* from the Spanish *pimienta.* Mediterranean influence brought in new ways of cooking. One important method was sautéing [*guisa*] with garlic, onions, and tomatoes. However, local taste created a new flavor. Local sautéing, according to Doreen Fernandez,[6] differs from the Spanish in its liberal use of shrimps and patis, both products of a riverine environment, and that Chinese condiment, soy sauce. This is evident, for instance, in the Filipino version of Chinese noodles, *pansit bihon guisado.* The Spanish form of beef stew, *mechado,* is flavored locally by combining tomato paste with soy sauce. Pre-Hispanic Filipinos most likely pickled their foods in vinegar, as in *paksiw.* So did the Spaniards, using peppercorn and plenty of garlic, as in *adobado.* The two traditions met together with Chinese soy sauce to form the highly popular *adobo.*

Relations of power may not seem obvious in cooking. But taste preferences have been used to advertise class and ethnicity.[7] Some Filipinos of European descent proudly proclaim that they do not care for bagoong. In Hawaii Filipinos' fondness for bagoong is mocked. However, in the Philippines, the cooking style that did triumph, both at home and at banquets, fuses together the Spanish, the Chinese, and the indigenous.

Dressing habits of both Spaniards and islanders changed over time. Pre-Hispanic Tagalog men wore a loincloth that had sufficient width to cover the hips and thighs. With this went a short-sleeved, collarless jacket [*cangan*] sewn in front and extending a little below the waist [*poco más de la cintura*] (Morga 1609, 173). The women, in turn, wore a wraparound tubular skirt tied together above the waist and a collarless jacket that could either be long- or short-sleeved and was tied in front with braids or cords of silk. Cotton or, in the women's case, silks were used (Quirino 1958, 348, 370, 372).

The galleon trade was the first commercial network to connect Asia, the Americas, and Europe together. During the seventeenth century, Manila was the entrepot of Asia and thus attracted many traders from other Asian countries—a fact many educated Filipinos today forget. Contact with outsiders inspired changes in the men's upper garment, the *baro* (fig. 9). The Chinese came in a loose, collarless tunic or jacket [*san*] which was slipped over the head and may be hip-level, knee-long, or ankle-level according to the occasion (Yarwood 1978, 86). This was worn over loose trousers [*koo*] (fig. 6). On the other hand, the Indian traders came in two costumes: (1) the jamah, also called *jamal,* and the (2) *kurta.* The former is a combination of tunic and shirt, worn over long drawers, and reaches to the knees. It may be worn sheer, thus revealing the drawers (fig. 7). The kurta is even looser in shape than the baro and is worn over loose drawers; it is collarless, has buttons but no cuffs. Often made of cotton, it can either be opaque or woven so lightly that it resembles the gauzy materials Filipinos love. It may be either plain or embroidered. Even when embroidered, it has no cutwork (Bhusan 1958, 36 ff.). The kurta has been popularized by Indians, whether Moslem or Hindu, all over Southeast Asia.

The Tagalog costume changed. Le Gentil ([1779–1781] 1964, 109) says that outside Manila (then Intramuros) men wore a shirt "made of cotton cloth, of silk, or of grass fiber." The latter two materials probably refer to two local innovations: piña from pineapple fibers, and to *rengue* and *pinukpok* from abaca (De la Torre 1986, 15). The sleeves were wide, the shirt floated in the air because it fell outside the pants. In Manila, however, the shirts were worn with cuffs with two or three gold buttons. A vest was worn over the shirt, again suggesting Indian influence. Chinese influence resulted in a

Figure 6. A nineteenth-century Manila Chinese shopkeeper in a loose jacket and loose trousers (Andrews, Charles W. 1850–1860, Chino de Escolta, *Ilustracion Filipina periódico quincenal* [1 March 1850–15 December 1860], American Historical Collection, Rizal Library, Ateneo de Manila University).

loose cotton shirt without collar or cuffs, appropriately called *camisa de chino* [the Chinese shirt]. From the Chinese also came the trousers of colored silk, with embroidery on the loose bottoms, that La Gironière ([1855] 1962, 16) describes as being the costume of both *indio* and mestizo. The classic form of the barong Tagalog of embroidered pineapple cloth—loose shirt, collar and cuffs, embroidery all

Figure 7. A seventeenth-century painting of an Indian in long jamah, long drawers, and "lamplike" slippers (Bhusan, Jamila Brig 1958, *The costumes and textiles of India*, plate 8. Bombay: Taraporevala's Treasure House of Books).

over—had crystalized by the 1800s and was worn by indios and mestizos alike, as shown by Damian Domingo's paintings or in Wilkinson's print (fig. 8). In the tropics, it is cooler to wear shirts out. The pre-Hispanic *cangan* hung over the waist. Moreover, the native gauzes look better and are more comfortable when floating. Gathered in, they can irritate. Nineteenth-century Western notions of propriety decreed that men's shirts should be of opaque materials and be tucked in. Filipinos, however, preferred see-through shirts worn loose.[8] We should research on what Western Europeans thought of shirts that exposed the male torso. It is unlikely that many Filipinos wore the cotton undershirt that today goes with the barong Tagalog. Would this daily semiexposure of the male torso have reinforced the Western European stereotype that people born in the tropics, creoles included, were sensual?

Figure 8. A Chinese mestizo couple, 1846 (*Philippines: Habitans de Manille.* The Pardo de Tavera Collection, Rizal Library, Ateneo de Manila University).

In some visual materials from the early nineteenth century, men are shown wearing slippers with curled tips (fig. 9). This suggests that at least in Manila our involvement with our Asian neighbors during the Spanish period was more extensive than we today imagine, and that we should start thinking of the affinities of the barong Tagalog cum pants with those of its neighbors.

Tagalogs of the eighteenth and nineteenth centuries are sometimes depicted wearing a jacket over their loosely hanging shirts. Is this proof that the Spaniards forbade tucking the shirts in? No, be-

Figure 9. A Tagalog in *baro*, embroidered trousers, and "Aladdin" slippers, 1836 (*Océanie: Habitans de Manille*. The Pardo de Tavera Collection, Rizal Library, Ateneo de Manila University).

cause this could have been influenced by visitors to Manila. Indians then and now wear vests over their tunics. Moreover, sketches of Manila by Juan Ravenet in the late eighteenth century suggest similar habits among the Chinese and Armenians. The Chinese wears a long shirt that droops below his jacket's hem while the Armenian's unbuttoned jacket reveals a shirt flowing past his waistline (*Filipinas Puerta de Oriente* 2004, 266, 267).

The women's costume was also transformed. Their chemises, like the male shirt, made use of either translucent pineapple or abaca fibers; they were worn loose over a cotton undergarment. They continued to wear a skirt (now given a Spanish term, *saya*) with a *tapis* over it (Le Gentil [1779–1781] 1964). In the eighteenth century, they donned an embroidered kerchief over the chemise (ibid., 111). In the next century the shawl assumed the same material as the chemise, that is semitransparent, to become the unique *pañuelo*. The women's costume defied Western European propriety, for both chemise and shawl were gauzelike, with a playful traceried embroidery. The street clothes of Western women of the eighteenth and nineteenth centuries normally concealed the upper torso and the arms with opaque materials. No wonder, Paul de la Gironière ([1855] 1962, 16), a French resident in 1820–1839, commented that "Nothing can be more charming, coquettish, and fascinating than this costume, which excites in the highest degree the admiration of strangers," particularly Europeans. Like Le Gentil, he remarks on the translucency of the bodice. Unlike the former, he is not shocked by its "indecency"; rather he exults to find the costume "covering, but not concealing a bosom that has never been imprisoned in stays" (ibid., 1855, 16). Within the context of that period, a costume that to us confines, on the contrary, liberates. Filipinas so preferred comfort that they wore gauzelike clothes, and they rejected European corsets.

In addition to the climate, gender roles exerted an active influence. Filipina women continued to inherit property, manage businesses, and assert themselves. Faced with the prospect that Ibarra might have been killed by the crocodile at the bottom of the lake, Maria Clara, in *Noli me tangere,* did not faint because, editorializes José Rizal ([1886] 1961, 122), "Filipino women do not yet know how to faint" [*Las filipinas no saben aun desmayarse*]. Of course, had they worn corsets, they might have.

In the houses the local imprint was likewise visible. Originally the Spaniards built in the grand manner that became popular in the coastal cities of Spain and in the new cities of Spanish America: tall palaces of cut stone with vaulted ceilings (De los Rios de Coronel [1621] 1903). But two seventeenth-century earthquakes collapsed these ambitions (Fayol [1647] 1903). The native system of frame constructions where the heavy roofwork was supported by pillars [*haligi*] that merely swayed with tremors now looked attractive, though the drawback was that light materials could easily burn. A new construction style appeared. The tiles and wooden roofwork were supported by pillars of the sturdy molave which, when dried, resists water (Vidal y Soler 1874, 167). Wood was preferred for the second story, stone was restricted to the first (Le Gentil [1779–1781] 1964, 78). As in the indigenous houses, entertaining, eating, and sleeping took place in the upper story away from the damp ground (Zialcita and Tinio 1980).

The relative informality of the local lifestyle shows in the fewness of the rooms even in the upper story either in the late seventeenth century or in the nineteenth.[9] Aside from two large rooms for entertaining guests and for dining, there were often only two or three bedrooms. In contrast, the grand mansions of Mexico during the eighteenth century had many rooms in all three stories. Each type of servant had his or her room. On the third floor where the family lived, aside from a room for receiving guests, there was a music room, a chapel, a study room, a throne room in honor of the viceroy who represented the king, a dining room, and several bedrooms (Rubio 1991, Macedo 1994). In Manila, bedrooms were few and sleeping space shared. The French scientist Le Gentil de la Galaisière ([1779–1781] 1964,

88) reports, in horror, that the Manila creoles were fond of spreading straw mats on the floor and sleeping thereon, "men and women alike side by side." This practice, where the entire family and their relatives and visitors sleep on a mat on the floor, continues to survive in the countryside today. It was another indigenous practice that contradicted eighteenth-century Western Christian notions of propriety.

Houses were situated along rivers or streams, as had been the millennial custom of Filipinos because the waterways were the main avenues of transport, the chief sources of protein, and were venues for one of the principal recreations of the Filipino: daily baths. Le Gentil ([1779–1781] 1964, 87) exclaimed that no city could be "more corrupt" than Manila. The reason? Because men and women bathed in the river, in thin clothes and in each other's company. Even the creoles were addicted to the pleasures of the bath. They had bathhouses constructed over the river where men and women in their light clothes could soak in privacy (ibid., 98). Le Gentil came from a Christendom that lost the habit of bathing often, following the Renaissance (*EUIEA* 1910, 573–74). In the tropics, however, the Spanish Lion became a Sea Lion.

Christianity superseded the ancient indigenous beliefs and practices. In the process, it was itself transformed by the older religion. This occurred even in rituals approved by the hierarchy. The voice of the Virgin Mary was heard coming from a tree at Manaoag; her image was found in a tree at Antipolo; and was propitiated at a pandan bush at Ermita, Manila. At Caysasay in Batangas and at Obando in Bulacan, her image was fished from the river. Before the images of Mary and the Child Jesus, people sing, gyrate, or hop to this day while in a trance at Obando, Pakil, Kalibo, and Cebu. For indigenous religion had revered trees, as the abode of spirits, and rock formations by bodies of water, and crocodiles (Chirino [1604] 1969, 61–62). Its officiants fell into trances and shook when possessed by a spirit during rituals under the balete tree (Alcina [1668a] n.d., 3, 216, 220–22). The native way of seeing the world transformed the new religion.

This, too, happened in the most popular and, seemingly, the most orthodox of our processions: the Santo Entierro on the evening of Good Friday. The tableaux illustrate the different personages and stages of the Passion and Death of Christ. The images may be of ivory or wood and are often clothed in brocade trimmed with gold and silver embroidery. They stand on floats of beaten silver decorated with flowers and globes of light. The climax are two well-beloved images: Christ in His Coffin and His Grieving Mother [Mater Dolorosa]. It all seems so Spanish. And yet the social organization is not. In Spain, processional images, according to Spanish friends, are owned either by the Church or by the confraternities [*cofradías*]. Here they are owned by wealthy private families. Indeed a Good Friday procession is really a who's who of the leading families of each town. The most prestigious images are those of the Santo Entierro and the Mater Dolorosa (Venida 1996). Often they belong to the oldest or wealthiest families in town. Moreover, the images, including the coffin, are kept at home in the bedroom. This again, plus the many and large religious images in Filipino homes, surprises Spaniards. Significantly enough, in pagan days, the body of a well-loved leader was mummified and kept in a small, inner room, according to Spanish missionaries (Alcina [1668b] n.d., 3: 261; Chirino [1604] 1969, 88). He was invoked in times of crisis. The Filipino habit of keeping life-size images in the bedroom reveals the persistence of this cult of the ancestors. The Christian missionaries must have seen how strong it was, and decided to substitute instead Christian icons, especially the Dead Christ. As practiced in the Philippines, the cult of the Holy Sepulchre reveals the limitations of the Church's power rather than affirms it.

The cult of the dead leader persists in the taboos surrounding Good Friday. True the missionaries, who were scandalized by the frequent baths of their parishioners, must have taken the occasion to ask them to avoid bathing on at least this one day. They must also have enjoined silence out of respect. And, of course, they insisted on prohibiting meat. However, it is significant that when a datu died among the pagan Visayans and Tagalogs of the sixteenth to the seventeenth centuries, all observed taboos. They could not bathe, nor even approach the water; they could not eat meat; they observed silence. Violations were severely punished with enslavement (Alcina [1668b] n.d., 3:255; Chirino [1604] 1969, 88–89). Perhaps the converts must have accepted the new taboos because they saw Christ as a new datu.

The island church developed its own style. While the missionaries taught the locals Western art, the latter made their own contributions using their own traditions (Javellana 1991, 54–55). Spanish and Mexican churches suggest tension, drama, and vertical striving. In contrast Filipino churches look spread out and relaxed. This seems the result of both environmental and cultural conditions. Because of earthquake conditions, Filipino churches tend to be lower than those of Spain or even earthquake-prone Mexico. The wide buttresses that flank the church on both sides, as in the Ilocos and Miag-ao, Iloilo, reinforce a sense of breadth rather than height. Most interiors are not vaulted. Instead they have wooden ceilings with often beautiful murals. They thus communicate a lightness of feeling that contrasts with the stone vaults and golden bas-reliefs of Mexican and Spanish churches. Perhaps this lightness can also be due to the Filipino temperament which seems more lyrical than dramatic.

There are other contrasts with Mexican and Spanish churches of the same period. Filipino towers do not rise to the sky as sheer four-sided angular structures. Instead they rise in tiers and seem rounded because, like the pagoda that inspired their Chinese mestizo craftsmen, they have eight sides. Octagons for the Chinese symbolize good fortune. While the tower may be built into the facade, they can also be built at a distance, as in the Ilocos and Bohol. Unintentionally this makes them look somewhat Italian rather than Spanish or Mexican. Moreover, the Filipino church exhibits a simplicity accented in parts with a discreet richness of ornamentation. One has only to see the Jesuit church at Tepotzotlan, Mexico, or the Carthusian Church at Granada, Spain, to realize that such interiors, which are covered from ceiling to floor with tightly woven swirling angels, saints and clouds, are alien to the Filipino consciousness. In terms of social space, Filipino churches again offer a contrast. As was noted above, they share custody of the major processional images with the principal families.

During the eighteenth to the nineteenth centuries, a civil culture emerged that wove together indigenous culture and foreign influences. Vigan, Taal, Silay, Carcar: by Asian standards, our old urban centers are infants. But they should mean much to us; in them, a genuine Filipino urban culture emerged at last.

Though the lowland Christian Filipino regarded Westerners as models, increasingly, out of pride, a distancing took place. For instance, because of services rendered during an epidemic, the painter Lorenzo Guerrero was visited in his studio by Spanish officials in 1880 to award him a medal. They asked if he could remove his native shirt and don European clothes for the occasion. He replied: "You may affix it to the bodice of this poor but honorable shirt. If you ask me to wear a suit, I shall be obliged to refuse the award" (*EUIEA* 1935, 196). The officials gave in.

Though this essay is about the Filipino and the Spanish model, something should be said about the other admired model.

The Other Foreign Model. The domination of American culture seems near absolute on the airwaves, in the choice of movies to see, in the names of subdivisions. High-level instructions and speeches by the government continue to be made in English even though most listeners, including Manileños, either do not know English or understand it poorly. Though not a linguistic purist, I am upset over the ease with which English words are adopted by Filipino language writers without benefit of respelling. More: Many educated Filipinos cannot admit that their ancestors once upon a time fought for their freedom against American invaders—and that this fight is a continuing one. During the grand Centennial Parade of 12 June 1998, there were floats that dramatized the struggle against the Spaniards, none against the Americans. The following year there was no public symposium on the war that claimed thousands of civilian lives.

There are reasons why the ordinary Filipino is dazzled by American culture. One is that it signifies wealth, power, and advanced technology. Another is that it represents urban sophistication in general. About the first reason: If it is some consolation, even the Japanese and Europeans closely follow trends in the U.S.A. About the second: If Filipinos were more aware of the achievements of their urban tradition, they might be less awed by American culture. Among Filipino migrants to Hawaii, I note a difference between those who have come straight from the farm to Honolulu, and those from an urban bourgeois background. The former praise all that they see and hear, and deprecate many things back home. They will even deny that they are Filipino. The latter are somewhat more critical and at the same time more self-confident, for they are able to look at urban America from the perspective of another urban society: Manila, Cebu, or Bacolod.

The nationalist, therefore, should not consider as colonial frivolity this growing interest in visiting old churches and houses. These are products of a civil culture in the urban centers, and moreover were made by local craftsmen. I have heard fellow Filipinos remark, upon seeing a Filipino silver frontal in roccoco style that "I thought this was only found abroad. I did not realize that our craftsmen are so able." The realization strengthens pride of self and confidence that the Filipino can compete with others. Our neighbors in Asia have long traditions of civil culture that they proudly project. In our case, our civil culture is not only much younger, many educated Filipinos are not even sure it is truly "ours." Moreover, it is derided for being elitist, as though the civil cultures of our neighbors were not also heavily influenced by urban elites. If we keep an open mind about Filipino civil culture, as elaborated during the eighteenth to the nineteenth centuries, it gives us a viewing balcony.

Nick Joaquin is pilloried for being so concerned with the "Hispanic past" or with Hispanic culture in general, to the detriment of the Filipino. He is misread. What he praises is not Spanish culture in general but rather the synthesis between the indigenous and the Spanish, which finds expression in things like the *adobo* and *pan de sal,* that the Filipino on the street assumes is truly Filipino and is part of his daily culture (Joaquin 1989, 35). For him, this synthesis creates a vantage point from which the Filipino can evaluate new influences coming from other urban traditions, especially from the U.S.A.[10]

In fact this Hispano-indigenous synthesis has been used by two dissimilar groups: particular writers in Tagalog, like the late Rolando Tinio, and Jollibee. Rolando Tinio wrote brilliantly in both English and Tagalog. His advice to us regarding adding new words was to first look for an indigenous equivalent. If there is none, then look for a Spanish equivalent. Only if neither an indigenous nor Filipinized Spanish term is available is the new word to be accepted. On the other hand Filipino taste has enabled Jollibee to carve out its own kingdom in the face of McDonald's challenge. Unlike the latter's bland hamburger, Jollibee's version has a mixture—a secret one of course—where soy sauce and spices seem to be present. Jollibee's version appeals to many Filipinos because, since the seventeenth century, meat dishes in the islands have been cooked not only with patis but likewise with soy sauce, onions, garlic, and spices. The fusion of Spanish, Chinese, and indigenous traditions has developed in the Filipino a tastebud that finds McDonald's Big Mac wanting.

A Double Standard

Friends who go to Indonesia come back regretting that "While they have retained their culture, we have not." In reality neither the Sumatrans, the Javanese, nor the lowland Christian Filipino have retained their original culture. The original lowland Sumatrans, Javanese, before the advent of Indian influence, must have been like what our ancestors were on the eve of conquest by Spain or like the Sumatran Bataks until the end of the nineteenth century: a pork-loving people living in villages independent of each other, fond of wars and of tattooes as emblems of bravery, and ready to accord women some measure of autonomy by recognizing their right to transmit property. Indianization, and later on Islamization, changed many aspects of this behavior. But while such changes in Java and Sumatra are regarded by educated Filipinos and foreigners alike as "natural," changes undergone by Filipinos in relation to Spain are bewailed as "unnatural." The double standard is the result of the universal habit of neatly dividing humankind into an "Asia" and a "West," each of which is believed to have unique qualities that ought not in any way to mix with each other. The fallacy behind this reasoning will be exposed by later essays.

Meanwhile a fallacy we have discussed in this essay is the belief that a desire to follow foreign models is wholly the result of colonialism. Independent societies supposedly look inwards rather than outwards. This has not been the case either in pre-nineteenth-century Germany (or Germanies) or in pre-fourth-century Java and Sumatra. All these societies negotiated the transition from what I call "primal culture" to "civil culture" using ideas and practices taken from the Latins, in the case of the Germans, and Indians, in the case of the Sumatrans and Javanese. For the transition from primal to civil culture is a difficult one. The latter culture intensifies and diversifies occupational specialization, it introduces a greater pooling of disparate skills, it divides the city from the countryside, it deepens a sense of the individual ego, and it creates a broader sense of community. It thus creates conditions that have no parallel in primal cultures. Hence societies that have made an earlier transition, or whose civil cultures have attained a high level of development, become models for those in transition. Even countries that have not been colonized politically may thus go through a period of quasi-cultural colonization. Also crucial is another factor: Societies look to those in the vanguard of knowledge, for fear of falling behind.

Nonetheless, as happened in other societies, the genius of the islanders modified and adapted foreign influences to local physical, social, and economic conditions to create a new culture, a new set of symbols that for many Christian Filipinos, whether in the countryside or the city, signifies being Filipino. Often, because authors have not looked at how other cultures have coped with foreign influences, Filipinos themselves are the first to dismiss their culture as "derived" or "imitative." Yet, normally when Filipinos, either here or abroad, celebrate their Filipinoness they organize a fiesta with processions, music, dances, costumes, and food whose ancestry is precisely this eighteenth- to nineteenth-century synthesis.

Notes

1. In the fourth century, the Germans shunned occupying Roman towns. Being nomadic, they regarded these as *munimenta servitii:* markers of slavery. Only six centuries later, claims the historian Gudeman (in Tacitus [1928] 1950, 211), did they overcome this repugnance under Henry I, founder of cities.

2. A surprising description of a people who are famous today for their group discipline. But this should not be surprising if we realize that cultures do change, for instance, under the impact of living in a state or in a city. Filipino culture has likewise changed, and will still change.

3. For German medieval history, I consulted Bartlett (1993), Heer (1968), Tenbrock (1968).

4. Chinese travelers to Sumatra before the fifth century report that the mountain peoples of Sumatra were much feared for their aggressiveness (Hall 1985); but this was necessary for survival. In the absence of a central authority, members of each village had to hold their ground against those of another. The situation recalls what the Spaniards found among Tagalogs and Visayans in the sixteenth century, most of whom lived in small barangays independent of each other.

5. The Chinese repeatedly invaded Vietnam in order to colonize it. The cultural differences were sharp. Chinese looked down on the Vietnamese because the latter chewed betel nut and thus darkened their teeth, used to tatoo themselves, and accorded women a higher status (Taylor 1983, 34; Le 1955, 209). The Vietnamese fought back. However, they accepted and reinterpeted Confucian ideology precisely to justify rejecting Chinese overlordship. In the same way there is an emperor of the North, so is there an emperor of the South (O'Harrow 1983, 169).

6. I have conversed often with Doreen Fernandez on the Filipino's culinary culture; see also Fernandez and Alegre (1988, 1991).

7. For instance, Spanish friends are surprised that Filipinos eat their rice unfried, with just a sauce or a spoonful of soup on it. For them, rice is tasteless without oil. Others cannot tolerate the mixture of soy sauce and ginger.

8. Sinibaldo de Mas ([1842] 1963) is sometimes cited as proof that there existed such a discriminatory law mandating a separate costume for the natives. As pointed out earlier, he was sent over by the Spanish government to check on the political conditions. In his 1843 Informe, he said that Spain had three options: either (1) retain the islands as a colony, or (2) consider their loss unimportant, or (3) prepare them for independence. Retaining the status quo would lead to the second option—their loss. If Spain wanted to keep it as a colony, then it was important to humiliate the *indio* and the mestizo by not educating them and by not allowing them to wear the same style of clothes as the Spaniard. If Spain envisioned independence, then she should treat the indio and the mestizo as full equals in everything. De Mas concluded by stating that he preferred preparing the islands for independence. His report shows that, on the contrary, no such sumptuary law existed. Also, if the indio and the mestizo had to dress differently, how could Rizal and company have dressed in the Western way in the Philippines without problems? Students at the University of Santo Tomas all had to wear a jacket over a shirt that was tucked in. Do Rizal and company ever refer to such a sumptuary law? I suspect this legend was concocted sometime during the early part of the twentieth century and caught on because of its cuteness.

9. For a detailed reconstruction of what a late seventeenth-century house in Intramuros must have looked like, we relied on Doña Isabel Navarro de Piñero's 1699 testament that inventories and measures in detail every structural part of her house in Intramuros (Zialcita and Tinio 1980, 242 ff.). The paucity of rooms is repeated in nineteenth-century houses both in Manila and the provinces.

10. A running theme in Nick Joaquin is that by the nineteenth century, the educated Filipino had thoroughly absorbed the refinements of the Spanish way of life, whether in food, wine, art, or in sensibility in general. They thus found the introduced American way of life too crass and materialistic. Their *hispanismo*—really *filipinismo* because of the fact that this had been assimilated—provided them with a spiritual shield against the onslaught of the new, invading culture. However, Nick Joaquin does not reject American culture either. After all, he loves jazz, T. S. Eliot, and writes in English. He welcomes the better aspects of American culture in the Filipino; he rejects the notion that if it is new and American, then it must be better than the old, especially if of Spanish origin. In his play, *Portrait of the Artist as Filipino,* he caricatures the unthinking *sajonistas* (Americanophiles) by making two sisters dance in their flapper costumes in front of the masterpiece of Don Lorenzo: Aeneas carrying Anchises while fleeing the burning Troy.

We Are All Mestizos

Fue el doloroso nacimiento del pueblo mestizo
que es el México de hoy.

It was the painful birth of the mestizo people
that is México today.
—Inscription at the Plaza de las Tres Culturas, México D.F.

TWO FEARS HAVE HAUNTED discussions of identity among thoughtful Filipinos since independence in 1946. One fear is that, like a house that has inner levels that do not match, Filipino identity is "schizophrenic." Another fear is that because the lowland Christian majority's way of life is the child of two different cultures, the Western and the Eastern, it must therefore be "illegitimate," that is, a "bastardized" culture. The assumptions behind these two popular interpretations of Filipino culture are not questioned. Yet they are problematic.

Consider the first fear, that Filipino Christianity suffers from a "split-level" identity.

Split Level or Syncretic?

Jaime Bulatao, SJ (1967), first coined the now popular expression "split-level Christianity" to expose the contradiction between ideal Christianity and the actual, day-to-day conduct of Catholic Filipinos. In the popular press, this gave rise to another equally popular expression: "cultural schizophrenia." "Split personality" and "schizophrenia" are psychological terms for madness: The individual cannot think coherently and cannot distinguish fantasy from reality. It is astonishing that educated Filipinos routinely use these terms to characterize their culture.

As an anthropologist, I have always objected to these terms. They reduce to the level of individual psychology a complex reality that is *cultural*. A culture is the product-in-process, over the course of time, of many individuals who may differ from each other in personality, social class, and religion. We cannot expect the result to be harmonious in every aspect. Culture, as the network of symbols, beliefs, and values, may indeed create common linkages. However, particular sectors will most likely interpret and use it differently according to their needs. The potential for disagreement increases with the size and openness of a society. In any complex society, we should expect to find two or more traditions coexisting together. In a class-based society, there is an elite tradition and a popular tradition: the Great Tradition and the Little Tradition that Robert Redfield (1956) speaks of. People who are educated or who live in the urban centers where complex ideas are being generated will look at the world differently from a farmer who has had only a few years of schooling. We can improve on Redfield by noting that either tradition may well not be fully unified. Within each tradition, imported practices may coexist with local ones: a particular practice may fuse components of different traditions together and thus represent a new synthesis while other imported practices may coexist with local ones in contradiction. What the terms "split level" and "schizophrenia" cast as abnormal may in fact be *normal*, for conflicts between sets of beliefs and practices are present in many complex cultures and may last for centuries.

As evidence, let us look at Islam among the Central Javanese and the Maranao, and Christianity among the Germanic peoples.

The Central Javanese. Islam criticizes Christianity for retaining vestiges of polytheism and idolatry in its icons, its cult of the saints, and its Triune God. And yet in Central Java, the heart of the world's largest Moslem nation, nominally Moslem peasants revere the "spirit of the rice," offer gifts to the founding spirit of their village, and fear certain places as the abode of spirits. Some of these are clearly survivals from the original animist religion (Geertz 1960, 16). Brahmanic practices that came in from India between the fifth and the sixteenth centuries likewise persist. Even in the 1950s, professed Moslems went to the great temple of Loro Jonggrang outside Yogyakarta to offer money, fruits, and flowers to the goddess Durga and her favorite animal, the goat (Vlekke 1960, 27).[1] Another tension point between Islam and the older Brahmanic tradition is the desire of many among the Central Javanese elite to seek mystical union with God through meditation. Islam has its own mysticism, but the more purist-minded Javanese Moslems consider it an error to think that God and man can become one (Geertz 1960, 317). Finally the treatment of the body is another arena for contending traditions. Orthodox Islam prescribes parts of the body that should be covered. Thus a woman should unveil her hair only to her husband, for this incites sensuality; and she should not leave her arms and shoulders uncovered, for this is nakedness. Yet, in accordance with the traditions of the Indianized courts, during weddings, aristocratic ladies expose and decorate their hair with gold ornaments and wear batik sarongs that do not cover their arms and shoulders.

Thus though Central Javanese find common grounds in Islam, they differ in their interpretation, according to social class. This has led to social and even political conflict (ibid., 357–64). The indigenous, animist tradition is strong among the peasants, the Brahmanic among the bureaucrats and the descendants of the nobility, and the rigorously Islamic among the traders.

The Maranao. Like Christianity, Islam emphasizes that, in case of an offence, only the individual offender should be held liable. God renders punishment and rewards according to the individual's sins and virtues, rather than to the behavior of his or her kin. Yet among the Maranao of Lanao—who became Moslems in the seventeenth century, two centuries later than the Taosug of Sulu—collective kin responsibility is a practice that still persists in parts. Should an individual commit a crime against another, even his innocent kin can be regarded as liable by the offended party and can be punished with death. The kin group is looked upon as One Moral Person. Feuds can thus last for years.[2]

The notion that the kin are collectively liable formed an integral part of the moral code of many Austronesian-speaking peoples[3] before the advent of the High Religions and of states with bureaucracies that could compel warring kin groups to an agreement. Certainly this has been a feature of the non-Islamic Manobos of Mindanao until fairly recently (Garvan 1931, Soledad 1997) but not of Sulu where a single sultanate imposed itself on all the local leaders (Kiefer 1972). Significantly enough there never was a single sultanate over the Maranao. Instead there are many autonomous local leaders supported by their kin, each claming to be a sultan (Mednick 1965). The Islamic notion of individual responsibility conflicts with the older kin-based collective notion.

The Germanic Peoples. Christianity was first accepted by the Franks in the fifth century; later on it spread among other Germanic peoples, at times through the use of force. The last Germanic peoples to accept Baptism were the Swedes in the eleventh century. Practices from indigenous, pre-Christian religion continued to persist, however. The horse was the totemic beast of the god Odin; after it was sacrificed, its flesh was eaten in a sacred meal. Though the consumption of horseflesh was forbidden by the bishops in the eighth century, the slaughter of horses as part of the funeral rite for kings and knights was reported for the fourteenth century in England, France, and Germany. Even monks and priests disobeyed Church prohibitions. When a monastery was founded at Konigsfelden in Germany in 1318, a horse was sacrificed. Horse skulls have been found in churches in England. As recently as 1897, a horse's head was buried when a new Primitive Methodist chapel was founded in Cambridgeshire (Jones and Pennick 1994, 139–40). Beneficial pagan deities were renamed by the Christian priests during the Early Middle Ages: Freya became Maria; Baldur, St. Michael; Thor, St. Olaf. In some medieval Christian churches in England and Germany, images of the Germanic gods and goddesses appear with their attributes. They are depicted in a respectful manner. In the sixteenth century, Istein in Germany had a temple to Jupiter Christus (Jones and Pennick 1994, 160–61). When freedom of worship became accepted throughout the West in the nineteenth century, neopagan cults seeking the return of the worship of the ancient deities sprang up throughout northern Germanic Europe and continue to do so to this day (ibid., 218–20).

Have the Germanic peoples ever been truly Christian? This question has been raised about Germany in particular because of the crimes committed by the Nazis. Looking back, we can note that sectors of even the educated elite who knew Christian dogma much better than the populace were of two minds about the older pagan religion.

Undoubtedly, beliefs and practices from pagan religion persist among Christian Filipinos: a proneness to see spirits in trees, a reverence for sacred mountains, the use of animal blood in consecrating structures, an ethic that tends to center exclusively on the kin group.[4] But the Christian Filipino is not unique in experiencing conflicting religious traditions. Even societies where a more abstract Universal Religion entered, not through colonialism but through the native rulers, experience such conflicts. This is shown by the examples above.

There are other problems with the concept of "cultural schizophrenia": (1) it ignores the possibility that tensions between opposing traditions may eventually be resolved over the course of centuries in a new synthesis; (2) it overlooks the possibility that the tension itself may give an institution complex but dynamic relationships.

An example of both is the conflict between centralization and localism that has been a running theme in German history for over a millennium. The monarchical state that governed what is now called Germany had as its ideal a centralized empire in the Roman style. But the lords on which the emperor depended, during the Middle

Ages, to govern localities were jealous of their rights and privileges. The bishops, dukes, and counts might swear allegiance to the emperor, but were careful to keep him away from the small, political formations over which they were masters. Only in the nineteenth century were the Germanies unified with force by Prussia. Still, the main architect of this union, Bismarck, complained of "the German urge to division into smaller groups" (Mayer 1960). Under the Nazis in the 1930s, the pendulum swung to the opposite: Germany became highly centralized, local autonomy was deemphasized. The Federal Republic, which arose on the rubble of Nazism, was a synthesis of the centralization of a nation-state and local autonomy. Each of the German states would have the freedom to decide its own economic, housing, health, and educational programs. Defense and foreign affairs would be the federal government's responsibility.

Had one visited the Germanies at any time between the 1600s and 1870, one might have concluded that the so-called German urge to division would be a permanent handicap and that it could never lead to an overarching unity. One might have believed, as many Germans did, that French centralism was more efficient. Yet developments since World War II suggest the opposite. Because federalism allows important decisions to be made at several levels below the nation-state, Germans are able to arrive at decisions more quickly than the French in a European Union where regions cooperate, bypassing the capital cities.

When we turn to the Philippines, the tension between Western elements and indigenous components has either led to dynamic syntheses has lead to unresolved conflicts.

Here, too, is a tension between centralization and local autonomy. Over hundreds of barangays that were small independent political units consisting of interrelated kin groups (Chirino [1604] 1969, Morga [1609] 1910, Alcina [1668a] n.d.), the Spaniards imposed an authority structure: a state whose center was Manila. This eventually succeeded in reducing the bloody conflicts that used to plague relations between barangays; it created a milieu where people from different parts of the Christian areas could peaceably work and study together. But the centralization created problems. Mayors and provincial governors were forever running to Manila for approval of their projects, for the national government controlled the purse. To resolve this problem, the 1991 Local Government Code has devolved functions, traditionally lodged in the central government, to the provincial, municipal, and barangay governments. Thus the municipal governments are allowed to retain a major share of the taxes they collect.

Is the tension between centralization and local autonomy another example of "cultural schizophrenia"? One where local forms of behavior subvert imported forms of organization? I see this tension rather as one that is both necessary and potentially creative in any nation-state. If centralization were to be completely ignored and all power turned over to the local governments, then the Filipino nation-state would cease to be. On the other hand if local autonomy were ignored, cities and provinces would continue to have little incentive to plan for their future. I am not suggesting that the Local Government Code is the ideal solution, I am merely stating that tensions may be inescapable when the institution is complex and that, when creatively handled, they can engender a new synthesis.

There are areas in Filipino culture where the fusion of indigenous and Western styles over the course of centuries has resulted in blends that draw on the strengths of both styles. One example is religious ritual.

As pointed out in the preceding essay, the procession of the Sacred Burial [Santo Entierro] on Good Friday represents a balance between the power of the Church and the power of leading families in a municipality. Doubtless the Good Friday procession is the one annual event in most Luzon and Visayan municipalities that draws massive popular participation. I ask: Would it do so if the church, as in Spain and Mexico, controlled ownership of the sacred images? Could it be that because of the dispersed ownership, the private owners and their followers gain a greater sense of involvement in the affairs of their church? Those who analyze Philippine reality in terms

of "cultural schizophrenia" and "split-level Christianity" are welcome
to interpret the Good Friday procession as one more instance of in-
coherence; but they will overlook that interplay between private
ownership (by families) and public management (by the parish
priest), which helps account for the widespread enthusiasm for such
processions. This enthusiasm surprises Catholics from Europe where
such processions are disappearing. Perhaps, in their case, this interplay does not exist anymore. There, Church authorities long ago
won firm control in what has become a Pyrrhic victory. Here, limited control by the priests has encouraged icon-owners to participate
and feel that the procession is theirs.

Rather than "split level," I would characterize Filipino Christianity as "syncretic," for it attempts to fuse two traditions, the
Christian and the indigenous, into one tradition. In the process,
tensions and conflicts appear between the two. But this is to be
expected in any culture. The history of Christianity itself in the
West is full of conflicts between official practices and local ones.

Another fear stalks educated Filipinos when reflecting on their
own culture: the fear of illegitimacy. Educated Filipinos themselves
characterize their own culture as "mongrel," "bastard," sometimes as
"half-breed," for Western influence permeates many areas of Christian Filipino culture whether in the countryside or in the city. For
instance: sautéing in garlic, onions, and tomatoes; dancing the fandan-
gos, jotas, and polkas; painting in oil; festivals like Christmas and Holy
Week; the Civil and Penal Codes; Spanish- and English-derived words
which account for over a third of the vernacular vocabulary.

Half-Breed, Mongrel, or Mestizo?

"Mongrel" contrasts the mixed with the pure-bred and regards the
former as inferior because of supposed incongruities; "bastard" refers to birth outside a formal union; "half-breed" denotes a fusion
that is awkward, for it does not fit in with any established category.
The Filipino cannot be faulted for harboring this fear. Other Asians
have traditionally looked down on both cultural and physical unions

that bring together East and West as "bastard." "Eurasian" connoted bastardy, for until fairly recently, Anglos (White Americans, Britons, and Australians) looked down on mixed marriages. Indeed there were laws in particular U.S. states (until the 1950s) and in apartheid-ruled South Africa (until the 1980s) that banned mixed marriages. Anglos extended this disdain to the cultural realm where the "truly Asian," the "pure indigenous," or even the "tribal" is deemed better than artifacts, like ours, which mix the indigenous and the Western. This unease with the "mixed" partly explains why many of our Asian neighbors (other than the Latinized Macanese and Goanese) and Anglos secretly look down on the lowland Christian Filipino and his achievements, whether of the past or of the present. Fortunately, over the past decade, there has been a sea-change in the English-speaking world. Some British Commonwealth authors, like the Indian expatriate Homi Bhabha (1994, 5–6), assert that "hybridity" is a common cultural condition. Suddenly, "hybrid," formerly a word that connoted "the unnatural/the artificial," has become fashionable. So likewise "fusion," as in "fusion cooking." But this is to get ahead of our story. I should address persisting concerns about "bastardy."

Bastard from Whose Perspective? Common but fallacious presuppositions are the following:

1. Intercultural unions between East and West are supposedly like interracial marriages: They produce "abnormalities."
2. Like interracial marriages during the colonial period, intercultural unions between East and West supposedly create "bastards."

Against presupposition 1, the following should be noted:

Intercultural mixing is not like marriages across racial lines. The realm of culture is symbolic; it is made up of codes invented by human beings. Its meanings therefore can change. There is no law of nature that forbids human beings from borrowing ideas from each other. On the other hand marriages across racial lines do involve the biological, a realm different from the symbolic, for here predetermined genes are at work. Regardless of what an individual may want, he or she inherits genes that determine skin color, hair color, and skeletal proportions. These physical characteristics are commonly called "race." But are interracial unions against nature?

The concept of "race" has itself become problematic. True, many physical anthropologists used to cluster all human beings into races. One scheme distinguishes the Negroid, the Caucasian, and the Mongoloid (Jolly and Plog 1978, 411). Most Filipinos are regarded as belonging to the southern branch of the Mongoloid, along with most peoples in Southeast Asia. Still, there are anthropologists who criticize even the concept of "race." They see this as only one way of classifying humankind on the basis of physical qualities. There are other ways. If, for example, blood type were used as the basis for classification, then peoples who differ in skin color will be found to resemble each other in their blood type while those who are similar in skin color may differ in blood type (Nelson and Jurmain 1985, 196 ff.; Campbell 1985, 479 ff.).

This critique is ignored in the Philippines, where "race" [*lahi*] and "culture" are often confused with each other, thanks to a long-discredited anthropological discourse inherited from nineteenth-century Europe. Authors routinely speak of the "Filipino race" or "Rizal, the pride of the Malay race." From the point of view of physical anthropology, there is no Filipino race, nor Malay race, nor, for that matter, a German or Japanese or Chinese race. But there is a Filipino or German or Japanese culture.

Granting that races do exist, interracial marriages are not contrary to nature, for the unions take place within one single species: *Homo sapiens*. Races are not species. They are merely variations within one species. Successful interbreeding between races is possible whereas members of a species cannot successfully interbreed with those of other species to produce a normal offspring (Nelson and Jurmain 1985, 106).

"Mongrel" and "half-breed" in English carry a history of prejudice against interracial and intercultural unions between Europeans
and non-Europeans. It is noteworthy that until the 1940s particular states in the U.S., like California, forbade intermarriage between
Whites and "Mongolians/Malayans" (Bulosan 1973, 143). True,
interracial and intercultural fusions have since become a common
pattern in coastal U.S. states and, above all, in innovative California.
But negative overtones continue to haunt the use of "half-breed"
and "half-caste." Meanwhile the term "Eurasian" has connoted bas-
tardies in countries like India.

These prejudices have posed as Modern Science. Herbert Spencer, the nineteenth-century British thinker who helped lay the
foundations for the emerging science of sociology, claimed that cultural development correlated with brain size and skin color. He also
asserted that because the half-caste inherits characteristics from two
ancestors, who are physically distinct from each other, he is "not
fitted" for either ancestor's institutions. No wonder, according to
Spencer (in Basave Benitez 1992, 92), contemporary Mexico and other
South American Republics were plagued with perpetual revolutions.
Though racism is no longer politically correct in Anglo-American
academe, I suspect that the prejudice against intercultural unions
between the Western and the non-Western lingers in some circles.

In contrast, despite its own checkered history, "mestizo," as
used today in the Spanish-speaking world, has gradually come to
mean merely a "mixture." This brings us to the second presupposition of many educated Filipinos. Because they have been cut off by
English from the Hispanic world and from their own Hispanic tradition, they imagine that interracial and intercultural unions in
Spanish America and the Philippines denoted illegitimacy. Many
assume that the exploitative Spaniards could not have contracted a
legally recognized union with native-born Filipinos.

Interracial Mixing. In fact interracial unions were recognized as legitimate as early as 1503 by the Spanish crown, when formalized

with a Catholic wedding (Benitez Basave 1992, 17).[5] An important factor was the scarcity of Spanish women (Garcia Bernal 1990, 177; Muñoz Perez 1988b, 155). Initially only one out of ten Spaniards who migrated to the New World was a woman. Moreover, the barriers between Amerindians and Spaniards were based more on social considerations; in particular, differences in customs and religion rather than on skin color. For the Spaniards themselves, being of mixed origins, exhibited different skin tonalities from white to dark olive. Remarks Alfredo Jimenez Nuñez (1989, 61), "The population of the Iberian peninsula has been historically mestizo (*es historicamente mestiza*)." It is worth noting that Northern Europeans have traditionally looked down on Latin Europeans, not only for being economically backward, but also for not looking fully white.

Over the course of three centuries, the fortunes of the mestizo in Spanish America, particularly Mexico, swung from acceptance in the sixteenth century to discrimination in the seventeenth and eighteenth centuries, then to respectability in the late nineteenth century. In the seventeenth century, the Spanish crown made the legal position of the mestizos, of European and Amerindian descent, unstable. It forbade the mestizos, along with the Spaniards, blacks and mulattoes, from living in Amerindian towns. At the same time it kept them from bearing arms and from holding either royal or public office and imposed restrictions on their entry into the religious Orders. The undesirability of having a mestizo offspring with uncertain legal status thus made illicit unions the common form of union between Spaniards and native women. During the eighteenth century, to be a mestizo was equated with being illegitimate even as the mestizos became more and more numerous (Garcia Bernal 1990, 180; Muñoz Perez 1988a, 658). The emphasis on legitimacy screened aspirants to the colleges even though there were indeed mestizos and mulattoes who did graduate with university degrees (Gonzalbo Aizpuru 1988, 112). In contrast the creoles, or local-born Spaniards, who went to the university, could become religious and could hold public office.

Nonetheless, while *indios* and Spaniards each had their own assigned quarters in Mexico City, this was not strictly observed. At the end of the seventeenth century, Spaniards with large stone buildings might reside in only one part of the building but they would rent out another part to indios and mestizos. Though social distance existed, strict segregation did not. Over time ties of friendship and compadrazgo formed across racial lines (Gonzalbo Aizpuru 2001).

The Wars of Independence against Spain in the early nineteenth century were waged by the creoles (Villoro 1976, 324). Initially, therefore, the privileged status of the creoles was maintained. However, the demographic reality was that the mestizos had become far more numerous. By the late twentieth century, three-fifths of Mexicans were classified as mestizo, one-fifth pure Amerindian, or indio, one-fifth creole. In the meantime, the revolutions in Mexico after 1810, that of 1858 and 1910, destroyed legal barriers to the upward mobility of mestizos and Amerindians alike, and thus made being mestizo respectable. Indeed, the ideology of the 1910 Mexican Revolution consciously exalted the notion of *mestizaje,* or the process of mixing race and culture, as will be shown.

What was the situation in the Philippines? Did "mestizo" by the eighteenth century connote illegitimacy? This is a question that surely needs more research.[6] Significantly, one of the most prestigious and wealthiest families at the turn of the eighteenth century, the Roxases, ancestors of the Ayalas, do not at all look creole in their portraits. They look mestizo. In Rizal's novel, *Noli me tangere,* as Nick Joaquin (1977) first pointed out, both Maria Clara and Crisostomo Ibarra are mestizos. But while the former is the bastard of a Spanish friar and a native, the latter is the formal scion of the Basque Eibarramendia who had opened a farm and had married a native woman (Rizal [1886] 1961, 50–51). Ibarra's background is ignored by those who use this novel to equate mestizo with bastardy. The relations between indios, mestizos, and creoles in the *Noli* are also worth reexamining. Despite interracial conflicts in the novel, peninsular, mestizo, and indio eat together at the same table (ibid., 11ff). In real life there were interracial conflicts as the German traveler, Jagor ([1875] 1965, 16), reported. However, the British consul of Hong Kong, Sir John Bowring (1859, 18–19), observed that the lines of separation between ranks and classes were "less marked and impassable than in most Oriental countries." Indeed "I have seen at the same table Spaniard, mestizo and Indian—priest, civilian and soldier."

For sure, snobbery imposed a social distance between these ranks and classes. Moreover, to borrow a phrase from the Mexican author Benitez Basave (1992), the "esthetic-erotic ideal" was white. However, as in Mexico City, strict segregation was not followed in Manila. By 1840, a government report (Merino 1987, 12) stated that half of the residents in Intramuros (then equivalent to Manila) were either indio or mestizo. They occupied more than a hundred houses, all the colleges, the Conciliar Seminary, sixteen holdings, and four lots [*solares*] where they lived packed together. On the other hand, Spaniards did reside outside the Walls in the neighboring suburbs of Quiapo and San Miguel. Quiapo's Calzada de San Sebastian (now Felix R. Hidalgo) was praised by a guidebook as "the best and most beautiful in all of Manila because its buildings are svelte and comfortable with well-made arcades" (Gonzalez 1875). Based on my own research as a Quiapense, at the street in the 1900s were the mansions of Manila's leading families. While the Paternos were Chinese mestizo, beside them was the mansion of Enriquez, a Spaniard. On the other side of the street lived the Legardas and the Aranetas. Though called "Spanish" because they can trace their ancestry to migrants from Spain, by the 1900s, they had become mestizo through intermarriage. An ancestor of the Legardas had earlier married into the Tuasons who began as Chinese migrants and had become socially prominent by the 1760s. The family tree of the Aranetas and Roxases shows unions with such Chinese mestizo families as the Chuidian, LaO, Locsin, Limsiaco, Tiongco (Araneta 1986, vol. 1). Directly in front of the Paternos was one of the several mansions of the Padillas who began as native-born entrepreneurs in the 1850s

(Legarda 1999, 314). Aside from being neighbors, ties of friendship linked these families together.

The role of Catholicism has been crucial. By the sixteenth century, it recognized that the dark-skinned peoples outside Europe were fellow human beings who should be saved.[7] This early acceptance of nonwhites into a moral community made interracial mixing more common in Catholic countries than in Protestant ones, says the non-Catholic historian, Arnold Toynbee (1948–1961, 1:211 ff.), for only from the nineteenth century onward would the Protestants proselytize among non-Europeans. When a black was holy, normal power relations were inverted among Catholics. The white recognized him as morally superior and sought his intercession with God, as in the case of St. Martin de Porres, a black Dominican laybrother from Peru. His cult was widely popular in Spanish America. Cults where Mary and Jesus are brown-skinned appeared by the sixteenth century. The most famous was the cult of Our Lady of Guadalupe who attracted and continues to attract indio, mestizo, and creole in Mexico (Lafaye 1976). Two of the most popular icons in the Philippines, the Black Nazarene of Quiapo and the Brown Virgin of Antipolo, were carved in seventeenth-century Mexico. Regardless of ethnicity, the Quiapo families mentioned above were devoted to these two icons.

Though places within churches were allotted preferentially according to social status, the church as ceremonial center was open to all ethnic groups. The obverse side to this acceptance of non-Europeans was that indios and mestizos were not admitted into religious Orders, like the Dominican, until the twentieth century (De la Rosa 1990, 21). If they were, initially they were not given high positions of responsibility.

In late-twentieth-century Spanish America, mestizo refers to people whose parents are of different races. It can also refer to things that are the product of a mixture of influences. Mestizaje on the other hand refers to the process by which this mixture has taken place. As used today in Spanish, mestizo does not have a negative ring.[8] In contrast, the term "hybrid," which some English-speakers abroad now use as a term for the increasingly common intercultural mixtures all over the world, still has an air of the forced and the unnatural about it.

Terms like "indio," "mestizo," and "criollo" have, over the course of time, become sociocultural categories in Spanish-speaking countries, particularly in Mexico and Central America, to the point that physical appearance is almost ignored, according to the American anthropologist Charles Wagley (1968, 52, 166). More important are criteria such as a person's language, custom, community membership, dress, and self-identification. For the Latin American today, an "indio" is someone who wears sandals, wears a "quaint costume," is a subsistence farmer, and has limited education; whereas a fellow who speaks elegant Spanish, has a university degree and a refined taste—but looks American Indian—is not indio. The same criteria apply to the Black. Because of intermarriage, there is a gradation in color from very dark to white, such that members of the middle and upper classes have Black and American Indian features. Wagley observed that the U.S. differed in that who is Negro and who is White depended almost exclusively on biological ancestry. In the U.S., even a fair-skinned individual whose occupation, manners, and economic position are middle to upper class in status is classified as Negro for as long as he has a remote Negro ancestor (ibid., 165). Today the respectable term is "Afro-American" rather than Negro; however, Wagley's observation still holds. For the rule of hypodescent prevails in the U.S (Kottak 2000, 139). This "automatically places the children of a union or mating between members of different groups in the minority group." Kottak (2000, 146–47) contrasts racial classifications in the U.S. with those in Brazil, another Iberian-influenced country, where he did his fieldwork. There, it is class status that affects one's racial classification. True, there is intense discrimination against poor, dark-skinned Brazilians. However, one who is light-skinned and poor tends to be perceived and classified as darker than someone who is colored but rich. Conversely, the dark-skinned professional is perceived as "light."

The advantage of both Spanish and Portuguese is that they have a concept of "mestizo." This the English language has not had. As evidence that "mestizo" has acquired a positive ring in Mexico, consider the inscription at the Plaza de las Tres Culturas in the district of Tlatelolco in Mexico City. The inscription commemorates the site where Cuauhtemoc, the last Aztec emperor, fell before the Spanish invaders. It ends with:

No fue ni triunfo ni derrota, fue el doloroso nacimiento del pueblo mestizo que es el México de hoy.

In English it would read:

It was neither a triumph nor a defeat, it was the painful birth of the mestizo people that is Mexico today.

Substitute "half-breed" or "hybrid" and the sentence becomes nonsensical.

Intercultural Mixing. Cultural *mestizaje*, as a desirable process, has a long tradition in Mexico. It gained early acceptance among the creoles. True, the Spaniards were shocked at the human sacrifice and cannibalism that formed an integral part of the Aztec's indigenous religion. Stamping out the "devilish rites" became an excuse to destroy the Aztec monuments and raise churches and palaces over them. This contemptuous attitude toward the indigenous has been one running theme in Mexican history down to the 1910 Revolution which, in addition to being a social and economic upheaval, was also a cultural one, for it affirmed the dignity of the Amerindian cultures. Yet the 1910 Revolution, as a cultural event, had predecessors.

The development of the humanities and fine arts in sixteenth-century Mexico City was mestizo in character, for they had two poles, the indigenous and the Spanish, whose networks and ideas interwove with each other. Indigenous intellectuals learned Latin, classical rhetoric, and Western philosophy; some became acclaimed authors on these topics. Spaniards, like the Franciscans, wrote on the glories of the fallen native empire with the help of native informants. Spanish plays were translated into Nahuatl, or written in it (Gruzinski 2001). By the late sixteenth century, the Spaniards who had elected to stay permanently in Mexico, in other words, the creoles, consciously used the Indian past as an heirloom to differentiate themselves from the peninsular Spaniard, the *gachupin*. The creoles formed the highest layer of the social order in Mexico and were highly educated (Manrique 1976, 364). Among them were writers, both lay and religious, who wrote with pride about the indigenous past. An example is Sor Juana Ines (1651–1695), often regarded as Mexico's greatest poet. The widely read nun knew of the bloody pre-Hispanic rites, yet she tried to show that the Aztec religion was essentially the "true" religion and, for this reason, evangelization was easy: The ancient Mexicans worshipped the Great God of the Seeds who had taken the form of food and was consumed (Manrique 1976, 368). However, the progress of cultural mestizaje was not a straight path. For reasons to be further studied, models more strictly European prevailed among educated creoles and peninsulars starting in the second half of the seventeenth century (Gruzinski 2001, 219).

The cultural life of seventeenth-century Manila, then Asia's entrepot because of the galleon trade, was vibrant and drew on diverse sources according to John Summers (1998). Festivals were common and required new music to compose. There were poetry contests; the poems were written on long paper scrolls and posted. Entries were in Castilian, Basque, Latin, Greek, Portuguese, Italian, Visayan, and Tagalog. There were entries in "Mexican"—most likely, Nahuatl, the language of the Aztec empire. There were non-European dances by the Chinese, Japanese, and Tagalogs. Two centuries later, in the nineteenth century, Manila experienced another flowering of the arts. This sprang up among the city's different ethnic groups. In an article to be published in a book on Quiapo's heritage, Santiago Albano Pilar shows how artists of indio, Chinese mestizo, and Spanish ancestry excelled in the visual arts and competed with each other in open competitions sponsored by the Spanish government.

The Affirmation of Mestizaje. The Mexican 1910 Revolution overturned the dictator Porfirio Diaz and sought to affirm Indian culture and rights to land (Basave Benitez 1992). The study of the indigenous tradition became more systematic and widespread. Though the Spanish contribution was critiqued, it was not rejected either. Nationalists realized that the fusion of traditions was what made Mexico itself and no other. A literature on mestizaje began to flow. Thus Octavio Paz says that the Christianity brought in by the Spaniards was itself syncretistic. It had assimilated the pagan deities and transformed them into saints and devils. The phenomenon was repeated in Mexico. The ancient beliefs and divinities took on a Christian veneer and continued to appear in popular religiosity. Mesoamerican civilization may have died a violent death; the religion, language, and political institutions of Mexico are indeed Western, but the Indian face of Mexico continues to be alive and to give her a different orientation.

The situation is different in the U.S. where the Indians who were not exterminated were forced into reservations. While the Indian dimension does not show in the U.S. on the national level, Mexico is a land "between two civilizations and two peoples" (Paz 1994, 442). In an analysis of cultural mestizaje and the baroque, Bolivar Echeverria points out that the Amerindians and Blacks of Latin America used the baroque style in a paradoxical manner. Instead of literally following the strict canons of Western art, they so played with these canons that they inverted their meaning. Mestizaje is "the natural form of all cultures." The usual biologistic metaphor of mestizaje as a "combination of qualities" is inadequate. Mestizaje is rather a "semiotic process," for the symbolic subcodes drawn up by various human groups do not just coexist. Faced with a new subcode, a symbolic subcode devours it and assimilates it (Echeverria 1994,

32). In neither of these authors does cultural mestizaje appear as an easy fusion of traditions. It is articulated in terms of tensions and oppositions which are accepted as part of being human.

A study of the emergence of the notion of cultural mestizaje in the Philippines has yet to be made. It would look at the union between traditions of the Mongoloid Austronesian-speaking peoples, who form the majority, and those traditions of both the earlier inhabitants, the Agtas, and later settlers, like the Chinese, Europeans, Mexican Indians, and Americans with an eye on both the fusions and tensions in the emerging culture.

Such a history should also examine conscious attempts by Filipinos to deal with these cultural unions either through rejection or through acceptance. Since a selective acceptance is what I personally espouse, I would look at the rationalizations of those who were proud of the 1896 Revolution yet were accepting, too, of what was best in the Spanish tradition. An example would be Cecilio Apostol (1941) who wrote that:

> *[S]abemos que, al principio, para pactar su alianza, juntaron y bebieron, a la nativa usanza, sus sangres, en un vaso, Legazpi y el Rajah.*

> [W]e know that, in the beginning, to seal the alliance, Legazpi and the Rajah came together and, following native custom, drank their blood from a common cup.

Judging from Juan Luna's painting of the blood compact between Legazpi and Sikatuna, the Blood Compact seems to have been an important image among Filipinos, from Rizal's time (and probably even earlier) down to Apostol's generation.

Then came the generation after. Outstanding was Claro Recto (1960, 10 ff.), who saw that to battle American cultural imperialism, it was important to firm up pride in the Filipino tradition, which has a strong Spanish component, and in knowing the literature of the 1896 Revolution, which was largely in Spanish. The crusade was continued by the much-misunderstood Nick Joaquin whose icon is, not only Nuestra Señora del Santíssimo Rosario, Our Lady of the Most Holy Rosary, Queen of the Sea Battles, but likewise the ecstatic female shamans of indigenous rituals.[9] But we must go beyond Joaquin. Though he talks about the fusion of the indigenous, the Chinese, the Spanish, and the American in the Filipino, he is silent on the potential contribution of the Negritos/Agtas.

Identity should be Interpreted Culturally

The question of identity, whether local or national, is also a cultural one. Yet it is often discussed solely in psychologistic terms; worse still it is approached in a biologistic manner that is unknowingly racist. The cultural identity of the lowland Christian Filipino is thus often conceived of in a pejorative manner. We need to go back to the concept of "culture" as articulated by twentieth-century cultural anthropologists and its difference from "race." Earlier, Franz Boas ([1948] 1955) had emphasized that there is no correlation between ways of thinking and body form. People think differently from each other because they grow up in a particular culture, each of which has its own way of interpreting the world. He said that it was normal for a culture to accept new ideas from other cultures but that these are inevitably filtered and transformed by the preexisting local tradition. He also posited that because of the unending inflow of new ideas, no culture can ever be fully integrated. His are basic ideas that many overlook today.

We should examine the lenses Anglos use when viewing lowland, Hispanized Filipino culture. True, Boas and the American Historicalist school liberated the study of culture from the biologism of the nineteenth century; however, I fear that this biologism continues to tint the lenses of many Anglos when they look at intercultural and interracial fusions between Europeans and non-Europeans, for instance in the Philippines. While they may respect the fusion of cultures in Java (Indian-Islamic-indigenous) or in Thailand (Indian-indigenous), a number look condescendingly on mixtures of Western and indigenous cultures and consider it inferior to either the purely Western or the purely indigenous.[10] Earlier, I cited overviews of Asian art where the achievements of lowland Christian Filipinos are either ignored or cursorily treated in comparison to the extensive treatment given other Asians, including our non-Hispanized brothers in the Cordillera and in Sulu-Mindanao. As an American colleague, an anthropologist who has lived in the Philippines, once put it: "Give me dances from the tribes or from Moslems. Your lowland dances are third-rate Spanish." (He was then enjoying Filipino dishes prepared by his Filipino girl friend. Mediterranean influence underlay the dishes, for they were sautéd in garlic, onion, and tomatoes). Unfortunately, because many Filipinos, including even some nationalists, think in English and use its categories, they too develop a condescending attitude toward their own culture. Hence their penchant for using adjectives like "mongrel," "bastard," "derivative," or "imitative" when describing their heritage.

A complicating factor is that many believe that since an "Asian" identity exists, the Philippines must be strange for not conforming to this idealized identity. I will show in the next essay that this "Asia" is in fact a Western invention.

We need to do more cross-cultural comparisons and analyses. Too often Filipino scholars believe they can examine the Filipino identity without trying to understand other cultures as well. In reality, they implicitly make cross-cultural comparisons without realizing it, as when they claim that other Asian cultures have retained their primordial identity whereas we have lost ours. This claim is doubtful if we do an explicit cross-cultural comparison that does not look at Western influence as the only extraneous influence. As mentioned above, Islam, too, was originally extraneous to the Maranao and the Javanese. It is significant that little is known about what Taosug, Maranao, and Maguindanao cultures were like before Islam. Surely they did not begin only with Islamization in the same way that Tagalog and Visayan cultures did not begin only with

Christianization. We hear that among Moslem Indonesians and Mindanaonons, ordinary people still propitiate spirits in the environment, eat raw fish, and, while avoiding domestic pigs, eat wild pigs. We should examine other Asian cultures with an eye on similar incongruities. In a previous essay, I have exposed these for Vietnam vis-à-vis Chinese influences (Zialcita 1996).[11] We can go beyond Asia. Mention was made of incongruities between Germanic culture and Latin influences. For all the English arrogance about purity of culture, theirs is a mestizo culture. The language itself, though Germanic in structure, has many Latin and French words. This heterogeneity results in inconsistent rules of pronunciation, making it difficult for the nonnative speaker to master these rules. Thus "-ain" in "mountain" because of French influence [*montagne*] is pronounced differently from "-ain" in "rain," which is of Germanic origin.

Finally Filipinos should reestablish contact with Spanish America, particularly Mexico. The Filipino is looked upon as an oddity by other Asians, by Anglo-Americans and by non-Latin Europeans for being in Asia and being, at the same time, Hispanized. Their reactions range from puzzlement to condescension to contempt. These reactions subtly act upon many educated Filipinos and make them apologetic about their culture. In Mexico and some other Spanish American countries, however, at least officially, the notion of cultural mestizaje is regarded as a given. While they emphasize the bonds created by a common Hispanic culture, they also articulate their differences from each other and from Spain—differences brought about in part by the ethnic mix in each country. Thus while Anglos question why we dance jotas, Spanish Americans want to know how our jotas differ from theirs: They look for the "thisness" of our cultural creations. Some Britons, Germans, and Australians deplore the Spanish influence on Filipino food and look in vain for that burning flavor that they equate with Southeast Asian cooking. But Argentines, according to the culinary expert Nora Daza (1965) who lived in Buenos Aires for some time, are fascinated by the novelty of Filipino cuisine: The tomato sauce that is omnipresent in all Latin cooking is flavored with soy sauce. My experience with Mexicans and Italians has been similar. While books on Asian art ignore the ecclesiastical and civil architecture of the sixteenth- to nineteenth-century Philippines, Dorta's overview on Hispanic architecture (1973) includes the Philippines and articulates its singularity vis-à-vis Spanish American countries. Within the last decade, a steady stream of Spanish and Spanish American art scholars has visited the islands; they praise the originality of the local visual styles.[12]

In Mexico and in Spanish America, tensions between races and ethnic groups no doubt exist. The integration of both the indigenous and the Spanish into a tradition open to all Mexicans is still going on and is fraught with conflicts (Benitez Basave 1992).[13] The same may be said for the Philippines where the creation of a national tradition should pay attention, not only to the lowland mixture of indigenous-Chinese-Spanish, but also to the cultures of the non-Hispanized uplands and of Mindanao-Sulu. The situation in Mexico is still far from ideal. Nonetheless, dialogues with Mexicans and other Spanish Americans should hopefully make us realize that we are not at all a cultural freak.[14] In Andersen's fable, the duckling, whom other ducks ridiculed for its long neck, found out, from swimming in the right company, that in truth it was a graceful swan.

Notes

This essay is a revision of "Culturally, We Are All Mestizos" which appeared in 1998, *Budhi* 2, no. 1:137–58.

1. Pujo Semedi, an anthropologist, told me that as a student taxi-driver in Yogyakarta, he once picked up the wife of a high-ranking government official. The couple were known to be Moslems. Nonetheless, she went to Shiva's temple at Loro Djonggrang, prayed inside, and asked to be driven home. In contrast another anthropologist from Sumatra refused to visit the Hindu and Buddhist monuments while at Yogyakarta on the grounds that they were "pagan."

2. Carter-Bentley (1985) reports a case given by Mamita Saber of the feud between Batuampar and Sorosong. The feud started with Sorosong kiss-

ing Batuampar's sister in 1898. In retaliation the latter killed the former. But Sorosong's allies killed Batuampar's two young male cousins and reduced Batuampar's sister to slavery. Still, Sorosong's grandson decided to take revenge in 1945 by slaying Batuampar's wealthy grandson and his entire family without their knowing the reason. Grant Carter-Bentley (1985) gives other cases of violent conflicts. One began over a quarrel over a card game and soon drew in kin groups. The following case from the 1990s was narrated to me by a colleague who runs a nongovernmental organization, specializing in legal cases, in a Mindanao city. "A Maranao woman had been kissed by Ali. His relatives agreed to have the matter brought to the Islamic court, the Shari'ah. A compensation in the form of audiovisual equipment was given to the woman's relatives. However, some of her relatives still sought revenge. They wanted to kiss a close relative of Ali. Foreseeing the violent consequences, the intended victim escaped from Lanao and sought help."

3. The literature on this is abundant. As an example for Northern Luzon, see the detailed ethnographies on the Ilongot of Nueva Vizcaya, for instance by M. Rosaldo (1980).

4. Scott (1994) reconstructs in detail the indigenous religious systems in each of the different peoples of the Philippines at Spanish contact.

5. The king's instruction to Governor Ovando was that Spaniards should marry indios so that the latter would become "people of reason" [*gente de razon*]. In 1514, Ferdinand the Catholic formally authorized mixed unions (Benitez Basave 1992, 17).

6. Clarita Nolasco (1969) studied the Filipino creoles from the sixteenth to the nineteenth centuries. A similar study is needed on the mestizos whether European or Chinese.

7. Thus the papal bull, *Sublimis Deus* of 1537, says that the devil inspires his minions to claim that the newly discovered Indians are brutes who were created to serve Europeans and who are incapable of receiving the Faith. "We know . . . that the Indians are true human beings" (Jimenez 1989).

8. As far back as 1917, the *Enciclopedia Universal Ilustrada Euopeo-Americana* (1917, 1091), under the entry for "Mestizo," says that:

> All cultures are characterized by a mixed combination (*combinación mestiza*) of cultural elements of diverse origin and have been preceded by greater or lesser proportions of *mestizaje* by blood.

In French, *métis*, which translates as mestizo, sometimes connotes inferiority vis-à-vis the purebred. Still, the Black French-speaking African writer, Leopold Sédar Senghor (1964, 395), reports that when De Gaulle was asked if African infusions would "pollute French blood," his answer was "The future belongs to *métissage.*"

9. The encounter between Christianity and paganism, interpreted as both opposition and fusion, is the theme of Joaquin's (1991) "Summer Solstice," and "Legend of the Virgin's Jewel." In other stories, like "Candido's Apocalypse," the synthesis of Hispanic and indigenous tradition is opposed to the intrusive American culture. But this, too, ends in a new synthesis. Candido accepts his Americanized nickname and self as part of his identity. Joaquin's essays (1989) embrace and justify intercultural fusions.

10. A miniencyclopedia on popular music around the world downplays contemporary Filipino music for being influenced by Spanish and American models (Broughton et al. 1994, 438–39). It discusses only Freddie Aguilar and yet ignores the Apo Hiking Society. Surprisingly it ignores Kontragapi and Joey Ayala's Bagong Lumad. Noteworthy is that in the ASEAN Music Festivals, Filipinos regularly win prizes. One suspects that these writers had preexisting biases against mainstream Filipino culture, for being mestizo, and were not willing to understand it in its particularity.

11. In Vietnam, Chinese impositions led to the substitution of patrilineal kinship for bilateralism. However, Vietnamese women have maintained a higher status than their Chinese sisters. The Chinese tried to ban betel nut chewing, but the Vietnamese practice it to this day!

12. Some of the architects who have visited within the last five years are Javier Galvan Guijo, Javier San Roman, Juan Porras (from Spain); Nelson Herrera (from Cuba); and Jorge Loyzaga (from Mexico).

13. Benitez Basave (1992, 143–44) asks if Mexico has a mere superposition of cultures rather than a true *mestizaje* where the *indio* substratum permeates the European layer imposed on it. Economic equality is needed as a prior condition. So likewise cultural equality. The indigenous past should be a source of inspiration in the creation of a contemporary culture. In this regard, the Philippines has an advantage: The continued use of the vernaculars inevitably refashions imported ideas.

14. Friendly Spanish Americans can understand one side of our identity: the very fact of our having mixed the European and non-European. But the other side, the Austronesian, is surely accessible only to fellow Austronesian speakers like Indonesians and Malaysians. I feel an affinity when mixing with ordinary Dyaks, Sundanese, Sumatrans, and Javanese.

PART III

Identity in the Global Village

As yet an Asian Flavor
does not Exist

The Philippines constitutes the only true end-point of the world.
—Pierre Chaunu 1960, *Les Philippines et le Pacifique des Ibériques*

JAVANESE DIP DEEP-FRIED and roasted foods either in sambal—a paste made from red chili peppers, garlic, salt, and sugar—or in *terasi,* a fermented shrimp/fish paste that may be studded with chopped red chilies. Tagalogs prefer dipping sauces with a sour base: palm vinegar with a lone crushed chili pepper pod; vinegar with slivers of onion with mashed garlic and pepper; chopped green camias and tomatoes; or small raw pickled mangoes mixed with tomatoes and coriander. Though the Javanese use some tamarind juice in their dishes, they complain that the Tagalog's sour dishes, especially those cooked in vinegar, upset their system. On the other hand while the Tagalogs use some chili pepper, many of them claim that sambal burns their stomach. Which taste is more authentically "Asian": the Javanese or the Tagalog?

Many assume that an identifiable pan-Asian sensibility exists in all domains, from philosophy to literature to music to cooking; and that while Javanese culture is authentic, because it conforms to this ideal norm, Tagalog culture is inauthentic because submission to Spanish colonization has alienated it from this norm. Thus, the writer Mariles Vitug (interview 1997) asked the culinary expert Doreen Fernandez, "The Philippines has been colonized twice. Did

239

this confuse the country's cuisine?" Note the loaded word "confuse." In an interview for the *Philippine Star*, Lorrie Reynoso, a chef-instructor at the prestigious New York Restaurant School, says that the consensus of Filipinos and American food editors and critics is that when Westerners think of Asian cuisine, "whether it is Thai, Burmese, Indonesian," they always associate it with indigenous spices "which Philippine cuisine does not have" (Martel 1997).

I question, however, whether a pan-Asian sensibility has ever existed—especially one that favors burning spices. For their dipping sauce, the North Vietnamese favor *nuoc mam*, which, like our *patis,* is an amber-colored fish sauce. On this they sprinkle a few slices of chili. Cantonese food, which has influenced Filipino sensibility, uses ginger, pepper, and soy sauce but not the variety of spices one finds in Java, certainly not the chili pepper that Szechwanese love. While Koreans love plenty of chilis and garlic, Japanese abhor their taste and their smell as low class. They prefer mustard (wasabi) and soy sauce. Who is more Asian: the Japanese who hate garlic and chili or the Szechwanese and Koreans who love these?

I also question whether indigenous pre-Hispanic, pre-Islamic Philippine societies participated in a pan-Asian passion for piquancy. According to my anthropology students, who have lived in the uplands of Mindanao, both the hitherto animist upland Bukidnon and Manobo only use salt for flavoring, and sometimes not even that because of the cost of transport from the coast. The town centers of Ilocos Norte were exposed to Hispanization from the late sixteenth century onward. But Ilocano farmers, among whom I stayed while doing field research, generally use only bagoong to flavor their everyday vegetables and occasional meats. Peppers appear when they fry and sauté [*guisa*], usually for feasts. Their term for black pepper is *paminta*, from the Spanish *pimienta*. It is hard to believe that their ancestors enjoyed spicy meals before the coming of the Spaniards. Or that contemporary Ilocano farmer taste is "confused."

As far back as the early seventeenth century, the missionary Alcina ([1668a] n.d., 3, 351) observed of the Visayans that "many times [they take] their roots or rice alone or with a little salt and not all have this always." The Boxer Codex ([1590] 1960, 364) said of the Visayans that "their ordinary food is a little rice boiled solely in water and some sun-dried fish." Neither author mentioned pepper and other spices. Just because we are close to the Spice Islands does not mean that a taste for black pepper was widespread here before Legazpi. Or that cardamom, cloves, cumin, and nutmeg were regular seasoning agents of Visayan and Tagalog food. Westernization supposedly resulted in the loss of piquancy. And yet the descendants of the Mexican Indians, who domesticated the chili before Columbus (Sabau 1992), came here during the galleon trade, bringing with them new plants, cooking styles, and the fiery fruit. In the rest of Asia, Portuguese traders introduced the chili.[1] That a taste for it spread like fire in other Southeast Asian countries, whereas it merely simmers among us, says something about the intensity of the Filipino sensibility.

I propose questioning a concept that is over two millennia old, namely, "Asia." Simplistic notions of what Asia is and should be in relation to the West have succeeded in marginalizing, on the international scene, the achievements of lowland Christian Filipinos, not only in cuisine, but in the other arts as well. They have also succeeded in making many educated lowland Christian Filipinos apologetic about their culture *when they reflect on it and have to articulate it before outsiders.* Often they assume that since the costume, the music, the architecture, and the literature of lowland Christian Filipinos have an obvious Hispanic component, they cannot be Asian, for to be Asian means to be non-Western. Therefore, they cannot be "authentic" either, for to be in Asia means thinking and behaving like a true Asian. Thus the anguish in defining the Christian Filipino's identity. The maps indicate that his country is in Asia but both fellow-Asians and Western authors (generally non-Latin) question his credentials as an "Asian." On the other hand, though Hispanic elements continue to be vivid in the Filipino's culture, Spanish as a spoken language has practically disappeared from his home, office, and school. This is a situation shared by the Filipino with the Guamanian. Hence, despite interest in the Philippines among educated Spaniards and Spanish Americans, and despite invitations to join their group activities, non-Spanish-speaking Filipinos shun such activities whether these be informal get-togethers or formal conferences. And while the educated Filipino is fluent in English, he cannot join either that club of English-speaking former colonials, the British Commonwealth, simply because he was colonized by the Americans rather than the British. He does not play cricket. In which gathering of nations is the lowland Christian Filipino fully accepted for what he is, given his unique history? This dilemma galls especially if we consider that in Filipino culture, one has to belong to a *barkada*—to a peer group. Who are our likely barkada mates in the assembly of nations?

Assumptions about "Asia" resonate in other fields, for instance, political economy. During the economic boom in Asia from the late 1980s to 1997, the Philippines lagged far behind. Citizens of the wealthier Asian countries and influential Filipinos conveniently explained this as the result of Westernization. Being individualistic, Filipinos supposedly do not have the "Asian sense of community-orientedness." They did not mention the fact that Laos, Cambodia, Bangladesh, and India were also behind. Or that North Korea, where the state owned the strategic resources and the important enterprises, in the name of the people, experienced famines because individual farmers had no incentive to increase or improve production.

In this article, I would like to show that the Filipino should not feel embarrassed about not being sufficiently "Asian," for this Western-invented construct has no clear content. He should not feel embarrassed either about being Westernized, for the West is a syncretism-in-process. The insistence on measuring Filipino achievements according to a supposed Asian norm has prevented many, including Filipinos themselves, from appreciating the originality of some of these achievements.

Asia or Asias?

Arnold Toynbee (1948–1961, 8:706 ff.) questioned the relevance of the terms "Asia" and "Europe" in his *A Study of History* which lists and compares the genesis of all known civilizations. Then followed John Steadman's *The Myth of Asia* (1969), an entire book which focuses on questioning the concept of an Asia. But these critiques have been largely ignored. It was Edward Said (1984) who popularized the notion of "Orientalism" by claiming that Westerners had created a simplistic and degrading stereotype of the Orient. By "Orient," he meant largely the Arab countries. I will sum up the arguments of Toynbee, since they are not known to the general public, and I will add my own observations regarding the philosophical systems and culinary traditions of the region. Moreover, I propose using a new term "Continentism" to refer to the habit of dividing the world into continents and imagining that each has an unchanging Platonic essence.

Every society has a system for classifying all human societies known to it. The Chinese regard their country as the Middle Kingdom [*zhung guo*]. Indeed they call it such today. In imperial times, the Chinese regarded their country as the center point of the world; all other peoples were outsiders in varying degrees of inferiority. Moslems on the other hand have classified people as either believers or infidels.

The ancient Greeks first used the terms, "Asia" and "Europe," to refer to both a continent and a way of life (Toynbee 1948–1961, 8:708 ff.). While Asia was "intuitive" and "emotional," Europe was supposedly "rational." Ironically, at this stage, the land mass that they called "Asia" was the Anatolian Peninsula whose coastline, like the Greek mainland itself, was then populated by Greek colonies. The Romans called Anatolia "Asia Minor" and the vast unknown realm beyond "Asia Major." They continued the Greek habit of imagining that Europe was "rational" while Asia was "mystical." But what was the basis for these pat generalizations? Did they send study missions to that vast realm to examine the way of life of the different societies in detail? None. It was left to one of their successor peoples, the Westerners, to do detailed, factual studies of the peoples of Asia starting in the eighteenth century. But while the Greek notion that the Sun revolved around the planet Earth was rejected by Copernican astronomy, the Greek habit of dividing the world into continents, each endowed with a Spirit, was retained. In the meantime another dichotomy, unknown to the Greeks, entered. This was the dichotomy between "West" and "East." The Roman Empire split up in the fifth century A.D. into two halves: the Western and the Eastern. Christendom divided accordingly. Western Christians acknowledged the authority of the pope in Rome; Eastern Christians respected the patriarchs, chief among whom was the patriarch of Byzantium/ Constantinople. Eventually with increasing secularization, Western Christians simply referred to themselves as "Westerners."[2] They saw themselves as the heirs to Graeco-Roman rationalism, in contrast to the supposedly mystical Easterners. One curious thing about this dichotomy is that it regards even the Byzantines, who spoke Greek and kept alive the Greek philosophical tradition, as "mystical," being Easterners, and therefore as less rationalistic than the Latin-speaking Westerners.

This dichotomy has made us forget that ideas have flowed from East to West and vice versa over millennia. Nothing can be more "Asian," we imagine, than those sculptures of serene, lifelike Buddhas dressed in robes with rippling folds. And yet it was Hellenic art which inspired sculptors during the second century B.C. in Buddhist-influenced Northwest India to interpret Buddhas and Boddhisativas realistically through an interplay of light and shadow. From thence the new esthetic spread to Java, Burma, Cambodia, and Siam (Zimmer 1955, 340 ff.). In the 1980s, under George Ellis, the Honolulu Academy of Arts opened at long last a small but permanent exhibit on Filipino santos. One of the best pieces is a wooden saint whose face and monk's robe are expressively sculpted. Understandably, Ellis located this exhibit in the Western rather than in the Asian wing. The truth is it could have been located in either wing.

At the same time Westerners easily forget their artistic debt to Asians. Gothic seems the quintessential Western style and a symbol of Christianity, for its pointed arches soar toward the infinite. And yet the pointed arch was invented in the Near East in the seventh century A.D., popularized in the ninth century (Briggs 1959, 13) and introduced into the West in the eleventh to the twelfth centuries by returning crusaders. When the Golden Mosque was inaugurated in Quiapo, Manila, in the 1980s, some commented that it had no relationship to the surrounding cityscape. In fact it did. The pointed arches related to another Quiapo landmark, the Neo-Gothic San Sebastian Basilica of 1891, while the dome connected to the dome of nearby Quiapo Church. Both Moslems and Christians inherited the dome, and other features of their civil culture, from the Romans.

That there has been no Asia can be shown if we examine the following: geography, race, language, and culture.

Geography. Toynbee (1948–1961, 8:708 ff.) questioned whether Asia and Europe can be neatly separated from each other in terms of physical geography. By convention the Ural Mountains running vertically across Russia divide Europe from Asia. But these are really low-lying hills. They have not barred the movements of empire-building pastoralists like the Huns and the Mongols. To use the language of the 1970s, the hills do not divide ecosystems from each other. The Russian steppes constitute a single ecosystem: the Black Earth. Another boundary is supposed to be the Hellespont between the Greek and Anatolian Peninsulas. Still another are the Suez marshes between Egypt and the Sinai. We may doubt whether the latter two boundaries do separate distinct ecosystems. On the other hand, Asia as currently defined, covers many contrasting ecosystems: tundras, steppes, fertile floodplains, the towering Himalayas, rain forests, tropical archipelagoes. We should ask: Why not cluster the Philippines with other Pacific Islands that fall outside "Asia"? Why does attention focus solely on what it has in common with the rest of an "Asia," which includes even the snow-capped Himalayas and the deserts of the Arabian Peninsula?

Race. We hear talk of an "Asian look." Supposedly this means being nonwhite. The fact is that representatives of the Caucasoid race, the same race to which Europeans and Americans belong, form the majority among Arabs, Jews, Pakistanis, Iranians, and Afghans. In India, the white-skinned Aryans constitute the upper castes while the dark-skinned Dravidians form the bulk of the lower castes. On the other hand there are the Mongoloids to which the Chinese, Japanese, and Southeast Asians belong. There is no Asian look.

Language. Often India and the West are sharply contrasted with each other, with India somehow representing the quintessence of "Asia" because of the wide influence of Hinduism and especially of Buddhism throughout the region. Juan Francisco (1985) says that before the sixteenth century A.D., Indian influence did indeed enter the Philippines, particularly the Visayas and Luzon; but this was in diluted form via visitors from Indonesia rather than from India. However, Filipino intellectuals like to believe that the Filipino spirit is closer to the Indian than to the Western. Be that as it may, it is worth emphasizing that the Indian, Iranian, and European languages all belong to the same family of languages, the Indo-European (Burrow 1955). The Aryans were a cattle-herding people who spread in all directions from a hypothetical heartland in Central Europe. Groups entered India, overcame the local kingdoms and constituted themselves as the priestly and warrior castes (Lincoln 1987). *Diwata* may seem so Filipino, but in fact it comes from *dev*, the Sanskrit word for god to which the Latin word, *divus*, is related. From divus came words like *dios*, *divino*, and "divine," which have entered common usage in the Philippines. Which indeed is more "Asian" and therefore more Filipino: "diwata" or "Dios"?

One of the West's sources of unity, despite the bitter wars among its member countries, are languages that transcend national boundaries. Latin was such a language, then French, and now English. In Islam, Arabic has played an even more important unifying role. But for Asia as a whole, we would be hard put looking for a unifying Asian-based language. There are different language families in Asia: the Tibeto-Chinese-Burmese, the Japanese, the Turkic, the Austroasiatic, the Austronesian, the Arabic, and the Indo-European. Arabic unifies Moslems; thanks to Buddhism, Pali and Sanskrit have influenced the languages of Tibet, Burma, Thailand, Cambodia, Java, Vietnam, China, Korea, and Japan; for centuries Japanese, Koreans, and Vietnamese read Chinese script and incorporated this into their languages. But historically no language from within the region has brought together Japanese Buddhist, Iranian Moslem, Chinese Confucian, and Hindu. The lingua franca of all four today is English.

Culture. There are societies that differ from each other in many aspects of their culture, but nonetheless share felt communalities because they all revere similar symbols in various fields such as art, law, literature, philosophy, or religion. They therefore constitute an *oikumene*—to use this Greek-derived expression: a universe of spiritual and cultural meanings revered by several societies (Toynbee 1948–1961, vol. 1; 1972). Oikumenes become possible when full-time occupational specialization is established in a society and a distinction is thus drawn between mental and manual labor. The fortunate privileged few are freed to speculate, plan, innovate, often in urban centers, and dialogue with their peers in other societies. Such a broad cultural community constitutes a "civilization" or what I prefer to call "civil culture." Unlike Tylor ([1832–1917] 1958) and some historians, Toynbee and Anglo-American archaeologists do not regard "civilization" and "culture" as equivalent terms. A civilization is a type of culture. It implies a state, indeed a "universal state," according to Toynbee—a state that embraces many diverse peoples. In most cases it has implied the existence of a city [*civitas*]. Moreover, at the heart of every civilization is a vision of how people of diverse backgrounds can relate to and live with each other (Toynbee

1972, 44). This vision is manifest in a particular artistic style (Toynbee 1972, 46). An example of an oikumene, or of a civilization, is Islam that transcends the boundaries of "Asia," "Africa," and "Europe." The community of believers extends from Lanao in Mindanao to Morocco in North Africa, from Uganda to Bosnia in the Balkans. Before the advent of nineteenth-century nationalism, any Moslem "entered, upon his arrival in a Muslim country, into the rights and duties of the local population" (Von Grunebaum 1955, 44). During the nineteenth century, the Barbary States in North Africa and Aceh in Sumatra both turned to the Ottomans, as brother Moslems, for help against the Western powers (Mehmet 1990).

For this article, my examples of ecumenical styles are drawn primarily from cooking, secondarily from philosophy.

Toynbee (1948–1961, vol.1) catalogues all the known "civilizations."[3] Of these, four are relevant to our discussion: the Islamic, the Indian-influenced, the Chinese-influenced, and the Western. The final essay in this book will point out that differences between them make it difficult to speak of "Southeast Asia" as an oikumene. Here I would like to stress that differences between the first three make the concept of an "Asia" questionable. The Prophet Mohammed's vision inspires Islam; Brahmanism animates India; Theravada Buddhism flourishes in Sri Lanka, Burma, Thailand, Laos, and Cambodia; Confucian ethics guides China, Korea, Japan, and Vietnam. To force these divergent traditions into one mold disfigures them.

Islam, for instance, stresses the Absolute Oneness and Otherness of the Lord. It bans representations of the divine in human form. And yet such representations play a vital role among Buddhist, Christian, and Hindu alike. Islam carries its quest for purity into the kitchen. In the name of God, it bans foods, like pork, as unclean (Ali n.d., 173). It prescribes slaughtering procedures to expel impurities; it requires that animal blood be drained from the meat. Brahmanism starts from the opposite direction. Unlike Islam and Christianity, it believes that the self must be reborn into several lifetimes and be purified before it can dissolve into Ultimate Reality. There are many gods and goddesses who dwell in the universe. Some can teach humans the path to ultimate union through meditation. While the Moslem preaches a universal brotherhood of all believers, Brahmanism divides society into castes and imposes a strict separation between them. Contact with lower castes pollutes, for these selves have been so reborn because of vices in a previous lifetime. Food prepared by them likewise pollutes. Ideally a Brahmin cooks his own food, especially at a large party (Cohn 1971, 131). To end the cycle of death and rebirth, Brahmins avoid killing and causing pain toward sentient life; they thus advocate vegetarianism. But meat, including beef, is basic to the Moslem diet. Unlike Brahmanism and Islam, Confucianism does not ask about the world's origins nor about what lies beyond. Instead it has concentrated on ordering social relations in the here and now: between elder brother and younger brother, between son and father, between subject and emperor. Thanks to this pragmatism, Confucians can tolerate the veneration of the many divinities of Mahayana Buddhism and of Taoism, as long as this does not threaten the integrity of the state. Thanks to it, too, the Chinese have been omnivorous. True, Confucius in Book 10 of the *Analects* enjoins the gentleman to avoid "fish that is not sound, nor meat that is high." But he adds that the gentleman "must not eat what has been crookedly cut, nor any dish that lacks its proper seasoning" (Confucius 1938, 148–49). Confucius's concern is for health and esthetics rather than for fulfilling a Transcendental Law laid down by a Personal Creator. There is no culinary world view that connects Islam, Brahmanism, and Confucianism together.

No doubt there is a culinary world view that creates a sense of community among all Buddhists, whether Mahayana (North/East Asia) or Theravada (South/Southeast Asia). This is the exaltation of vegetarianism as the ideal practice because it respects animal life as equally sentient. Many Buddhists may not be vegetarian, but this ideal is present as a horizon. The world view underlying vegetarianism connects Buddhism and Brahmanism together. However, it is not an ideal of either Islam or Confucianism.

The "Asian" taste to which Filipino cuisine should aspire is vague. Indian and Indianized Southeast Asian cooking blend together cardamom, mace, nutmeg, cinnamon, black pepper, chilies. This is not true of Cantonese or Japanese cooking, nor indeed of the cooking of traditional upland Filipinos, such as the Bontoc or the Manobo. Moreover, the heavy use of milk products in everyday Indian and Arabic cuisine has not been echoed by Chinese-influenced and even Indian-influenced Southeast Asian cuisine, because of lactose intolerance.

In contrast there is a unity to the West both in cooking and in the realm of thought. The West has a common moral vision that its member countries share despite bitter internecine wars. In my view, its version of Christianity interprets God as both Transcendent and Immanent: God is beyond the ordinary, material world yet is present within it because of the Incarnation and the Indwelling of the Spirit. Thus the paradox: a stress on ascetic self-denial and at the same time a preoccupation with improving this world, affirming human rights, and advocating responsibility to all human beings. The Christian vision of the self, communing with God, as spirit to spirit, made food taboos unnecessary from apostolic times. No doubt restrictions on the consumption of food, especially meat, during periods of penance like Lent have been imposed by the Catholic Church. But these have been seasonal restrictions rather than taboos. And it is significant that even these restrictions have faded away in the late twentieth century because the Church has recognized that the inner attitude matters more. But can one speak of a common vision in the face of a division into a Catholic South and a Protestant North? In answer, let us note that when the split occurred, during the fifteenth century, a secularizing attitude began to appear, has since triumphed and, save in pockets like North Ireland, has made these differences largely unimportant. Moreover, particular cities like Catholic Paris and Protestant London, became focal points for all of the West. For instance, over the past three centuries, the Parisians introduced a table protocol that became pan-Western: the fork and the knife; food courses served in sequence with light foods leading to heavier ones; sauces where reduced meat and vegetable juices are melded together with butter-and-flour mixtures (Jacobs 1979, Guy 1962). In addition, within the West particular regional cooking styles create a sense of communality. Unlike Northern Europeans and Anglo-Americans, Mediterraneans (Spaniards, Provençals, and Italians) all love garlic. They also combine this with onions and tomatoes, and at times sauté in it. Tagalogs, Pampangos, and Visayans have adopted the fork, spoon, and knife; have developed recipes using sauces with butter-and-flour mixtures; and relish the classic trio of garlic, onions, and tomatoes when sautéing.

It is hard to believe that a common "Asian" style of thinking and feeling so underlies Islamic, Indian, and Chinese civilizations that the Chinese Buddhist can easily understand Islamic philosophy, while the Arab can readily identify with the Rig Veda. In contrast in the West, despite bitter wars, German and French can converse with each other because Descartes has played a central role in the development of German philosophy, as Kant and Hegel continue to do in modern French philosophy. Indeed French and German can converse at table because of a common menu and etiquette. Thus far no analogous thinker or menu brings together Moslems, Brahmins, and Confucians.

Two objections will be made against my position: First, that while Westerners are rationalistic and this-worldly, Asians are one in being mystical and supernaturalistic; and second, that Asians, unlike Westerners, are familistic. Thus, there supposedly exists a common Asian vision of the world. To the first, I answer that an other-worldly mysticism has thrived in the West in the same way a pragmatic, this-worldly rationalism has been active in Asia. Nineteenth-century Vietnamese Confucians mocked Noah's Flood and the Tower of Babel as irrational (Woodside 1971, 288). The dogma that Bread and Wine are the Body and Blood of Christ repelled seventeenth-century Buddhists in Sri Lanka not only because they were vegetarians, but also because symbolic blood-drinking struck them as cannibalistic (Roberts 1989, 71). Christianity's espousal of the Trinity, the God-Made Man, and the cult of the saints shock the Moslem as polytheistic. The notion, too, that men and women in the prime of their life should forsake marriage and torment the flesh with severe mortifications is, for the Moslem, irrational. And yet through the centuries thousands of Catholics have taken vows of poverty, chastity, and obedience; contemplatives have forsaken legitimate pleasures, such as those of the table, and have entered the Dark Night of the Soul on the way to union with God. On the other hand Steadman (1969) cautions against generalizing about "Asian mysticism." China has indeed had Taoism and Mahayana Buddhism, both of which espouse separation from the everyday, secular world. But it also has Confucianism that dismisses metaphysical and theological debates as irrelevant, and prefers to concentrate instead on mundane matters like the running of the state. China, too, has a long empirical tradition that enabled its technology to surpass that of the rest of the world until just three centuries ago when the Scientific Revolution took place in the West (Needham 1954, vol. 3).[4] Since the advent of modern science in the seventeenth century, Westerners have summoned every institution, be this the legal order, the economy, or Christianity before the Tribunal of Reason. But this mentality has since been assimilated by particular Asian countries, like Japan, Korea, Taiwan, and Singapore, and is one explanation for their economic success. Indeed, when it comes to managing cities or to developing science and technology, our neighbors are more Westernized than us.

Regarding the second objection, namely, that concern for the family is uniquely Asian and is not Western: In truth familial concern has been strong among Latins. Latins and Latin Americans are visibly close to their mama; even after they have left home, they come home frequently for leisurely family meals, and enjoy close links with their siblings and cousins. Traditionally, many Latin households have been extended families. Indeed family corporations continue to be common in Spain and Italy, as in the Philippines. At the same time let us not forget that kinship systems in Asia vary widely. The Chinese prefer patrilineality: Only the sons inherit and transmit property; only the father's relatives are recognized as the self's relatives. When a woman marries, it is understood that her husband's relatives should henceforth command her primordial loyalty. In contrast, the system among Indonesians, Malays, and Filipinos is bilateral, as is the case among Western Europeans.[5]

There is a Western tradition, despite differences between member cultures. There, too, is an Islam. From an outsider's perspective, there seems to be a tradition shared in by Chinese, Korean, Japanese, and Vietnamese. But we can conclude that there is no single, definable, coherent cultural tradition that embraces all the Asias together. When people, therefore, say that the Filipino is confused because Westernization has altered his pristine Asian identity or that he is a strange animal because he is neither Asian nor Western, we should ask what being "Asian" means in the first place. Often it is simply understood as that which is not Western. On the other hand what many mean by "Western" is not that clear either. The West is supposedly materialistic and indifferent toward family ties. As shown above, this is simplistic. Because of unwarranted generalizations, the West is defined as the negative of "Asia"—a concept that, in the first place, is nebulous. Ironically, the "West" has become the shadow of "Asia," a phantom it created. Because the West's wealthier members have dominated the world for over two hundred years and, as colonialists, have warred against indigenous cultures, the "West" has become a favorite bogeyman. I, too, resent this dominance that has led to exploitation and bullying. At the same time, however, I propose that the West is not a monolithic culture. In the process of spreading and conquering other peoples, circumstances have compelled it to recognize local traditions.

Westernization, Indigenization, and Asianization

Let us look closer at what Toynbee means by "the West." First of all, Toynbee does not confuse civilization with continent; he distinguishes between Western Christendom and Europe. The latter is a continent. Eastern Orthodox Christendom is also in Europe but is not the same as Western Christendom. His reasons for so distinguishing would take us far from this topic. Secondly, Toynbee takes Western Christendom to mean that synthesis of the Hellenic heritage (he prefers this term to "Greco-Roman") and Latin Christianity that emerged in the ruins of the Western part of the Roman Empire. Western Christendom was born along an axis extending from the mouth of the Rhine down to the Tiber and the Po in the eighth century, expanded to include the rest of Western Europe, and leapt overseas to take in the Americas, Oceania, and the Philippines (Toynbee 1948–1961, 1:37–38, 11:maps 4 and 66). Components of the Western tradition that form part of the Filipino's discourse today are Roman-inspired civil law; Greek, Scholastic, and Modern Philosophy; art styles like the Baroque and the Neo-Classical; art forms like the sonnet and the sonata; and economic theories from liberalism to its opposite: socialism. One cannot dismiss all these as negative.

It is true, of course, that over the past two centuries Western capitalist powers colonized the rest of the world—which is why the "Asia" versus "West" dichotomy became popular. The U.S. annexed the Philippines in 1898 and supported the Marcos dictatorship almost until the end in 1986. Indeed we must look out for our own interests. But Western states are not the only colonizers; some of our neighbors have been. The Asia-West dichotomy can play tricks. Despite the Philippine experience of 1942–1945, the subjugation of Korea by Japan in 1910–1945, or the Chinese invasion of Tibet, prominent Filipino intellectuals claim that Japan and China pose no threat because they are "fellow Asians."

In safeguarding our independence of spirit vis-à-vis the Western powers, let us advert to a key word in Toynbee, "syncretism," which refers to the fusion of different cultural traditions to form new ones. For Toynbee, many civilizations are syncretistic. An example is Western Christendom itself that sprang from the union of two seeming incompatibles: Hellenism and Christianity. This synthesis fused in turn with the Germanic and the Celtic. After it crossed the seas, it merged with American Indian cultures to give birth to Mexico, Peru, and other Latin American societies that differ both from each other and from Spain. On the other side of the Pacific, it united with the indigenous cultures of the Philippines. A receiving society is not necessarily passive. Even as it receives, it transforms because indigenous patterns persist. Toynbee (1948–1961, 8:565) notes that the Spanish conquerors of the Philippines and Peru were "more eagerly concerned to impart their Christian religion than to propagate their Castilian language." By using the vernacular languages in the Catholic liturgy, they enabled these to become literary languages that resisted the spread of Castilian. In other domains a spiritual distancing likewise occurs because of syncretism. Consider cooking. In Mexico, the Spanish sauté was baptized with chili peppers, which are "anathema" to many Spaniards (Feibleman 1969, 10). In the Philippines (Fernandez 1996), shrimps are thrown in together with spoonfuls of *patis*, fermented fish sauce. Sometimes bagoong or fermented shrimp paste is itself sautéed. Both patis and bagoong are equally anathema to sensitive Spanish noses. Thus while a Filipino prefers Spanish cooking to, say, Pakistani or Indian cooking as more familiar, nonetheless even vis-à-vis the former, he experiences some distance. At times he will look for those heady marine fragrances that recall home. This interplay between the local and the foreign, the familiar and the imported, should be used in such a way that while we remain open to the West, we will feel spiritually distinct.

The pervasiveness of Western literature and philosophy in the Philippine world is such that we cannot understand some of the Filipino's more outstanding works without referring to Western literature and philosophy. *Florante at Laura*, Balagtas's long romance, can indeed be read as a veiled attack on colonialism. And yet that poem is thick with references to Greco-Roman antiquity and Western history. The same can be said of the novels and poems of Jose Rizal. Western philosophy played a key role in the movements that led to the foundation of the Filipino nation: the Propaganda and the Revolution of 1896. The notions of Rizal, Del Pilar, Bonifacio, Jacinto, and Mabini concerning the need for democracy were clearly influenced by the spirit of the Western Enlightenment, which focused the light of reason on the social order. In the case of Mabini, the Moslem scholar Cesar Majul (1960, 98–99) sees the presence of an even older Western philosophical tradition, Scholasticism, which Mabini was exposed to in the Dominican University of Santo Tomas. The second half of the twentieth century and the opening decades of the twenty-first is an exciting period: To protect the environment, promote gender equality, and advance social justice, activists question the established order. Though they often blame Western influence for problems, nonetheless their theoretical framework and methodology are Western in inspiration. This is not surprising, for the quest for both rationality and empirical validation has defined the Western spirit since the Enlightenment.

On the other hand, the complete triumph of the Western sensibility has been checked by a variety of factors. One is local taste. Sautéing may be commonplace among the Tagalog farmers of Bulacan where I stayed. But my farmer-hosts in distant Ilocos generally sauté in garlic and onion only for feasts. They eagerly export the garlic from their fields to the Tagalogs for cash. As some Ilocano farmers complain about garlic, "It stinks!"

Another factor, as Toynbee correctly points out, is the persistence of the vernaculars. The very grammar and vocabulary of a language compels its users to abide by its logic, its implicit interpretation of the world. For this reason it is important for us to know the mythology of Austronesian peoples, past and present, that is to say, the mythology of our ancestors and of our upland siblings. Some of these myths can be shown to be still at work among the lowland Christian majority and have been transmitted via the vernacular. Knowing these myths will help develop a philosophy that is truly rooted. Unfortunately, the term "Asianization" has confused matters because it is equated with "indigenization."[6] Just as bad, the latter term is haphazardly used among us Filipinos. Thus philosopher-friends argue that, as Filipinos, they are "Asian" and should, therefore, study Indian or Chinese philosophy. Yet, they ignore the myths of the Ifugao and other peoples of the Philippines. Island myths (see, for instance, Barton 1946; Magos 1986) give us a balcony from which to appraise ideas from the West and elsewhere. Somehow, these philosopher-friends seem to imagine that by understanding Confucian family-centered ethics, they gain access to the indigenous Filipino mind "which is Asian."

Indigenization and Westernization are not necessarily contradictory processes. Sometimes they have complemented each other. While crushing particular indigenous habits, Westernization may have actually enabled others to survive and flourish among Catholic Filipinos rather than among their Moslem brothers. The pre-Islamic, pre-Christian Filipinos drank wine; ate pork and raw fish; and most likely (as in the Cordillera) they fancied dog meat. Whereas these have disappeared among Moslem Filipinos and strict Moslem Indonesians, they thrive among Ilocanos, Tagalogs, and Visayans because Christianity has not made a moral issue out of them. Notable, too, is that the local relish for sour flavors may have received a boost from the Mexicans who pickle [*adobar*] meats in spices with some lemons (Fernandez 1994, 195). In another realm, that of costume: Pagan Filipino women showed off their hair and, depending on class and ethnicity, either covered their breasts with a blouse or else exposed them. This ran counter to the Islamic insistence on covering a woman's hair and figure and—in some places—her face. Even as Catholics, Filipino women wear shorts and sleeveless blouses. And they let their hair fly in the wind.

Nor is Westernization incompatible with the Filipino's Asianization—if by this we mean connecting with our neighbors. Sinicization intensified from the sixteenth century onward—precisely after Legazpi. Though the Chinese had been trading with Filipinos since the tenth century, they really settled in large numbers only with the arrival of Spaniards willing to pay in coined silver.

"Native Philippine products were of limited variety and value, and handling them was not enough to attract a resident Chinese colony" (Scott 1994, 207). In 1570 there were only a few Chinese residing in Tondo, consisting of political refugees and recent arrivals. Thirty years later "the Chinese quarter had four hundred shops and eight thousand residents" (ibid., 207). It took some time for popular Chinese foods like *bihon, hopia, mami,* pansit, and pechay to become part of the culinary landscape. They are not mentioned by seventeenth-century dictionaries (ibid., 208). Nick Joaquin (1989, 28) thus says that our pansit-and-*lumpia* culture really dates back only to the Spanish period.

On the other hand Spanish influence brought in Arab practices. Often forgotten is that a major part of Spain was under Arab and Berber influence for eight centuries. Many practices we consider Spanish are thanks to this influence. For instance, the Spanish fondness for flavoring and coloring rice with spices, like saffron, and mixing scraps of food with it, as in paella, has affinities with Near Eastern styles of treating rice. Thus, while the Maranao acquired the habit of coloring their rice yellow from fellow Moslems coming in from a geographically western direction, we got ours from the Spaniards who sailed in from the rising sun, the Americas. In the realm of thought, let us remember that Moslem scholars preserved the Greek texts of Aristotle and transmitted them to Spain and to the rest of Western Christendom with their own commentaries. Thomas Aquinas dialogues with ibn Sina (Avicenna) and the Spaniard ibn Rushd (Averroes) throughout his *Summa Theologica.*[7] As a result, such Moslem philosophers may be relevant to us Christians but not necessarily to the Buddhist. Curiously, while Filipino philosophers advocate Chinese and Indian philosophy, they have negected the study of Arabic philosophy despite the strong presence of Islam. Once more the Asia-West dichotomy confuses. Since, when reading Saint Thomas, one cannot but know something as well about Avicenna and Averroes, a Filipino philosopher-friend asks in conversation: "But are they Eastern thinkers? They seem Western."

An Unappreciated Originality

I come to my third point: The insistence on measuring the Filipino's achievements against supposed "Asian" norms makes it difficult to appreciate the lowland Christian Filipino's originality. Those who identify "Asia" with complex seasoning find Tagalog or Visayan cooking "uninteresting" because of the restrained seasoning; worse still, as unoriginal. Unfortunately, they overlook the distinguishing feature of lowland Christian Filipino cuisine particularly the Tagalog, which is not the seasoning, but the fondness for sour flavors. On one level there is an interplay between the salty and the sour. The sea is evoked by the fermented shrimps and fish; the flavor of young gardens by the green fruits. On another level, the sour is used as a foil against the texture of fats and oils. *Adobo* and *paksiw* both pickle meat and fish in vinegar, pepper, and garlic before cooking them. *Kinilaw* is raw fish soaked in green mangoes or limes and flavored with raw onions, ginger, and a dash of pepper. Cebuanos roast fish stuffed with green tomatoes to produce an exquisite tart flavor. As in other parts of Southeast Asia, we have broths [*sinigang*] that are cooked with green tamarinds. However, we have added tomatoes to this plus substitutes for tamarinds: sandor (santol), green mangoes, guavas, and *catmon*. Green chili peppers are cooked into the broth, though sparingly. Possible dipping sauces are either fermented fish sauce [patis] or tiny fish (*dulong*). In the fifty-one Tagalog dipping sauces that Dez Bautista and Mila Enriquez list for Fernando (1992, 57), 90 percent are either sourish or sour. Recipes imported from China, Spain, and Mexico are transformed by the taste for the sour. Manileños dip their Chinese-inspired spring rolls in a vinegar sauce where chopped raw onions and pepper soak. Ilocanos do the same for their Mexican-inspired empanadas, which are fried crepes, of rice in the Ilocos rather than corn, stuffed with mashed mung beans where a raw egg has been mixed while cooking. The Manila puchero is derived from the Spanish *cocido,* which is a stew of chicken, beef, sausages, chickpeas, and leafy vegetables. What differentiates the Manila version is its dipping sauce of broiled and peeled eggplants soaked in black pepper, raw onions, and vinegar. The Tagalog style of preparing beefsteak dips thin slices of beef in pepper, soy sauce, and *calamansi* juice before sautéing them, Spanish-style, in garlic and onions. Paradoxically, a mild sourness seems cheerful, for it stimulates a glad expectation.

While the pleasure of a Javanese meal derives in part from the ornate medley of spices, the pleasure of a Tagalog or Visayan meal is more subtle. The faint sourness does not totally hide the natural flavor of the fish or the meat. It half reveals the juices, half conceals them. This quality that I call "translucency" appears as well in our other art forms. Even the houses of wealthy nineteenth-century Filipinos do not have the gold-encrusted, junglelike lushness of the carved screens and walls of Javanese and Balinese palaces. Instead interior wall transoms have strips of lacelike tracery, often in natural finish, and exterior walls with sliding window panels whose flat *capiz* shell panes half-reveal, half-conceal the landscape while catching its shadows. Our traditional textiles in Luzon and the Visayas do not have the silk, the gold, or the ornate vegetation of batik. Rather they are delicate gauzes, as in piña, jusi, and sinamay, which tease the beholder's eyes, particularly when they have cutwork embroidery. Filipino paintings of the twentieth century, be this the late Cubism of Manansala, the stylized Realism of Carlos Francisco, or the gauzy Abstractions of Chabet, Albor, and Olazo, echo this diaphanousness. Whoever expects the visual and gustatory spectacle that characterizes particular Southeast Asian art forms will be disappointed by Filipino art. This is not the case, however, if he relishes the subtle play of overlapping filmlike surfaces whether in food or in the visual arts. Or if he enjoys seeing light hovering, in its various moods—around the body, in a room or on canvas.[8] The theme of translucency runs through nineteenth- to early twentieth-century Filipino couture and architecture; it is also manifest in twentieth-century painting since Amorsolo. This should be explored.

The Philippines is original for a second reason. The French economic historian Chaunu (1960, 18) remarks that "the Philip-

pines constitutes . . . the only true end-point (*bout*) of the world."
Here the westward expansion of the Atlantic world and the eastward
expansion of the Mediterranean world, of which Islam forms a part,
meet each other again. "Men of races and cultures, that are basically
opposites to each other, had never before met together, in a more
reduced area or within a more reduced period of time" (Chaunu
1960, 23). Aside from the indigenous populations, there are the
Spaniards, the Chinese, and the Japanese (ibid.). As mentioned above,
saffron entered the archipelago from both directions: east and west.
Particular Filipino dishes reveal an encounter between distant cultures. *Pansit bihon guisado* is Chinese noodles sautéd Spanish-style
in garlic and onions and flavored with soy sauce, a Chinese-Japanese
invention, and patis, a Southeast Asian innovation. *Champurrado* is
rice cooked in chocolate, following Mexican fashion, mixed with milk
which was introduced from Western Europe, and is then sprinkled
with a Southeast Asian favorite: tiny fried fish. In both dishes the
sea's tang is vividly present. Lately "fusion" cooking, or cooking that
brings together flavors from East and West, has become popular in
English-speaking countries. Unfortunately, because of our preoccupation with having an "Asian" flavor, we hesitate to project our cuisine
as an example of fusion cooking. But, as Joaquin (1989, 31) asks:
"Why want to be East or West or North or South when we can be
our own singular self as culture or history have shaped us?"

"Continentism" has worked against the lowland Christian Filipino, whether peasant or urbanite. While many Asian intellectuals
see him as an intruder, non-Latin Westerners regard him as unexotic
and unoriginal.[9] And therefore as inauthentic. Even when Filipinos
sing in Tagalog, his songs are subtly stigmatized. Because some
Americans and British hearers find his style of singing familiar—it is
not pentatonic and the pitch is defined—they dismiss it as derivative. I use the expression "non-Latin" because, from my personal
experience, I find Italians and Spaniards to be more appreciative of
many aspects of the Filipino's cultural products. They are not as
concerned that his food, music, or architecture be "exotic." In com-

parison, based on my visits, until the 1970s, museum exhibits by Americans on Filipino art tended to emphasize primarily either the upland tribal or the Moslem. While the high art of our neighbors was on display—silks, porcelains, Buddhas—a favored specimen from the Philippines on exhibit was the headhunting axe. The assumption was that the Christian Filipino's artifacts would be out of place in the Asian wing. This has begun to change. Pasadena Museum in California has featured Philippine oil paintings and ivory carvings. In 2003, the Honolulu Academy of Arts opened a new wing that featured Philippine art in all its variety.

But prejudice persists elsewhere. In a guidebook (Peters 1997, 29–36) dedicated exclusively to the Philippines, there are detailed drawings of the different types of houses in the Cordillera, none on the variations of the *bahay kubo* in the lowlands, none either on the gentry's wood-and-stone house. The lowland Christian Filipino should be bothered. To project his culture, must he ignore his farmers' houses with their various weaving styles, his graceful nineteenth-century houses and churches, and for that matter his meat pies, stews, and pastilles, to live up to the image of what an Asian is supposed to be? Paradoxically, this means surrendering to a disguised form of cultural imperialism imposed by the non-Latin Westerner. Eager to be accepted as "Asian," many Filipinos apologize about their Western-influenced heritage.

Flavors beyond Asia

To appreciate Filipino culture in its singularity, we should suspend our preoccupations with what is or is not Asian and reflect on our concrete experience of particular Filipino artifacts. This way we can better appreciate unique features of our people's achievements. Moreover, like Chaunu, we should assume that, on a globe, influences can move in any direction. Hence it does not matter from where the influence came: north or south, east or west.

Realistically speaking, however, the Greek-inspired dichotomy of Asia versus Europe will probably never disappear. It persists for several reasons. First, it is one way to bond different societies that have historically been bullied by the U.S. and Western European powers. Though the Japanese are themselves a power, they, too, resort to that discourse when they feel pressured by the U.S. They speak of their affinities with other Asians while projecting themselves as the spokesman of Asia vis-à-vis wealthy Western powers. Second, it is a convenient way to classify cultures and societies in a diverse world even though the dichotomy is simplistic and, therefore, misleading. In the meantime an entire network of academic departments, institutions, and journals has arisen internationally, using the term "Asia." It would be too costly to scrap the term.

Nonetheless, alternatives are possible. We could restrict the use of Asia to mean a physical zone of the globe and articulate instead other bases for cross-cultural comparisons, as well as for cross-cultural cooperation. In other words, let us treat Asia as a continent, albeit with fuzzy, arbitrary boundaries, but not as a single cultural unity. Instead of "Asian civilization," it is better to speak of "Asian civilizations." Perhaps, in the future, because of increased interaction between Asians, a strong sense of Asian identity will emerge. An Asian flavor may emerge. Fine. In the meantime, however, let us be wary of a priori definitions that exclude Lowland Christian Filipinos.

Other bases for cross-cultural comparisons and cooperation are the following:

Austronesia. The Philippines, like Malaysia and Indonesia, belongs to a language family that takes in Madagascar and covers most of the Pacific Islands. Because of the longing to belong to a prestigious Asia of sophisticated civil cultures, Filipinos have forgotten their links with a major part of this cultural region. And yet they share myths, seafaring lore, and a crafts tradition with other Pacific Islanders. The ancestors of Micronesians and Polynesians sailed for their new homes millennia ago from the Philippines and Indonesia (Bellwood 1985). They also partake of a widespread cooking style. In Hawaii, as in

Bicol, they mix pork, fish, taro, and taro leaf together and steam the package. However, they flavor it only with salt, not with chili, as in Bicol. During the nineteenth century, Spanish documents often referred to the Philippines as "Oceanía española." Together with the Carolines and the Marianas, it formed an administrative unit.[10] Today some anthropologists and travel writers prefer to locate the Philippines within Oceania rather than Asia because, unlike most of Southeast Asia, it has not been deeply influenced by Indian ideas, social practices, and art.[11] I should add that since the nineteenth century, Oceania, like the Philippines, has become a member of Western civilization.

Southeast Asia. The Philippines is situated in a tropical region characterized by inland seas, large islands, narrow river valleys, an extensive mountainous terrain, and deep forests (Winzeler 1976). There are four civilizations present in the region, the Chinese-influenced, the Indian-influenced, the Islamic, and the Western, and four language families, the Austronesian, the Austroasiatic, the T'ai, and the Tibeto-Burmese. Yet if one looks at the region as a particular type of ecosystem requiring a particular response, it indeed forms a unity, though not as a single civil culture. Throughout the region, because of the preference for living by or on the water where the main sources of protein are found, wooden houses are built on stilts. Food, in the lowlands at least, is flavored with fish/shrimp pastes and fish sauce and often has fish as the main course. If religious prejudices on both sides be suspended, Christian Filipinos, Moslem Malays, and Moslem Indonesians can easily be comfortable with each other because of linguistic and other affinities.

The Hispanic World. The Philippines was the westernmost extension of the Spanish Empire. However, Spain ruled it through the viceroyalty of Mexico; after 1821, Spain ruled it directly. Ideas came in that are common to all Spanish-influenced countries; at the same time some ideas were Mexican in origin. Conversely, the Philippines influenced the Mexican West Coast. Baroque art entered the islands; in exchange Manila workshops exported exquisite ivory saints to all of Spanish America and Spain. Mexican soldiers and missionaries brought in fruits and vegetables (chicos, squash, cacao, tomatoes, guavas) and flavoring agents (chilies, annato seeds). They inspired the making of cakes mixing peanuts and cereal paste as in tamales or cooking with a paste of ground peanuts mole-style. Filipino migrants reciprocated by bringing in the mango and the coconut wine, which continues to be called tuba on the Mexican West Coast. There, too, vegetable dishes cooked in coconut milk are called *ginatan*—from *guinataan,* reports Jorge Loyzaga (1996), a Mexican architect interested in this exchange of influences. A pan-Spanish way of cooking present in all Spanish-influenced countries are such habits like sautéing in garlic, onions, and tomatoes or stewing (puchero, cocido) greens, tubers, meats, and sausages together.

Shared habits foster sympathy. During my travels abroad, I keep meeting ordinary Spaniards and Spanish Americans whose remarks reveal much reading on the Philippines. Sympathy in turn can lead to a helping hand. At a parish in Hamburg, I met non-Spanish-speaking Filipino workers who had been invited by Spaniards and Spanish Americans to join their club on the grounds that they were brothers in spirit.

There are other taste clusters that the Filipino kitchen participates in. The Chinese-influenced cluster, with its ginger and soy sauce, is one; the Arab-influenced, with its saffron, another. Filipino cooking has thematic flavors that give it coherence; at the same time, like a poem, it alludes to other culinary worlds. Surely this opens advantages on a shrinking planet.

Notes

This essay is a new version of "Why Insist on an Asian Flavor?" which appeared in *Philippine Studies* (fourth quarter 2000).

1. Hutton (1996, 8) explicitly says: "The Spanish were responsible for the introduction of chilies, which they discovered in the New World and carried to the

islands of the Philippines. These fiery fruits swept throughout Southeast Asia and India." A lesson to be drawn is that we cannot assume that the order of things that we see in other Southeast Asian countries today has always been there or is truly indigenous.

2. Following Toynbee, I distinguish between "Europe" and the "West." Europe is a continent from the Western Christian perspective. But it has been home to three civilizations: Western Christendom, Eastern (or Orthodox Christendom), and Islam. Only since Peter the Great, in the eighteenth century, did Russia seek Westernization. The nineteenth-century debate between the "Westernizers" and the "Slavophils" about the appropriateness of Westernization reveals that there was in fact a difference between the two Christendoms. Toynbee (1972, 401 ff.) sees the twentieth-century attempts of the Soviets to set themselves up as the world capital of a new orthodoxy, using Marxism which they imported from the West, as another chapter in a centuries-old rivalry with the West. On the other hand Western civilization crossed the seas to embrace the Americas, the Pacific Islands, and the Philippines.

3. Toynbee (1948–1961, 1:130–32) identifies some of the following pertinent "Societies," which he uses interchangeably with "civilization," when the former is *spelled with a capital "S."* These are (1) the Western, (2) the Orthodox Christian, in both Russia and the Balkans, (3) Arabic, (4) Hindu, and (5) Far Eastern (China, Korea, and Japan). Years later, Toynbee (1972, 72) modifies some of these terms. He prefers "civilization" to "Society." He lists Orthodox Christian, Western, and Islamic civilizations as "affiliated to" both Syriac and Hellenic civilizations; the Korean, Japanese, and Vietnamian civilizations as "satellite" civilizations of the Sinic; and South-East Asian civilization as "satellites" first of the Indic, then, in Indonesia and Malaya only, of the Islamic. By "affiliated to" he means born from and have become totally independent. While "satellite" means that those civilizations "developed their loans . . . on lines of their own that are distinctive enough to entitle them to rank as separate civilizations."

4. Needham (1954, vol. 3) attributes the Chinese failure to develop higher forms of mathematics to the fact that foreign trade under the Qing was gradually deemphasized. The advent of statistics in the West was stimulated by the challenges of trade. Thankfully he does not fall back on the cliché of a "mystic, intuitive, non-rationalistic Asia."

5. Often what is meant by "Western" may be "American." For instance, a Filipino friend who grew up in Hawaii came over and enthused: "What I like about Asians is that they touch each other a lot when talking. It's so unlike Westerners." Arabs and Filipinos do pat and hug, but Japanese, Chinese, or Javanese? These are no-touch societies. On the other hand, while White Americans squirm

when touched by just anybody, Spaniards and Italians do love to touch. As popularly used, "Western" is a catchall for all that is negative.

6. The false supposition that all indigenous, pre-Western cultures in the Philippines are the same has led to artifacts that insult Islam. Filipino painters of the 1930s and 1940s painted wedding scenes set in pre-Hispanic Philippines where the dancing girls display their naked breasts. In one corner is a pig's head for the banquet. They would call such "Moslem Wedding"! The famous Carlos V. Francisco was guilty of this (see Duldulao 1988, 132–33). A news item about a Sinulog Festival in Cebu in the early 1990s says that a float carried women "who represented Moslem princesses offering gifts to idols"! One of the organizers of the Pamulinawen Festival in Laoag, Ilocos Norte, tells me proudly that they had a similar tableau. The P1,000 bill of the Philippines features on one side the rice terraces, stone idols, and a *langgar*. The last is a sacred place of worship for Moslems. Why should this be featured along with a stone idol, which is the very antithesis of Islam? "Asia" is a catchall for all that is supposedly non-Western.

7. The distinction between contingent being and necessary being, between being that does not have to exist (like plants, animals, humans) and being which must exist (like God) entered Scholasticism from Islamic theologians. This close relationship between Islamic and Western Christian thought is overlooked by those who see all "Asians" as the same, and as sharply different from the Westerners.

8. Lor Calma designed a towering sculpture for the Fort Bonifacio complex. It is made of translucent sheets of glass lit from within. Why so? he was asked. His reply illuminates: "It's more Filipino, *mas malambing* (more tender and caring)."

9. Just how arbitrary "Asia" is can be seen when we consider an adjacent continent, "Oceania." Another term is "Pacific Islands." It covers several clusters: Micronesia (Guam and the Marianas, and the Carolines), Melanesia (Fiji, Papua) and Polynesia (Tahiti, Samoa, the Marquesas, Hawaii, Easter Island). This continent is often represented as semiaboriginal: grass huts, half-naked women, angular ancestral idols, seafood with simple seasoning. And yet Westernization, which became pervasive since the nineteenth century because of conquest, is often accepted as part of the cultural landscape by Westerners themselves. Despite an independence movement in Tahiti, Americans tend to look at Tahiti's Frenchness, particularly its cuisine, as part of its appeal. Nor would Americans consider Guam and Hawaii as unnatural because of their heavy Americanization. However, the lowland Christian Filipinos are seen as unnatural because they live west of the supposed boundary between "Asia" and "Oceania" rather than east of it.

10. Because of this preoccupation with our links with Asians, who admittedly are more prestigious, we have neglected our links with Guam, which used to be administered by the governor-general of Spanish Philippines and by the archbishop of Cebu. The national costume of Guam is a *traje de mestiza* of the 1930s: a *saya* and a *baro* made of gauzy *arenque* with butterfly sleeves—without the *pañuelo*.

11. For instance, Lavenda and Schultz (1987, 200), when citing facts about the Ilongot of the Sierra Madre, locate them in the Philippines, which they classify with Oceania. The Ilongots' belief that by cutting off the head of a victim, they can make a servant out of the spirit finds parallels elsewhere in Micronesia and Polynesia. This used to justify going to war: Some guidebooks I have seen group the Philippines together with Guam, Fiji, Ponape, Tahiti, and Hawaii: under Oceania rather than under Asia because there are no ancient pagodas and Brahmanic temples here. All these positions make sense.

Southeast Asia is a Collage

"It looks like a Bornean longhouse!"
—Budhi Gunawan, an anthropologist from Sunda, West Java

A SIXTEENTH-CENTURY MOSLEM could leave the Strait of Gibraltar, travel through the Middle East and northern India, cross over to the Malay Peninsula, go down to northern Sumatra and journey upward along the west coast of Borneo to Sulu without leaving the world he cherished and was familiar with. This was a world defined by the mosque and the minaret, the Sacred Book and its commentaries, a legal tradition based on Roman law and the Sacred Book, a philosophical system that drew inspiration from Aristotle, and an art that sought inspiration in abstractions and Arabic script. Though modern Islam never was a political unity and today, in fact, covers many independent nation-states, nonetheless, it constitutes a felt unity. During the recent civil war in Bosnia, Malaysians (brown-skinned and speaking an Austronesian tongue) offered asylum to Bosnians (white-skinned and speaking an Indo-European tongue) because they were fellow Moslems.

Emotive, meaningful symbols that are shared together create an *oikumene*, a moral and aesthetic community that embraces diverse cultures and races. This has been Toynbee's (1982) insight as shown earlier. Islam is an oikumene. So obviously is the West which began as the Western half of a Christendom that had split along the fault lines of a collapsed Roman Empire. Though the West expanded overseas to include new cultures, it continues to constitute a world with shared symbols: Christianity, whether Catholic or Protestant; the philosophical, political, and legal heritage of the Greeks and Romans; and art styles from Gothic down to Modernism. Do Chinese-influenced countries constitute an oikumene? To an outsider like me, it seems that they do. Despite bloody conflicts in the past and recent present, there is a community of symbols that they share: Confucian ethics, Taoist metaphysics, Mahayana Buddhist soteriology, Chinese script, roofs with high ridges and upturned corner eaves, noodles, and chopsticks. I find it easy to understand why in Hawaii, far from the ancient rivalries in Asia, Chinese, Japanese, and Koreans prefer each other's company to that of other Asians.

Has Southeast Asia been an oikumene? What communalities link Southeast Asians together? What place does the Westernized Philippines have in this emerging community? The questions are not of mere passing interest. Since World War II, there has been a continuing attempt to create a political and economic community in Southeast Asia with the European Union as the model. Inevitably, questions about cultural communalities embracing the entire region arise. There are also questions about the "Southeast Asianness" of the Christian Filipino. It is often pointed out that whereas both the aboriginal culture of the uplands and the Islamized culture of Sulu and Mindanao have obvious links with the rest of the region, the majority culture, Hispanized in many ways, has little. Indeed up until the 1960s, scholars hesitated to include the Philippines in cultural studies on Southeast Asia (McCloud 1986, 5; Osborne 1983, 12).

To answer these questions, we should note four things. First, the concept "Southeast Asia" is a new term that previous generations would not have understood. In centuries past, the Chinese referred to the "Region of the Southern Seas" as Nanyang; while the Japanese referred to it as Nanyo and the Indians "Farther India" (Fifield 1958, 2; Osborne 1983, 12). The vague, catchall Chinese and Japanese terms point to a mere place. On the other hand, there is a cultural dimension to the Indian term. The region is seen as an extension of India. But would Indians have included both Sinicized Vietnam and animist Philippines in "Farther India"? This is doubtful. As for Southeast Asians, they seem not to have had a common term for the region. "Southeast Asia" was coined by Westerners during the twentieth century, and this became popular at the close of World War II when the Allies organized a Southeast Asian Command (Tilman 1987, 16).

When George Coedès's book on the region first came out in 1944, the original title was *Histoire ancienne des États hindouisés d'Extrême-Orient* [Ancient History of the Indianized States of the Far East]. The third edition in 1964 was called *Les états hindouisés d'Indochine et d'Indonésie* [The Indianized States of Indochina and Indonesia]. However, when it was translated and published in 1968, its title had become *The Indianized States of Southeast Asia.*

Second, we should make a distinction that is often overlooked when discussing "the unity of Southeast Asia." There are different ways of clustering cultures together. The common threads that link Southeast Asians at present are not of the same order as those linking Western Europeans together. Despite internecine wars, Western Europeans share an oikumene defined by powerful, emotion-charged symbols. Thus, on one of the anniversaries marking the end of World War II, the French government asked that a Beethoven symphony be played in Paris. Though Beethoven is German, the French and other Europeans regard the music of Beethoven and, for that matter of Bach, Haydn, and Mozart, as belonging to all of them. Significantly, the European Union chose Beethoven's Ninth Symphony as its anthem. Are there similar symbols that appeal to all Southeast Asians? At this point in time, the answer is "no." The Ramayana does indeed appeal to Indianized Southeast Asians but not yet to the northern Vietnamese or to Filipinos. Nonetheless, there are commonalities that do link most Southeast Asians together because there are other ways by which they form a culture area. These may not be as powerful as the symbols of an oikumene, but they could well be in the future.

Third, we should be careful of projecting our aspirations for a future unity to the distant past. Because Indian influence has been pervasive in the region, fellow Filipinos imagine that whatever was in Cambodia and Java must have been present in Luzon and the Visayas. If they have stupas, we must have had them. If they have the Ramayana, our ancestors must have chanted this in Luzon and the Visayas until the iconoclastic friar came. Let us go back to Francisco (1987, 48, 51), whose lifelong specialization was the study of Indian influences in Filipino culture. He asserted that the limited Indian influences in Luzon and the Visayas entered not directly from India but via the filter of the Indianized kingdoms in Indonesia. The verb he used was "percolate."

Finally, we should note that significant aspects of Hispanized Filipino culture in fact link it to other cultures in the region. Indigenous elements persist, even in artifacts and institutions that seem to be Hispanic. I will establish this by examining the Filipinos' basic food habits, their national costume, their supposedly "Spanish" houses, and the Good Friday procession to show how indigenous elements link them with the rest of the region.

Ways of Grouping Cultures

Cultures can be grouped in different ways. To illustrate each of these, I will give non-Southeast Asian examples, then follow with a discussion of Southeast Asia in relation to each type of grouping.

A Family of Languages. Societies with related languages share common myths because they had a similar livelihood and social organization when they first appeared as a small group. Thus there is an Indo-European family of languages which includes Celtic, Germanic, Latin, Hellenic, Slavic, Iranian, and Indian languages. Within these languages, myths centering on the sky gods and on cattle rituals are important (Lincoln 1987), for the Indo-Europeans began as cattle herders. However, for the average speaker of those languages today this linguistic and mythological unity that scholars have unearthed means little. Though linguistically related societies differentiate from each other in terms of social structure in response to political, economic, and ecological factors, there is a wide gap between India, Russia, and England.

Responses to a Common Ecosystem. Societies, which are faced with similar challenges from the ecosystem, tend to respond similarly, according to cultural ecologists, because their basic options are limited by the climate, topography, and resources surrounding them. There is a Mediterranean environment characterized by extended summer droughts, mild rainy winters, a relatively uniform temperature, and "a close interdigitation of mountain, valley and sea" (Pitkin 1963, cited by Gilmore 1982, 77). In terms of settlement patterns, therefore, a common response throughout the Maghreb, southern Spain and France, Italy, coastal Croatia, and Greece has been to form compact, isolated towns located near sources of water. To this I would add the preference for stone houses with flat, rather than steeply pitched, tile roofs.

Again it is doubtful whether the similarities of these responses would mean much to ordinary Mediterranean residents. Historically, they have been divided into three oikumenes: the Eastern or Orthodox Christian, the Western Christian, and the Islamic. Though the Western Christian and the Orthodox Christian have drawn close to each other in this century, ancient suspicions and hatreds divide them, as can be seen in the former Yugoslavia where Catholic Croat and Orthodox Serb have bitterly fought each other, even though their languages are mutually intelligible, though differing from each other in the script. Croats use the Roman script, Serbs the Cyrillic.

An "Oikumene" United by a Shared Great Tradition. As explained above, cultures in an oikumene are wedded together by a vision of the world that is reinforced by communalities in ethics, law, politics, or art.[1] According to the anthropologist Robert Redfield (1956), the cultural tradition in preindustrial states and cities has a dual character. The literati and power holders in urban centers have the resources to commission the best talents to work for them; moreover, they specialize in mental work. They thus develop a tradition which is more intellectual, more sophisticated, and more refined than that of the peasants and urban laborers. The latter two have little time for speculation, for they are immersed in poorly compensated manual work. Besides, in pre-nineteenth-century societies, there was no obligatory universal education from which they could have benefited. Temples, churches, and palaces embody the Great Tradition; wayside shrines and huts manifest the Little Tradition. The Great Tradition defines the ideals for the Little Tradition, but fashions and forms from the Little Tradition may also enter the Great Tradition and transform it.

Most Great Traditions have been influenced by even older and more prestigious Great Traditions. For this reason a common universe of discourse tends to unite clusters of Great Traditions. Morocco, Egypt, Iran, and Aceh in Sumatra each have their own distinctive Great Tradition, thanks in part to the influence of the Little Tradition in each place. But there are common elements that unite them because of Islam which originated in Arabia. Similarly the Great Traditions of Italy, Spain, France, England, and Germany, though different from each other, share a bond because they all partake of that fusion of Greco-Roman law and philosophy, Christian ethics, and Germanic customs that is commonly called "Western."

Communalities created by a shared Great Tradition are highly meaningful to those who share them, for, at the deepest level, they refer to the "basic and indubitable" in the realm of religion, ethics, philosophy, and the arts. Like everything human, however, this sense of the "basic and indubitable" is in fact culturally constructed. The myths created by a Great Tradition have this advantage over those created by a family of languages; they are propagated by highly organized institutions that enjoy legitimacy: the state, religious organizations, and schools. Moreover, their symbols are highly visible: the Crescent and Star for Moslems, the Latin Cross for Western Christians. They give those who share the Great Tradition a sense of fellowship vis-à-vis those who do not. Nonetheless, they have not prevented bitter wars among peoples who share a Great Tradition because the desire for dominance does upset these relations. Thus the wars among Western European countries, or the wars of liberation by the Arabs against the Turks, their fellow Moslems.

These are but some of the ways to classify cultures according to their common features.[2] These types do not coincide with each other in their boundaries. Thus, a country or a culture may well participate in one type of culture area but not necessarily in another. For instance, Southern Italy shares much with India in language and myth, for both belong to the Indo-European family of languages. However, if responses to a particular ecosystem be the criterion, then it shares communalities only with countries within the Mediterranean zone, be they Western Christian, Orthodox Christian, or Islamic. Finally, in terms of a shared Great Tradition, the communalities most valuable to Southern Italians would not be any of the above but those linking them to the rest of the Christian world, including Catholic countries in the Americas and Asia.

The question therefore is, Which of these ways of grouping cultures applies to Southeast Asia?

Southeast Asia as a Unity

Many languages of Southeast Asia, like Malay, Sundanese, Javanese, Taosug, Cebuano, and Tagalog, belong to what is called the western subgroup of Austronesian languages. But this grouping within Austronesia does not coincide with the boundaries of Southeast Asia. Because of ancient migrations, peoples in Madagascar and in Micronesia also speak Western Austronesian languages. Other languages on the mainland, like Mon (Burma), Khmer (Cambodia), and possibly Vietnamese, belong to the Austroasiatic family (Bellwood 1985, 125). Austronesian and Austroasiatic share similar myths and motifs: a dualism that emphasizes oppositions between female and male creators or between forces of the mountain and forces of the sea; and a tree of life from which male and female sprang (Keyes 1987; Fox 1987; Taylor 1983, 8). The hornbill bird and the crocodile have sacred status in both groups.

Then there is a third cluster of languages, the Tibeto-Burmese family of languages, including Lao and Burmese. It also includes Chinese, and seems very different because of the use of tones. The linguistic expert Paul Benedict posits that Thai and other Ta'i languages were originally related to both Austroasiatic and Austronesian (Bellwood 1985).

Southeast Asia can also be conceived of as sharing communalities because of ecological factors. Mountains predominate; flat lands are confined largely to "intermountain river basins, valleys, coastal fringes, and river deltas" (Winzeler 1976, 625). An extensive tropical rain forest covers many areas from Thailand and Malaysia to Indonesia and the Philippines while a tropical deciduous forest environment characterizes Laos and Vietnam. Temperatures are high and the air humid throughout the year (Hutterer 1976, 224). In addition to all these, E. L. Jones (1991) proposes that, compared to early Japan and Europe, there may be higher rates of disaster such as famines, floods, wars, and the spread of malaria.

Because of this common environment, certain forms of behavior are found throughout the region. Since waterways are more efficient avenues of transport and since bodies of water rich in marine life are present, many settlements are located beside them. As a protection against the humid ground and frequent floods, wooden houses raised on stilts have been present throughout the region. Even in Vietnam, houses used to be on stilts, as shown by bas-reliefs on the drums of Dongson dating back to the fifth century B.C. However, because Chinese influence from the first century A.D.

onward emphasized building houses on raised platforms, the style is found only in a few riverside settlements and in the village communal hall: the *dinh*. Turning to food, ordinary Southeast Asian food is flavored with fermented shrimp paste and fish sauce. Basic flavors, therefore, taste of marine life.

We come to the question: Does Southeast Asia form a single oikumene with a shared Great Tradition? To answer this, qualifications need to be made.

Let us ask if such a universe ever existed in Southeast Asia. Indian influence appears to have come in via traders and priests starting with the first century A.D. and to have spread from Funan (southern Vietnam) to Java, Sumatra, the Malay Peninsula, and to what are now Cambodia, Thailand, Laos, and Burma. It played a crucial role in the formation of the newly emerging kingly states and urban centers in the region, for it provided organizational and ideological models for organizing monarchies and their sacred cities. It preached that the king was an incarnation of a divinity, Shiva, Vishnu, or Buddha, and, therefore, worthy of reverence by all, including rebellious nobles; it showed how to construct buildings of stone and metal: stupas guarding Buddhist relics and "mountain towers of stone" at Brahmanic temples; it popularized the Mahabharata, the Ramayana, and an aristocratic literature that glorified and justified the exploits of warriors and kings; it taught new dance gestures and a style of dressing that wrapped cloth of varying sizes and shapes around the body. The ideology was provided by various forms of Brahmanism and Mahayana Buddhism. Centuries later another less esoteric form of Buddhism, Theravada, entered Laos, Cambodia, Thailand, and Burma, and replaced the Mahayana (Coedès 1964, 2, 453 ff.; Harrison 1966, 18; Wolters 1982, 10–11). However, even then, from the fifth to the fifteenth centuries, large areas of what is now Southeast Asia were left out of this sphere of Indian influence: northern Vietnam, Borneo, the Moluccas, and the Philippines. True, Mahayana Buddhism found favor in the Vietnamese court. But, as in other Chinese-influenced cultures, this coexisted with Confucian ethics. Eventually the court preferred the latter because it provided a vision and framework for managing the state (Ho Tai 1985, 28). Moreover, the script, literature, music, architecture, costume, and etiquette of China, rather than those of India, became the models of the Vietnamese (Woodside 1971).

In the case of the Philippines, Indian influences entered Mindanao and Western Visayas, most likely through the agency of traders from either Sumatra or Java, rather than through visiting Indian traders and priests. The Philippines was too far to the north away from the spice route and too far to the east away from the main trade route between India and China (Francisco 1987, 50–51). But some of the influences can be seen, albeit in diluted form. Thus the notion that the universe is made up of layers above the earth and layers below found currency in Mindanao and Western Visayas. Traditional Bukidnons of the Mindanao highlands believe that there are seven layers ascending skywards, and seven layers descending to the underworld (Unabia 1986). Most likely, this is their interpretation of the Hindu-Buddhist notion that the soul must undergo several cycles of purification, seven heavens and seven hells, before attaining union with the One. In the Visayas which are further to the north, ordinary people, now Christians, believe that the entire universe has only seven layers (Magos 1986). But this diffusion of Indian influence was not accompanied by the formation of monarchies whose king incarnated Vishnu or Siva, nor by the erection of monasteries where the Vedic or Buddhist texts were studied.[3]

Around the fourteenth century, Islam entered Southeast Asia, again via Indian traders, and slowly gained adherents in the Malay Peninsula, the Indonesian Archipelago (even in Sumatra and Java) and Southern Philippines. In the following century, Christianity came in with the Portuguese, followed by the Spaniards in the sixteenth, and gained a foothold in Malacca, Flores, the Moluccas, and in much of the Philippines. Then came the Dutch, the British, the French, and the Americans to trade and to colonize. During the seventeenth to the nineteenth centuries, the Chinese migrated southwards, not merely as traders but as migrants. They brought with them their world view, their ethics, and their arts; and established enclaves that persist to this day.

There is thus not one Great Tradition that covers all of Southeast Asia today, but four: the Chinese (Vietnam, Singapore), the Indian (Laos, Cambodia, Thailand, Burma, Bali, and, to a continuing extent, the aristocracy of Central Java),[4] the Islamic (Sulu, parts of Mindanao, Malaysia, most of Indonesia), and the Western (Singapore,[5] Philippines, Flores, East Timor). True, there are commonalities in myth and behavior because of the related languages (Austroasiatic and Austronesian); there are also commonalities created by a similar physical environment. But there are no highly charged symbols that are universal throughout the region. This is not to say that no such symbols will appear in the future. I refer to the situation at present.

There are laudable efforts to create a Southeast Asian consciousness on the basis of similarities in art-form. In general we can notice these tendencies:

An emphasis on commonalities shared by aboriginal art forms in the region. Thus, the jewelry and the sculpture of the peoples of the Cordillera who have hitherto been animists can be shown to have continuities with those of animists in other parts of the region. The same can be shown for their weaving.

An emphasis on commonalities given by two Great Traditions: the Indian and the Islamic. The Ramayana epic has been dramatized throughout the Indianized lands through puppets and courtiers' dances. A Ramayana festival involving the participation of those countries has been organized. On the other hand close contacts between Moslems take place through schools and exchanges.

A deemphasis of art shaped by the two other Great Traditions: the Chinese and the Western. Courses on "Southeast Asian theatre" or on "Southeast Asian architecture" at the University of Hawaii, during my stay in 1981–1987, ignored Northern Vietnam and the Philippines. The focus was on Indianized cultures, with nothing on Islamic influence on architecture. However, during my final year, I was asked to give a talk on Philippine theater. In entries on Southeast Asian arts for the *Encyclopedia of Asian History* (Wicks 1988, O'Connor 1988) the emphasis was on Indian-inspired art. The Chinese-inspired temples and palaces of central and northern Vietnam were not mentioned. This is strange. As stated above, the Chinese presence in northern Vietnam goes back to the first century B.C., and is thus older than Indian influence on other countries of the region. Little or no mention is made either of Islamic influence. This did arrive later, around the thirteenth century, but it has since altered the landscape of Malaysia, Indonesia, and the Philippines. As may be expected, there is complete silence about Filipino stone churches and their statuary from the seventeenth to the nineteenth centuries.

To conceive of Southeast Asia purely in terms of Pagan, Sukhotai, Angkor, and Prambanan is to close doors rather than to open them. The prevailing tendency is to imagine "Southeast Asia" as a piece of a larger jigsaw called "Asia," that is, as a bounded cultural unity with definable boundaries that neatly set it apart from other cultural unities in the world jigsaw puzzle. It may be better to imagine it as a collage whose different materials cluster and overlap with each other, while extending into the surrounding space.

Hispanized Yet Southeast Asian

Many foreigners and even educated Filipinos imagine that the Philippines' artistic links to the rest of Southeast Asia are constituted solely by the art of aboriginal groups in the uplands of Luzon and Mindanao and the art of Islamized societies in the South. The art of the Hispanized Filipinos is deemed "out of place" in "Southeast Asia." But so, likewise, is the art of the Sinicized Vietnamese. Forgotten is that both Islamic and Indic influences were also originally intruders centuries earlier; eventually they fused with indigenous traditions. The same thing has happened to Hispanic influence in the Philippines and to Chinese influence in Vietnam.

Cooking. Allegedly, what defines the Southeast Asian flavor is the heavy use of chili pepper. Thus Northern Vietnamese and Filipino cuisines, with the exception of Christian Bicolano and the Moslem Taosug cooking, seem out of place and are likely to disappoint outsiders who have an a priori notion that authentic Southeast Asian cooking ought to be "spicy." I am told that in Amsterdam, a Filipino restaurant uses plenty of chili to cater to this preconceived notion of Dutch customers.

As was pointed out earlier, however, the fact is that the chili pepper was domesticated in Mexico centuries before the Europeans came and may have first entered Southeast Asia via the Manila Galleon. The chili pepper (*Capsicum annuum L., Capsicum frutescens L.*) was thus itself intrusive once upon a time. If we have to find commonalities in taste, they should be sought on an even more basic level: the frequent use of shrimp paste and fish sauce, and the fondness for rice and aquatic food. These are universal in both Northern Vietnamese and Filipino food. In the case of the latter, marine-derived condiments acquire new dimensions because they are mixed in with another cooking tradition. As noted previously, Filipinos love to sauté fish or meat in garlic, onions, and tomatoes, as in the Mediterranean and Latin America. Sometimes they flavor this with fish sauce to create a bouquet, or they sauté the shrimp paste itself in the classic trio.

Thus, solidly Spanish recipes like *cocido madrileño* (called *puchero* in Manila), which is a stew that mixes together chickpeas, cabbage, string beans, sausages, and scraps of chicken and beef, now have a Southeast Asian bouquet because of the infusion of *patis* (fish sauce). On the other hand that favorite Tagalog dipping sauce—*ginisang bagoong*, fermented shrimp paste sautéed in garlic, onions, and tomatoes—combines the best of two worlds: the burnt oil, garlic, and onions amplify the pungency of shrimp paste, while the saltiness of the shrimp paste counterbalances the sweetish flavor of cooked tomatoes and onions.

Costume. When people think of linkages between the Philippines and the region in terms of costume, they think of either tribal costumes or the costumes of the Moslem ethnic groups. The costume of Hispanized Filipinos supposedly does not fit in. In a recent book on world costumes (Kennett 1994, 129), the section on the Philippines, classified under "Southeast Asia," featured the costume of the Ifugao but not that of the lowland majority. Nor was there mention of Vietnamese costume under "Southeast Asia" and the (Sinicized) "Far East."

In fact the costumes of the Hispanized majority do fit in. As was mentioned in an earlier essay, the barong Tagalog, as a loose shirt worn over long pants, relates to two traditions: the Indian and the Chinese. Today Indonesians and Malaysians, too, wear their national costume, their batik shirts out. However, as Teruo Sekimoto (1997) points out, these first appeared only during the 1960s. Before that the educated urbanites wore Western-style trousers, jackets, shirts, and ties. On the other side of the ocean, Mexicans and Central Americans wear their cotton shirt [*guayabera*] out. Collared, long-sleeved and cuffed, its distinctive characteristic is that it has a column of vertical pleats running down the front with occasional embroidery on both sides of the buttons, with no cutwork. Some Mexicans say that their shirt may have been influenced by the Filipino shirt which came in via the yearly Manila Galleon, which in turn may have been influenced by the Indian.

The lowland Christian Filipina women's costume became one-piece [*terno*] only during the 1930s (Bernal 1992, 51). Before that and during the centuries before Spanish rule, it was a two-piece garment consisting of a skirt and a blouse [*baro*] with sleeves that extend to a little past the elbow. There are obvious similarities between this two-piece garment and those of the Bukidnons, Mandayas, T'bolis, Taosugs, Maranaos, Javanese, Malay, Thais, Laos, and Cambodians. One major difference that made the Hispanized Filipina's costume unique is that, before the 1930s, her blouse was semitransparent being of gauze-like textiles (sinamay, jusi, or piña). Underneath was a cotton undergarment. Moreover, the shawl/kerchief found throughout the region was draped around both of her shoulders only to become the pañuelo which, in the 1850s to the 1930s, was as semitransparent as the bodice.

It is unfortunate that in two fairly recent books on textiles in Southeast Asia, there were no colored photos of the piña in all its embroidered finery. Instead the visuals of the Philippine section focused on textiles by either Moslems or hitherto tribal peoples (Fraser-Lu 1988, Maxwell 1990). The unstated assumption seems to have been that piña with its dainty, monochromatic, cutwork embroidery "does not fit" into their preconceived notion of what Southeast Asian textiles should look like, namely, rainbow-colored and non-Western. (Interestingly enough, neither were there photos of Vietnamese textiles, perhaps because they look too Chinese?) But the piña was invented by Filipino artisans in Southeast Asia, not outside the region, even though the pineapple fruit did indeed come from the Americas. We must be careful of preconceived notions about what Southeast Asia is supposed to be.

While our men and women's costumes have shared motifs with those of our neighbors, nonetheless they do stand out for being different. They are ecru in hue, are semitransparent, and are delicately embroidered. Moreover, they feature cutwork embroidery [*calado*] which has a teasing quality about it. Should the fact that we stand out be a cause of shame? Or should we not take it as one more evidence of our originality?

*Houses.*Filipinos and some foreigners think of either tribal houses or houses of Moslem communities as the bridges to Southeast Asia. The traditional houses of wood and stone that developed from the seventeenth to the early twentieth centuries in Luzon and the Visayas are regarded as "Spanish houses" (fig. 10). And yet the curious thing is that visiting Spanish and Mexican architect-friends keep asking: "Why are they called Spanish?" Then there was a student of mine, Budhi Gunawan, a Sundanese anthropologist, whose instant reaction to one of them was, "It looks like a Bornean longhouse!"

In his overview of the house in Southeast Asia, Dumerçay (1987, 53) has only a paragraph on the Philippines and on the supposed house-type of Negros.

> Walls are made of split bamboo or palm fronds, but the materials are rarely woven. Between the outer and inner parts of the wall a filling of palm leaves or some other leaf material is inserted, making the overall appearance of the house rather primitive.

We may quarrel with his notion that "the materials are rarely woven." But that can be taken up in another context. For now, what galls is that nowhere in his overview does he inform the reader that this archipelago, whose large population alone makes it difficult to ignore, has a wide variety of house styles by region and by class. Proof of the latter is the island of Negros itself where houses and mansions from the nineteenth and early twentieth centuries are hardwood frame constructions whose subtlety of proportions and detail are certainly not "primitive." We Filipinos must beware of constructions of "Southeast Asia" by so-called experts. Their narrow notions of what is "authentically" Southeast Asian exclude a priori the best achievements of the lowland Christian Filipino.

The indigenous house at the time of Spanish contact had a steep roof that rested on posts, rather than on the walls. Floors were raised above the ground as a precaution against floods and insects. Like their peers elsewhere in the region, Filipinos love living by or over bodies of water. The house of the Visayan chief was a longhouse with walls of timber that was ornamented with carvings and had a thatch roof. His followers' houses were smaller and lower huts of either hardwood or woven bamboo (Alcina [1668b] n.d., 4:43–44). After the foundation of Spanish Manila in 1571, a synthesis of two building traditions emerged. The heavy roof was carried by wooden posts dug deep into the ground. These could sway freely during a tremor, whereas stone walls could not. The resulting house is thus low by Spanish and Mexican standards, for it has only two stories rather than the classic three. The upper story has wooden walls; the ground story stone walls. Both are mere curtains. Often the great posts are exposed within the house or are made to stand freely be-

Figure 10. Early-nineteenth-century house in Luzon

side the stone walls (fig. 11). In comparison with Mexico, Spain, and the rest of Southeast Asia, these traditional houses have long windows that extend almost from post to post with an additional small window (*ventanilla*) between the window sill and the floor sill (see Zialcita and Tinio 1980). The roof could be of thatch or tile, depending on the owner's preferences. In the nineteenth century, metal roofs became common alternatives.

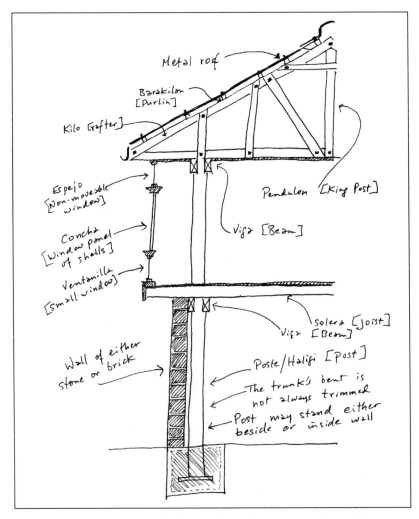

Figure 11. Cross-section of a house from the 1890s to the 1900s

Budhi Gunawan was thus correct in likening the wood-and-stone house (*bahay na bato at kahoy*) to a longhouse (fig. 12). The construction system of the wood-and-stone house is a wooden frame, as in Borneo: The stone walls carry no load. Living quarters are in the upper story. There are different types of Bornean longhouses. Closest in spirit is a two-story longhouse of timber with a long external gallery that I saw at Macong in East Borneo in 1997. The airiness reminded me of our nineteenth-century houses. In general though, all longhouses are similar in their pronounced horizontality: a corridor runs through the center with small apartments on both sides for the several families and households that live under one roof. This contrasts with the classic Javanese house which consists of single-storied pavilions with separate roofs and intervening courtyards arranged in a cruciform manner around the house proper. Budhi, who comes from West Java, was struck by the horizontality of the Taal wood-and-stone house: The structure is long and has a continuous roof. Moreover, both the second story of our wood-and-stone houses and the longhouse cantilever, and thus seem to float above the ground. In contrast the classic single-storied Javanese house is earthbound.

Figure 12. A longhouse in Sarawak, Borneo

The wood-and-stone house can be looked at as a longhouse with a stone skirt around the wooden legs of its ground story, a row of shell windows to close its verandas in the upper story, and a hat of either tiles or thatch as roof.

This house has four other connections in the region: to (1) the *rumah gedung* of Indonesia, (2) the Arabic *mashrabiyya*, (3) the translucent window/doors of the Sinicized world, and (4) the traceried transoms common in the region.

A close Indonesian cousin of the wood-and-stone house is the rumah gedung ["office building house"] of the historic center of Jakarta and of Southern Sumatra which has a conventional hip roof of tile over a wooden upper story and stone ground story. The roof rests on wooden pillars dug into the ground. The stone wall is but a curtain. The connections between this and our style of construction should be explored. There was direct commerce between Dutch Java and Spanish Manila during the galleon trade (Legarda 1999, 162, 247).

Figure 13. A *mashrabiyya* from Cairo, Egypt

The Arabs gave Spain the custom of constructing cantilevered, grilled wooden balconies called "mashrabiyya," also *rowshan* (fig. 13). The 3-meter high balcony rests on wooden consoles embedded into stone walls protruding 60 centimeters from the building. It has its own roof and a decorative entablature on its roof line. Residents can peer into the street in privacy through the grilled balcony; while in an adjoining room, they can enjoy the air circulating through the grilles (Earls 1997a, 1997b). This wooden balcony became popular in particular regions of Spain and of the New World, such as Lima, Peru. The Spanish term, *ajimez*, is of Arab origin. According to the Spanish art historian Enrique Dorta (1973, 403), the ajimez's final form is the Filipino *galeria volada*, the flying gallery that runs along the length of the house front to protect it from sun and rain (fig. 14).

Figure 14. The *volada* in San Juan de Dios, Intramuros (destroyed during World War II)

In contrast to the rest of Southeast Asia and to Mexico and Spain, the wood-and-stone house has long, horizontal windows. Moreover, these are closed with wooden lattice work panels that carry translucent materials that are not glass. Since the eighteenth century, windows in Spain and Spanish America have been narrow but tall French doors opening onto a projecting balcony (fig. 15). Until now in Thailand, Malaysia, and South Sumatra, windows are likewise full-length doors. In their case, however, the two wooden leaves are pushed out to flap over the facade. A wooden railing on the same plane as the wall keeps the insider from falling out of the window (fig. 16). In contrast China, Korea, and Japan have latticework panels with thick rice paper pasted onto one side and which, therefore, allow light to filter through. The Philippines substitutes flat *capiz* shells (*Placuna placenta*) which likewise create a distinct but comfortable glow (fig. 17). Chinese artisans migrated to the Philippines from the opening of Spanish rule. Presumably they may have seen possibilities in using shell as a substitute for paper and for the (then) expensive glass. However, unlike in China, but like in Japan, the panels do not push out but slide in grooves on a sill.

Figure 15. Open balcony with French windows, in Mexico and Central America, Spain

Figure 16. Window and balustrade with push-out shutters, in Thailand, Malaysia, Singapore, Indonesia

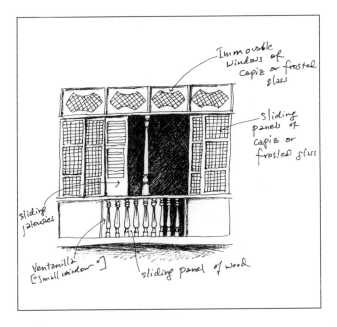

Figure 17. The two-part window with sliding panels, in the Philippines

The Japanese came during the early seventeenth century as merchants and refugees from religious persecution—in 1603, there were 1,500 Japanese in the Manila suburb of Dilao (Delacour 1994). They returned as migrants from the 1880s to the early 1900s. Japanese friends who have visited Filipino houses remark on the similarity between the local shell-paned panels, designed in grids, and their own shoji panels (fig. 18).

During the nineteenth century, Chinese artisans appear to have popularized wooden transoms with cutout and carved flowers and birds throughout Southeast Asia. So did Japanese artisans in the Philippines who brought in adaptations of their *ranma*, or pierced transoms. Indeed, according to oral tradition, a master craftsman who carved some of the best traceries at Silay, Negros Occidental, in the 1900s was called Kitai. This seems to me to have been a Japanese

Figure 18. Shojis, sliding Japanese wooden lattices with rice paper

family name. These traceried panels have a functional purpose in the Filipino wood-and-stone style. Situated between ceiling and interior walls, they help wind and light circulate.

It is thus unfair to insist that wood-and-stone Filipino houses are "Spanish" copies that have nothing to do with either Southeast Asia or Asia in general. Yes, they are Hispanic, but also Southeast Asian.

Indeed, in comparison to Java and Northern Vietnam, the millennial tradition of building on stilts has persisted longer in Filipino cities and villages, partly because of the wood-and-stone style. As a Filipino, I am always struck by the fact that many Javanese houses, whether in the city or the countryside, are single-storied and of stuccoed brick rather than wooden houses on stilts. And yet in earlier centuries, Central Javanese houses were built on stilts, as suggested by bas-reliefs at Prambanan. In Vietnam, a Chinese preference for ground-level houses seems to have led to the near-disappearance of building wooden structures on piles. At Hanoi's Museum of Ethnology, there is a telling contrast. The indigenous longhouses still in use in the aboriginal uplands stand on stilts. However, the houses of the lowland Sinicized Vietnamese, who constitute the majority, follow Chinese custom in raising their one-story houses on a stone platform. It is noteworthy that Hanoi sits at a confluence of rivers and lakes, its ground is therefore humid. Houses on piles would have been more appropriate. In Central Java, residents shifted to building with floors on the ground around the thirteenth or fourteenth century (Schoppert 1997, 32). Reid (1988, 62) suggests that in Northern Vietnam and Java, large timbers had become scarce by the sixteenth century in the most densely populated areas. In some aspects of culture, the Hispanized Filipino is more traditionally Southeast Asian and Austronesian than some of his neighbors.

One criterion, therefore, for defining a Southeast Asian architectural communality would be the use of the house on stilts. But this criterion could be broadened to include as well all responses to the physical environment and to the preexisting traditions in the region. Thus defined, Vietnamese temples and palaces can be regarded as fitting the tropical landscape. Though influenced by Chinese ideals of architecture, they differ in not having ceilings and interior wall dividers (Bezacier 1955, 34). Rafters and interior columns are well-articulated, perhaps as a response to the need for maximum ventilation in the tropics. Even Filipino sixteenth- to nineteenth-century churches, often termed "Spanish," may after all be "Southeast Asian." Because of the frequency of earthquakes, they tend to be relatively low in height. Their ceilings are of wood rather than of stone. At times the trapezoidal woodwork of the roof is exposed in Mudejar fashion. Moreover, Chinese motifs appear in the treatment of clouds and garment folds in statuary and in the belfries. In Spain and Spanish America, towers are integrated into the facade and are four-sided. In contrast Philippine towers are often polygonal from base to dome, may rise in tiers, and are sometimes separated from the church as free-standing structures. They thus evoke the pagoda, as Javier Galvan (2004, 85 ff.), a Spanish architect and expert on Hispano-Filipino churches, points out in a paper on the octagon in Filipino towers and the Chinese world view. In some way, too, these octagonal church towers evoke the "corn cob" towers of Khmer temples.

Religious Rituals. Processions are essentially demonstrations where the faithful pray while accompanying religious images along a determined route. The most popular procession in many Filipino towns and cities is that of the Santo Entierro [Sacred Burial], or Christ in the Coffin. This takes place on Good Friday evening every year to mark the anniversary of Christ's death on the cross.

At first glance, the procession could not possibly have any connection with Southeast Asia. Not only is it Hispanic, it is a symbolic funeral procession. But it has, for, as mentioned earlier, the procession has continuities with the cult of the ancestors. Upon his death, the pre-Hispanic chief was mummified and his body kept in a coffin in the innermost part of the house together with family heirlooms (Chirino [1604] 1969, 88). The belief was that his spirit would protect the house from intruders. The Ifugao of the Cordillera Mountains would keep the ancestral corpse in a sealed coffin underneath their houses (Barton 1946). In pagan times, the Batak of Sumatra kept the dried corpse of their ancestor in a boat-shaped coffin hanging from the eaves outside their house for one to ten years (Sibeth 1991, 70–71). The custom of keeping the dried remains of the ancestor inside or close to the house may have been widespread in Indonesia before, but is no longer so because of Indian-introduced cremation. Cremation has caught on even among non-Indianized groups in the outer islands, for instance, among the Dyak of Borneo who burn the remains of their ancestor in a large ceremony called *tiwah* (Bambang and Prijanti 1990, 61).

Despite centuries of Hispanization, some rural Bicolanos keep the bones of their ancestors. After these have dried up and have been exhumed from the first burial, they are wrapped with cloth into a bundle and hung from the rafters for their power to protect (Cannell 1991). For ancestors were revered and prayed to in pagan times all over Southeast Asia; indeed they are prayed to even today by mainstream, lowland Christian Filipinos. Among Ilocanos in Northern Luzon, people lay aside a portion of any newly prepared roast meat or sweet meat for the deceased ancestors of the house. While such offerings do not take place in Metro Manila, friends confide that they do pray once in a while to a deceased grandparent or parent for help. Or consider this: A highly educated lady from Manila had her mother cremated. She keeps some of the ashes in a powder case that she carries around with her in her handbag.

Processional statuary is owned and kept at home by Filipino families. In Spain and Spanish America, they are owned and kept either by the Church or by confraternities. Locally, the icons are referred to with parental terms. Mary is "Ina" [Mother]; while Christ, the Son of God, is called "Ama" [Father]. The last, "Christ Our Father," is strange from the point of view of official theology. Are these icons unconsciously looked upon as symbolic ancestors by particular families? This could be explored. For now, I should mention that in Tagalog and Pampango families, these icons are given titles to orchards and rice lands to ensure their maintenance in perpetuity.

They have thus become part of the family. Moreover, they are bathed and dressed regularly. Much like the corpse of the pre-Hispanic datu, these icons are regarded as protection against intruders. "My family feels safer because of our life-sized Cristo de la Paciencia [Christ Resting after the Scourging]" confided my dentist, the late Dr. Mario Villacorta. Indeed he would drape his dental jacket over it. Another lady, the owner of a famous nineteenth-century mansion in Bulacan, said that every night, she would take out the life-sized image of Christ-in-the-Coffin, place it on her bed and hug it for protection.

One other connection with Indonesia that should also be explored is the investment of time and resources in funeral processions. The ornate funeral processions of the Balinese are well-known. So are the funeral rituals among the Toradja of the Sulawesi. The anthropologist Shinji Yamashita (1997), who is familiar with the Toradja, pointed out that their funerals not only honor the dead, they also affirm the high status of both the dead and the living before the local community. Among Filipinos, the possession of a processional tableau, above all of Christ-in-the-Coffin and of His Grieving Mother, both indicate and validate a long lineage, current economic prosperity, and high social standing. Dr. Villacorta once told me that as a struggling student, his dream was to own a processional tableau. When finally he became a successful dentist, he had one made, and eventually two more depicting particular scenes from the Way of the Cross. However, the honor of owning the Christ-in-the-Coffin and His Grieving Mother in his town of Meycauayan, Bulacan, stayed among families of older social standing.

The Good Friday procession fits into a regionwide tendency to pray to the ancestors, to hold on to some of their remains, and to celebrate their funeral with a grand, public ceremony.

Our Place in an Invented Region

Because ASEAN exists, and exchanges among Southeast Asian countries are growing, the question "What is Southeast Asia?" has become an important one. People look for symbols that can make them feel that they share an identity vis-à-vis the rest of the world. As a starting point, we should avoid projecting our present desires to the past. A "Southeast Asia," conceived as a felt unity, like "Western Europe" or "Islam" has never existed. Historically, the latter two have been oikumenes with vivid, deeply felt, shared symbols. Countries within the presently denominated boundaries of Southeast Asia have not formed a single oikumene. At present these countries participate in four different Great Traditions: the Indic, the Sinic, the Islamic, and the Western. It would be a mistake to develop a Southeast Asian identity only around commonalities derived from a common Indic heritage; or conversely, only around aboriginal elements that lie outside these Great Traditions. Either option effectively excludes Sinicized Central and North Vietnam and Hispanized Luzon and the Visayas. They may also alienate devout Moslem Malaysians, Filipinos, and Indonesians. It is better to highlight various commonalities:

- Responses to a similar environment, for instance, fish sauce or the house-on-stilts.
- Motifs brought about by common myths and behavior generated by membership in closely related languages, Austroasiatic, Austronesian, and Thai, such as the cult of the ancestors or the relatively higher status of women compared to men's.
- Influences of the four Great Traditions which create a sense of community. Necessarily this will emphasize subclusters within the overall cluster that is Southeast Asia. Aside from Malaysia, Indonesia, and southern Philippines, there are pockets of Moslems in southern Vietnam, Cambodia, southern Thailand, and Burma. They will naturally feel an affinity for each other. On the other hand, the widespread use of English as a literary medium creates bridges among Filipinos, Malaysians, and Singaporeans.
- Influences from the outside that create a common ground but which thus far have not fostered an all-embracing oikumene. For instance, the pervasive influence of Chinese migrants has created a common culinary symbol throughout the region;

the noodle, and a common motif of turn-of-the-century houses, such as traceried woodwork. But both have not been accompanied by the transmission of Chinese script, classics, and temple architecture to the ordinary Southeast Asian.

Highlighting these commonalities creates space for Chinese enclaves like Singapore, whose traditional shop houses, with their Chinese roofs, Corinthian pilasters, and Portuguese tiles, obviously combine several traditions together.

It is also important to take a more inductive approach in imagining "Southeast Asia," as was done, for instance, by Anthony Reid (1988) in his synthesis. Instead of assuming that the defining characteristic of Southeast Asia is Indianization, he sorts out different aspects of Southeast Asian life: the material culture, social organization, festivals and amusements, and he articulates the patterns cutting across them. His approach is rich in data and detail. Moreover, it embraces both the Philippines and Vietnam. Hopefully, someone in the future will show how these commonalities have been changed by, and at the same time have changed, the four Great Traditions. At present the world is conceived of as a giant jigsaw wherein each part has a defining essence. In the same way "Asia" is supposed to have an essence, so likewise is its subregion, "Southeast Asia." It is more realistic to imagine the latter as a configuration of cultural traditions of different shapes and textures overlapping and connecting with each other.

Highlighting commonalities while using a more inductive approach creates space as well for us Hispanized Filipinos in Southeast Asia. While many of our characteristic artifacts and rituals do indeed link us to the Hispanic world, they link us as well to Southeast Asia. Our cooking style, national costume, traditional urban houses, and even our Good Friday ritual bridge two worlds: Southeast Asia and the Hispanic World. Such a Southeast Asia would have space for the Sinicized Vietnamese, too. In some American graduate schools, one favorite question is: "Does Vietnam belong to Southeast Asia or to the Far East?" This parallels the question raised for the Philippines: "Does it belong to Southeast Asia or to the Hispanic World?" My answer would be a counterquestion: "Why not to two or more worlds?" Malaysia and Indonesia belong to both Southeast Asia and the Islamic world. This is not questioned. We should aim to feel at home in both Mexico and Indonesia, Spanish America and Southeast Asia.

The Philippines began to emerge as a distinct community transcending the narrow confines of kin and locality during the late sixteenth century when, for the first time in universal history, the world was experienced as a globe. One result of this is that domains in the lowland culture of Luzon and the Visayas mix and fuse together influences that came in from north and south, east and west since the sixteenth century. Though Filipinos should be proud of their uniqueness, many are apologetic about this for several reasons: (1) all that is Spanish is currently demonized, (2) a prevailing reductionism prioritizes the indigenous while confusing "race" with "culture," and (3) that binary "Asia versus the West" has become a metaphysical indubitable. In the meantime, however, international politics and economic imperatives have created a grouping of nation-states broader than the Association of Southeast Asian Nations. This new grouping is the Asia-Pacific Economic Cooperation (APEC) which embraces Southeast Asia, China, Japan, and other nation-states fronting the Pacific Ocean, notably Australia, Canada, the U.S., and Spanish American countries. We now hear talk of a common history linking the peoples of the great sea. Eventually, efforts to promote a common identity for the member states will surface. Because of its unique history, the Philippines has an identity that connects together both sides of the Pacific Ocean. But will we be proud of this and be sensitive to the opportunity it offers?

Because of blinders imposed by our popular history books, the Philippines has missed opportunities to be the first in building bridges across the Pacific to Latin America. Malaysia, not us, opened the first air route linking a Southeast Asian city, Kuala Lumpur, with a Latin American city, Mexico D.F. We nearly missed hosting the first forum that brought together the foreign ministers of East Asia and Latin America. The idea of establishing the forum was raised by the Singaporean Pres. Goh Chok

Tong during a meeting with President Frei of Chile in 1998 (editorial of *Philippine Panorama*, 25 Jan. 2004, 3). Luckily, we are told, his advisers suggested Manila as the natural venue for this historic encounter. And so the forum took place in Manila and Tagaytay on 28–31 January 2004. Hopefully in the future, we will be more alert to the opportunities that our affinities in several neighborhoods of the global village create for us.

Notes

1. The exact term for this type of culture in both Arnold Toynbee's work and the Anglo-American tradition of archaeology is "civilization," that is, a culture where the state [*civitas*] and the city [*civitas*] are both present as institutions and which can embrace a wide variety of cultures to create an *oikumene* (see Toynbee 1972, 43 ff.) However, this precise use of "civilization" as a type of culture is not observed by many writers. Instead they use "civilization" and "culture" interchangeably. To avoid confusion, I prefer not to use the term in this essay.

2. "Culture area" is much used in American anthropology. I have not used it because it tends to connote a bounded geographical area where different cultures share similar traits. So defined, it is similar to common responses to an ecosystem and is only one way to classify cultures together.

3. The copper plate unearthed in Laguna has an Old Malay text in the Early Kawi script that was used at one time in Bali in Indonesia, Thailand, and Champa in Central Vietnam (Postma 1992). Dated to around 900 A.D., it raises anew the question: To what extent did Indianizing influences penetrate northward? And still another: Why did this influence, if present, not lead to the formation of a monarchy? Also why did the script fall into disuse?

4. Still, one has to qualify what this Indian Great Tradition would mean today. Over the course of centuries, participating cultures have become isolated from each other. First because of the advent of Islam and its conversion of Java and Sumatra; second, because Western colonialism created new political boundaries. As a result, Bali has gone on its own separate course. Perhaps the Indian Great Tradition no longer exists as an all-embracing tradition but as several autonomous traditions. In contrast, Islam may be diverse, but there are focal points in the tradition, like the pilgrimage to Mecca, which creates a vivid sense of universal community.

5. Singapore is both Sinic and Western. Its unequalled efficiency suggests that it has internalized Western notions of public and business administration far more than its neighbors, including the Philippines.

References

Abbreviations

B and R   Blair, Emma and James Robertson
EUIEA   *Enciclopedia Universa Ibeor-Europeo-Americana*
MER   *The Marxist-Engels Reader*
MRF   *Marx et la Revolution francaise*

Abella, Domingo. 1977. The mission school. In *Filipino heritage: The making of a nation* 4, 953–56. Alfredo R. Roces, editor in chief. Manila: Lahing Pilipino.

Abraham, Edru. 1993. Professor in dance and music at the University of the Philippines at Quezon City. Personal communication.

Adams, Robert MCormick. 1966. *The evolution of urban society: Early Mesopotamia and pre-Hispanic Mexico.* Chicago: Aldine Press.

Agoncillo, Teodoro A. 1956. *The revolt of the masses and the story of Bonifacio and the Katipunan.* Quezon City: University of the Philippines.

—————. 1960. *Malolos: The crisis of the Republic.* Quezon City: University of the Philippines.

Aguinaldo y Famy, Emilio. 1954. Lineas proemiales. In Francisco Zaragoza, *Marella: la inquietud romántica de la revolución.* Postscriptum by Claro Mayo Recto. Manila: [General Printing Press].

—————. 1967. *My memoirs.* Translated by Luz Colandrino-Bucer. N.p.

Alcina, Francisco Ignacio. [1668a] n.d. *The Muñoz text of Alcina's history of the Bisayan Islands.* Books 1–4. Transliteration by Victor Baltazar from a microfilm of the Spanish text. Chicago: University of Chicago, Department of Anthropology, Philippine Studies Program.

—————. [1668b] n.d. *The Muñoz text of Alcina's history of the Bisayan Islands.* 3 vols. Preliminary translation by Paul S. Leitz. Chicago: University of Chicago, Department of Anthropology, Philippine Studies Program.

Alejandrino, José (Gen.). 1933. *La senda del sacrificio: Episodios y anecdotas de nuestras luchas por la libertad.* Manila: [s.n.].

————. 1949. *The price of freedom: Episodes and anecdotes of our struggles for freedom.* Translated by Jose M. Alejandrino. Prologue by Teodoro M. Kalaw. Manila: M. Colcol and Company.

Ali, Yusuf A. N.d. *The Holy Quran: Translation and commentary.* Jeddah, Saudi Arabia: Dar al-Qiblah for Islamic Literature.

Alonso, Ana Maria. 1994. The politics of space, time and substance: State formation, nationalism, and ethnicity. *Annual Review of Anthropology,* 23:379–405.

Alvarez, Santiago. 1992. *The Katipunan and the Revolution: Memoirs of a general.* With the original Tagalog text. Translated into English by Paula Carolina S. Malay. Introduction by Ruby R. Paredes. Quezon City: Ateneo de Manila University Press.

Alzona, Encarnacion, ed. 1964. *Julio Nakpil and the Philippine Revolution, with the autobiography of Gregoria de Jesus.* Translation by Encarnacion Alzona. Manila: The Heirs of Julio Nakpil.

Anderson, Benedict. 1983. *Imagined communities: Reflections on the origin and spread of nationalism.* London: Verso.

Apostol, Cecilio. 1941. *Pentélicas (Poesías).* Prologue by Claro Mayo Recto, anthologizing by Jaime C. de Veyra. Manila: Gráfica, Inc.

Araneta, Antonio S., ed. 1986. *1030 R. Hidalgo.* 2 vols. Mara, Inc.

Armillas, Pedro. 1968. Urban revolution. *International Encyclopedia of the Social Sciences* 16:18–21.

Augustinian Memoranda. [1573] 1903. In B and R, 34:273–84.

Azurin, Arnold Molina. 1994. Pagkaraan ni Cristobal Colon: Ang diyalektika ng kolonisasyon/dekolonisasyon sa Ilokos. In *Katipunan: Isang pambansang kilusan.* Edited by Ferdinand Llanes. Quezon City: Trinitas Publishing.

Baer, Hans A. 1986. The concept of civilization in anthropology: A critical review. In *The burden of being civilized: An anthropological perspective on the discontents of civilization.* Edited by Miles Richardson and Malcolm C. Webb. Atlanta, Georgia: The University of Georgia Press.

Baetiong, May Czarina A. 1999. Urban planning lack hounds business breaks throughout the years. *BusinessWorld,* 29 Dec., 15.

Bambang Harsrinuksmo and Prijanti Pakan. 1990. Adat dan tata cara penguburan. *Ensiklopedi nasional Indonesia.* Vol. 1. Jakarta: Cipta Adi Pustaka.

Bartlett, Robert. 1993. *The making of Europe, conquest, colonization and cultural change, 950–1350.* Princeton, New Jersey: Princeton University Press.

Barton, Roy. 1938. *Philippine pagans: The autobiographies of three Ifugaos.* London: G. Routledge.

————. 1946. *The religion of the Ifugaos*. Menasha, Wisconsin: American Anthropological Association.

————. 1949. *The Kalingas: Their institutions and custom law*. With an introduction by E. Adamson Hoebel. Chicago: The University of Chicago Press.

————. [1919] 1969. *Ifugao law*. New foreword by Fred Eggan. Berkeley: University of California Press.

Basave Benitez, Agustin F. 1992. *México mestizo: Análisis del nacionalismo mexicano en torno a la mestizofilia de Andres Molina Enriquez*. Mexico, D.F.: Fondo de Cultura Económica.

Bautista, Basilides. 1999. Specialist in religious processions and statuary. Personal communication.

Bellwood, Peter. 1985. *Prehistory of the Indo-Malaysian archipelago*. Sydney: Academic Press.

Berger, Peter. 1989. Moral judgment and political action. *Dialogue* 84 (Feb.): 2–7.

Bezacier, Louis. 1955. *L'Art vietnamien*. Paris: Editions de l'Union Française.

Bhabha, Homi. 1994. *The location of culture*. London:Routledge.

Bhusan, Jamila Brij. 1958. *The costumes and textiles of India*. Bombay: Jal Hirji Taraporevala.

Blair, Emma and James Robertson. 1904–1907. *The Philippine Islands, 1493–1898*. Cleveland: Arthur H. Clark Company.

Bloch, Marc. 1961. *Feudal society*. Vols. 1 and 2. Translated by L. A. Manyon. Chicago: The University of Chicago Press.

Blum, Jerome. 1978. *The end of the old order in rural Europe*. Princeton, New Jersey: Princeton University Press.

Boas, Franz [1948] 1955. *Race, language and culture*. New York: The Macmillan Co.

Bobadilla, Diego de. [1640] 1990. Relation of the Philippine Islands. In *Documentary sources of Philippine history*, 4:329–43. Edited by Gregorio Zaide. Manila: National Bookstore.

Bowring, Sir John. 1859. *A visit to the islands*. London: Smith, Elder and Co.

Boxer Codex. [1590] 1960. The manners, customs and beliefs of the Philippine inhabitants of long ago, being chapters of "A late 16th century Manila manuscript." Transcribed, translated and annotated by Carlos Quirino and Mauro Garcia. *The Philippine Journal of Science* 87, no. 4:325–453.

Braudel, Fernand. 1986. *L'Identité de la France: Espace et histoire*. 3 vols. Paris: Arthaud-Flammarion.

Brenan, Gerald. 1940. *The Spanish labyrinth*. London: Cambridge University Press.

Briggs, Martin S. 1959. *Everyman's concise encyclopedia of architecture.* London: J. M. Dent and Sons, Ltd.

Bronson, Bennet. 1977. Exchange at the upstream and downstream ends: Notes towards a functionalist model of the coastal state in Southeast Asia. In *Economic exchange and social interaction in Southeast Asia: Perspectives from prehistory, history and ethnography,* 38–52. Edited by Karl Hutterer. Ann Arbor, Michigan: Center for South and Southeast Asian Studies, University of Michigan.

Broughton, Simon, Mark Ellingham, David Muddyman, and Richard Trillo. 1994. *World music: The rough guide.* Contributing ed. Kim Burton. London: The Rough Guides.

Brumfiel, Elizabeth. 1992. Distinguished lecture in archeology: Breaking and entering the ecosystem—Gender, class and faction steal the show. *American Anthropologist* 94, no. 3:551–67.

Bulatao, Jaime. 1967. Split-level Christianity. In *Brown heritage,* 16–33. Edited by Antonio P. Manuud y Gella. Quezon City: Ateneo de Manila University Press.

Bulosan, Carlos. 1973. *America is in the heart, a personal history.* Manila: A. S. Florentino.

Bureau of Records and Archives Management (BRAM), Manila, Philippines. [s.d.]. Real Cedula de 2 de febrero, 1818. Ereccion de Pueblos, Ilocos Sur 1808–1817, bk. 2.

Burrow, Thomas. 1955. *The Sanskrit language.* London: Faber and Faber.

Cabilao-Valencia, Minda. 2001. Sociologist at the Ateneo de Manila University. Personal communication.

Camar, Usopay. 1970. The Bayanihan: How authentic is the repertoire? *Solidarity* 5, no. 11:45–51.

Campbell, Bernard, ed. 1985. *Humankind emerging.* Boston: Little, Brown and Company.

Cannell, Fenella. 1991. Catholicism, spirit mediums and the ideal of beauty in a Bicolano community, Philippines. Ph.D. dissertation, University of London.
———. 1999. *Power and intimacy in the Christian Philippines.* Quezon City: Ateneo de Manila University Press.

Carneiro, Robert L. 1981. The chiefdom: Precursor of the state. In *The transition to statehood in the new world,* 37–75. Edited by Grant D. Jones and Robert R. Kautz. Cambridge: University Press.

Carr, Raymond. 1966. *Spain 1808–1975.* Oxford: Clarendon Press.

Carter-Bentley, Grant. 1985. Dispute, authority and Maranao social order. In *Dispute processing in the Philippines,* 51–72. Edited by Resil B. Mojares.

Quezon City: Bureau of Local Government Supervision, Ministry of Local Government.

Caruncho, Eric S. 1999. Inner journey. *Sunday Inquirer Magazine*, 31 Oct., 6–7.

Casal, Gabriel. 1978. *T'boli art: In its socio-cultural context*. Makati: Ayala Museum.

Casiño, Eric. 1982. The Philippines: Lands and people, a cultural geography. In *The Filipino nation 2*. Edited by Jim Haskins. New York: Grolier International.

Castillo, Gelia. 1981. *Changing rural institutions and participatory development: A review of the Philippine experience*, Pt. 1. Makati: Philippine Institute for Development Studies.

Cerezo, Saturnino Martin. 1946. *El sitio de Baler*. Prologue by Azorin. Madrid: Editorial Biblioteca Nueva.

Champion, Timothy et al. 1984. *Prehistoric Europe*. London: Academic Press.

Chaunu, Pierre. 1960. *Les Philippines et le Pacifique des Ibériques (XVIe, XVIIe, XVIIIe siecles)*. Introduction méthodologique et indices d'activité. Paris: S.E.V.P.E.N.

Childe, Vere Gordon. 1955. *Man makes himself*. New York: New American Library.

Chirino, Pedro, S.J. [1604] 1969. *Relación de las Islas Filipinas/The Philippines in 1600*. Original Spanish text, translation by Ramón Echevarría. Manila: Historical Conservation Society.

Cipolla, Carlo M. 1969. *Literacy and development in the West*. Baltimore: Penguin Books.

Coedès, George. 1964. *Les états hindouisés d'Indochine et d'Indonésie*. Paris: Editions E. de Boccard.

———. 1968. *The Indianized states of Southeast Asia*. Honolulu: East-West Center Press.

Cohn, Bernard S. 1971. *India: The social anthropology of a civilization*. Englewood Cliffs, New Jersey: Prentice-Hall.

Cole, Fay Cooper. 1922. The Tinguian: Social, religious and economic life of a Philippine tribe. *Field Museum of Natural History*. Anthropology Series 14:231–493.

Colín, Francisco. [1663] 1900–1902. *Labor evangélica, ministerios apostólicos de los obreros de la Compañia de Jesus, fundación y progresos de su provincia en las Islas Filipinas*. 3 vols. Edited and introduced by Pablo Pastells. Barcelona: Imprenta y Litografía de Henrich.

Col. Zialcita, 86: Revolutionary hero, Quezon friend, dies. 1955. The *Evening News*, 7 Feb.

Confucius. 1938. *The analects of Confucius.* Translated and annotated by Arthur Waley. London: George Allen and Unwin Ltd.

Conklin, Harold C. 1957. *Hanunoo agriculture: A report on an integral system of shifting cultivation in the Philippines.* Rome: Food and Agricultural Organization of the United Nations.

————. 1980. *Ethnographic atlas of Ifugao: A study of environment, culture, and society in Northern Luzon.* New Haven: Yale University Press with the American Geographical Society of New York.

Conquest of the Island of Luzon. [1572] 1973. Manila, 20 April 1572. In B and R, 3:141–71.

Consejo de la Hispanidad. 1943. *Recopilación de las Leyes de los Reynos de las Indias.* 3 vols. Madrid: Consejo de la Hispanidad.

Constantino, Renato. 1975. *The Philippines: A past revisited.* With the collaboration of Letizia R. Constantino. Quezon City: Tala Publishing Services.

————. 1978. *Neocolonial identity and counter-consciousness: Essays on cultural decolonization.* Edited, with an introduction by István Mészáros. London: Merlin Press.

Corpuz, Onofre D. 1965. *The Philippines.* Englewood Cliffs, New Jersey: Prentice-Hall, Inc.

————. 1989. *The roots of the Filipino nation.* 2 vols. Quezon City: Aklahi Foundation.

Crow, John A. 1985. *Spain: The root and the flower, an interpretation of Spain and the Spanish people.* Berkeley: University of California Press.

Cruz, Romeo V. 1989. Nationalism in nineteenth-century Manila. In *Manila: History, people and culture. The proceedings of the Manila Studies Conference,* 57–70. Edited by Wilfrido Villacorta et al. Co-sponsored by De La Salle University and the Philippine Studies Association. Barrio San Luis Complex, 11–12 April 1986. Manila: De La Salle University Press.

Cunanan, Belinda. 1996. Biggest winners: FVR and Gordon. *Philippine Daily Inquirer,* 6 Nov.

Cushner, Nicholas P. 1976. *Landed estates in the colonial Philippines.* New Haven: Yale University, Southeast Asia Studies.

Darnton, Robert. 1984. *The great cat massacre and other episodes in French cultural history.* New York: Vintage Books.

De Bertier de Sauvigny, G. and David H. Pinkney. 1983. *History of France.* Translation by James Friguglietti. Arlington Heights, Illinois: The Forum Press, Inc.

De Casparis, J. G. and I. W. Mabett. 1992. Religion and popular beliefs of Southeast Asia before circa 1500. In *The Cambridge history of Southeast Asia.* Vol.

1. *From early times to circa 1800*, 276–339. Edited by Nicholas Tarling. Cambridge: University Press.

De la Rosa, Rolando V. 1990. *Beginnings of the Filipino Dominicans: A critical inquiry into the late emergence of native Dominicans in the Philippines and their attempt at self-government.* Quezon City: Dominican Province of the Philippines.

De la Torre, Visitación. 1986. *Barong Tagalog: The Philippine national wear.* Photos by Rene Mejia. Manila: A. Bautista Press.

De los Reyes y Florentino, Isabelo. 1888. *Artículos varios sobre etnografía, historia y costumbres de Filipinas.* With a critical prologue by Cesareo Blanco y Sierra. Manila: J. A. Ramos, ed.

————. 1890. *Historia de Ilocos.* 2 vols. Manila: La Opinion. Chicago: Newberry Library Photo Duplication Service.

De los Rios de Coronel, Hernando. [1621] Memorial y relación para su Magestad. In B and R, 19:183–297.

De Mas y Sans, Sinibaldo. [1842] 1963. *Informe secreto de Sinibaldo de Mas/Secret report of Sinibaldo de Mas.* Translated by Carlos Botor. Revised by Alfonso Felix Jr. Introduction and notes by Juan Palazon. Manila: Historical Conservation Society.

De San Agustin, Gaspar. [1698] 1975. *Conquistas de las Islas Filipinas (1565–1615).* Edited by and with an introduction, notes and indices by Manuel Merino, OSA. Madrid: CSIC.

Delacour, Catherine. 1994. Des guerriers japonais. In *Le San Diego: Un trésor sous la mer.* Edited by Dominique Carre, Jean-Paul Desroches et Frank Goddio. [Paris]: Association Française d'Action Artistique, Ministère des Affaires Etrangères.

DeVries, Jan. 1956. *Altgermanische Religionsgeschichte* 1. Berlin: Walter de Gruyter.

Doeppers, Daniel and Peter Xenos, eds. 1998. *Population and history: The demographic origins of the modern Philippines.* Published in cooperation with the University of Wisconsin-Madison Center for Southeast Asian Studies. Quezon City: Ateneo de Manila University Press.

Dorta, Enrique Marco. 1973. *Ars Hispaniae: Historia universal del arte hispánico, Arte en America y Filipinas.* Vol. 21. Madrid: Editorial Plus Ultra Sanchez Pacheco.

Dozier, Edward P. 1966. *Mountain arbiters: The changing life of a Philippine hill people.* Tucson, Arizona: The University of Arizona Press.

Duby, Georges. 1971. *Histoire de la France: Dynasties et revolutions de 1348 à 1852.* Paris: Librairie Larousse.

Duldulao, Manuel. 1988. *A century of realism in Philippine art.* First rev. ed. Quezon City: Oro Books.

Dumerçay, Jacques. 1987. *The house in South-East Asia*. Translated and edited by Michael Smithies. Singapore: Oxford University Press.

Earle, Timothy K. 1989. The evolution of chiefdoms. *Current Anthropology* 30:84–88.

Earls, Michael W. 1997a. Mashrabiyya. *Encyclopedia of vernacular architecture of the world* 1:467–68. Edited by Paul Oliver. Cambridge: University Press.

————. 1997b. Hijaz (Saudi Arabia, W). *Encyclopedia of vernacular architecture of the world* 2:1452–53. Edited by Paul Oliver. Cambridge: University Press.

Echeverría, Bolivar. 1994. El ethos barroco. In *Modernidad, mestizaje cultural, ethos barroco,* 13–36. Edited by B. Echeverria, Mexico, D.F.: Universidad Nacional Autonoma de Mexico: El Equilibrista.

Ekadjati, Edi S. 1995. *Kebudayaan Sunda (Suatu pendekatan sejarah)*. Jakarta: Pustaka Jaya.

Ember, Carol R. and Melvin Ember. 1999. *Anthropology*. Singapore: Prentice-Hall International, Inc.

Enciclopedia Universal Ibero-Europeo-Americana. 1910. Baño. *EUIEA* 7:570–85. Madrid: Espasa Calpe, S.A.

————. 1925. Instrucción. *EUIEA* 28:1735–40. Madrid: Espasa Calpe.

————. 1935. Guerrero y Leogardo (Lorenzo). *EUIEA* 27:196. Madrid: Espasa Calpe, S.A.

Enciclopedia Universal Ilustrada Europeo-Americana. 1917. Mestizo. *EUIEA* 34:1090–94. Madrid: Espasa-Calpe, S.A.

Encyclopedia of Asian History. 1988. Embree T. Ainslie, editor in chief. New York: Charles Scribner's Sons.

The Encyclopedia of Religion. 1987. Mircea Eliade, editor in chief. New York: Macmillan Publishing Company.

Engels, Friedrich. 1890. To Joseph Bloch, 21–22 September 1890. In Tucker 1972, *MER*, 640–42.

Ergang, Robert Reinhold. 1966. *Herder and the foundations of German nationalism*. New York: Octagon Books.

Fast, Jonathan and Jim Richardson. 1979. *Roots of dependency: Political and economic revolution in nineteenth-century Philippines*. Quezon City: Foundation for Nationalist Studies.

Fayol, Fray Joseph. [1647]. Affairs in Filipinas, 1644–1647. In B and R, 35:212–75.

Featherstone, Mike and Scott Lash, eds. 1999. *Spaces of culture: City, nation, world*. London: Sage Publications.

Feibleman, Peter S. 1969. *The food of Spain and Portugal*. New York: Time-Life Books, Inc.

Fernandez, Doreen. 1994. *Tikim: Essays on Philippine food and culture.* Pasig, Metro Manila: Anvil Publishing, Inc.

———. 1996. Author of books and articles on Filipino cuisine. Personal communication.

Fernandez, Doreen G. and Edilberto N. Alegre. 1988. *Sarap: Essays on Philippine food.* Woodcuts by Manuel D. Baldemor. Manila: Mr. and Ms. Publications.

———. 1991. *Kinilaw: A Philippine cuisine of freshness.* Makati, Metro Manila: Bookmark.

Fernando, Gilda Cordero. 1992. *Philippine food and life.* Drawings by Manuel D. Baldemor. Pasig, Metro Manila: Anvil Publishing, Inc.

Fifield, Russell Hunt. 1958. *The diplomacy of Southeast Asia: 1945–1958.* New York: Harper and Brothers, Publishers.

Firth, Raymond William. 1971. Morality, primitive. *Encyclopedia Britannica* 15:821–22. Chicago: Encyclopedia Britannica.

Flannery, Kent V. 1972. The cultural evolution of civilizations. *Annual Review of Ecology and Systematics,* 3:399–426.

Florescano, Enrique and Isabel Gil Sanchez. 1976. La época de las reformas borbónicas y el crecimiento económico, 1750–1808. In Tucker 1972, *MER,* 183–301.

Foreman, John. [1906] 1980. *The Philippines: A political, geographical, ethno-graphical, social and commercial history of the Philippine archipelago, embracing the whole period of Spanish rule, with an account of the succeeding American insular government.* Manila: The Filipiniana Book Guild.

Foster, Robert J. 1991. Making national cultures in the global ecumene. *Annual Review of Anthropology,* 20:235–60.

Fox, James F. 1987. Southeast Asian religion: Insular cultures. *Encyclopedia of Religion,* 13:520–27. Mircea Eliade, editor in chief. New York: Macmillan Publishing Company.

Fox, Robert. 1952. The Pinatubo Negritos, their useful plants and material culture. *The Philippine Journal of Science* 81, nos. 3–4:1–173.

———. 1965. A preliminary glottochronology for Northern Luzon. *Asian Studies* 3:103–13.

Fox, Frederick and Juan Mercader. 1961. Some notes on education in Cebu province, 1820–1898. *Philippine Studies* 9, no. 1:20–46.

Foucault, Michel. 1977. *Discipline and punish: The birth of the prison.* Translated by Alan Sheridan. New York: Pantheon Books.

Francisco, Juan R. 1987. *Indian culture in the Philippines: Views and reviews.* Fourth Sri Lanka Endowment Fund lecture delivered at the University of Malaya on Friday, 18 October 1985. Kuala Lumpur: University of Malaya.

Fraser-Lu, Sylvia. 1988. *Handwoven textiles of Southeast Asia.* Oxford: University Press.

Fried, Morton. 1967. *The evolution of political society: An essay in political anthropology.* New York: Random House.

Furet, François. 1986. *Marx et la Revolution française.* With texts by Karl Marx, compiled, presented, and translated by Lucien Calvie. Paris: Flammarion.

Furet, François and Denis Richet. 1973 *La Revolution française.* Paris: Fayard.

Galende, Pedro G., OSA. 1987. *Angels in stone: Architecture of Augustinian churches in the Philippines.* Metro Manila: G. A. Formoso Publishing.

Galvan Guijo, Javier. 2004. La arquitectura filhispana como síntesis de culturas. *Filipinas Puerta de Oriente: de Legaspi a Malaspina,* pp. 83–93. San Sebastian, Spain: Sociedad Estatal para la Acción Exterior. Legaspi: V Centenario V. Mendeurrena 2003, Sociedad Estatal Commemoraciones Culturales, Donostiako Udala/Ayuntamiento de San Sebastian, San Telmo Museoa/Museo San Telmo, ZumarragakoUdala, Ministerio de Asuntos Exteriores, Ministerio de Educacion, Cultura y Deportes.

Garcia Bernal, Maria Cristina. 1990. La población de la America Hispana en el Siglo XVI. *Historia de las Americas* 2:153–82. Coordinated by Luis Navarro Garcia. Madrid: Alhambra Longman, Universidad de Sevilla, Secretariado de Publicaciones, Sociedad Estatal para el Quinto Centenario.

Garna, Yustinus. 1987. *Orang Baduy.* Kuala Lumpur: Universitas Kebangsaan Malaysia.

Garvan, John. 1931. *The Manobos of Mindanao.* Washington, D.C.: United States Government Printing Office.

Gatmaytan, Augusto. 1999. Conflicts in construction: Manobo land and resources: Praxis and state legislation on tenure. M.A. thesis in Anthropology, Sociology-Anthropology Department, Ateneo de Manila University, Quezon City.

Gebhardt, Bruno. 1955. *Handbuch der deutschen Geschichte, vol. 2. Von der Reformation bis zum Ende der Absolutismus. 16 bis 18 Jahrhundert.* In cooperation with Max Braubach et al. Edited by Herbert Grundmann. Stuttgart: Union Verlag.

Geertz, Clifford. 1960. *The religion of Java.* London: The Free Press of Glencoe.

————. 1963. *Agricultural involution: The process of ecological change in Indonesia.* Berkeley: University of California Press, for the Association of Asian Studies.

Geertz, Hildred. 1963. *Indonesian cultures or communities.* New Haven, Connecticut: Human Relations Area Files Inc.

Giddens, Anthony. 1982. *Profiles and critiques in social theory.* London: The Macmillan Press.

Gilmore. David D. 1982. Anthropology of the Mediterranean area. *Annual Review of Anthropology* 11:175–205.

Gloria, Heidi. 1987. *The Bagobos: Their ethnohistory and acculturation.* Quezon City: New Day Publishers.

Goldman, Irving. [1937]1961. The Ifugao of the Philippine Islands. In *Cooperation and competition among primitive peoples,* 153–79. Edited by Margaret Mead. Boston: Beacon Press.

Gomez, Lourdes Rausa. 1967. Sri Vijaya and Madjapahit. *Philippine Studies* 15, no. 1:63–107.

Gonzalbo Aizpuru, Pilar. 1990. *Historia de la educación de los criollos y la vida urbana.* México, D.F.: El Colegio de México.

———. 2001. *Convivencia, segregación y promiscuidad en la capital de la Nueva España. Actas del Tercer Congreso Internacional Mediadores Culturales. Ciudades mestizas: Intercambios y continuidades en la expansión occidental Siglos XVI a XIX,* 123–38. México, D.F.: Centro de Estudios de Historia de México.

Grant, Michael. 1960. *The world of Rome.* New York: The New American Library.

Grégoire, Franz. 1958. *Etudes hégéliennes: les points capitaux du systeme.* Louvain: Publications Universitaires de Louvain.

Gruzinski, Serge. 2001. La ciudad mestiza y los metizajes de la vida intelectual: El caso de la ciudad de México, 1560–1640. *Actas del Tercer Congreso Internacional Mediadores Culturales. Ciudades mestizas: Intercambios y continuidades en la expansión occidental Siglos XVI a XIX,* 201–20. México, D.F.: Centro de Estudios de Historia de México.

Guerrero, Amado. 1980. *Philippine society and revolution.* 4th ed. Oakland, California: International Association of Filipino Patriots.

Guerrero, Fernando. 1952. *Crisalidas.* Manila: Philippine Education Foundation.

Guerrero, Milagros C. 1977. Luzon at war: Contradictions in Philippine society, 1898–1902. Ph.D. dissertation in History, University of Michigan.

Guichard, Pierre and Jean-Pierre Cuvillier. 1996. Barbarian Europe. In *A history of the family.* Vol. 1: *Distant worlds, ancient worlds,* 318–78. Edited by André Burguière, Christiane Klappisch-Zuber, Martine Segalen, and Françoise Zonabend. Introduction by Claude Lévi-Strauss and Georges Duby. Translation by Sarah Hanbury Tenison, Rosemary Morris and Andrew Wilson. Cambridge, Massachusetts: The Belknap Press of Harvard University Press.

Guy, Christian. 1962. *An illustrated history of French cuisine: From Charlemagne to Charles de Gaulle.* Translated by Elisabeth Abbott. New York: The Orion Press.

Hall, Kenneth R. 1976. State and statecraft in early Srivijaya. In *Explorations in early Southeast Asian history: The origins of Southeast Asian statecraft,* 61–

105. Edited by Kenneth R. Hall and John K. Whitmore. Ann Arbor: Center for South and Southeast Asian Studies, the University of Michigan.

————. 1985. *Maritime trade and state development in early Southeast Asia.* Honolulu: University of Hawaii Press.

Hall, Stuart and Paul du Gay. 1996. *Questions of cultural identity.* London: Sage Publications.

Hally, David J. 1996. Platform-mound construction and the instability of Mississipian chiefdoms. In *Political structure and change in the prehistoric southeastern United States,* 92–127. Edited by John F. Scarry Gainesville: University Press of Florida.

Harris, Marvin. 1968. *The rise of anthropological theory: A history of theories of culture.* New York: Thomas Y. Crowell Company.

————. 1979. *Cultural materialism: The struggle for a science of culture.* New York: Random House.

Harrison, Brian. 1966. *South-East Asia.* London: Macmillan.

Heer, Friedrich. 1962. *The medieval world: Europe, 1100–1350.* Translated by Janet Sondheimer. Cleveland: World Publishing.

————. 1968. *The Holy Roman Empire.* Translated by Janet Sondheimer. New York: Frederick A. Praeger.

Ho Tai, Hue-tam. 1985. Religion in Vietnam: A world of gods and spirits. In *Vietnam: Essays on history, culture and society,* 22–40. Edited by David W. P. Elliott et al. New York: The Asia Society.

Holmes, George. 1992. With Dora Jane Janson. *The Oxford history of Medieval Europe.* Oxford: University Press.

Horvatich, Patricia. 1992. Mosques and misunderstandings: Muslim discourses in Tawi-Tawi, Philippines. Ph.D. dissertation in Anthropology, Stanford University.

Huizinga, Johan. [1950]1955. *Homo ludens: A study of the play element in culture.* Boston: Beacon Press.

Hutterer, Karl L. 1976. An evolutionary approach to the Southeast Asian cultural sequence. *Current Anthropology* 17:221–42.

Hutton, Wendy, ed. 1996. *The food of Indonesia: Authentic recipes from the Spice Islands.* Recipes by Heinz von Holzen and Lother Arsana. Singapore: Periplus eds. with the Grand Hyatt Bali.

Ileto, Reynaldo Clemeña. 1979. *Pasyon and revolution: Popular movements in the Philippines, 1840-1910.* Quezon City: Ateneo de Manila University Press.

Inwood, Michael. 1992. *A Hegel dictionary.* Cambridge, Massachusetts: Basil Blackwell Inc.

Jacobs, Jay. 1979. *Gastronomy.* New York: Newsweek Books.

Jagor, Fedor. [1875]1965. *Travels in the Philippines.* Manila: Filipiniana Book Guild.

Janson, H. W. 1972. *History of art: A survey of the major visual arts from the dawn of history to the present day.* Englewood Cliffs, New Jersey: Prentice-Hall, Inc.

Javellana, Rene, S.J. 1991. *Wood and stone for God's greater glory: Jesuit art and architecture in the Philippines.* Quezon City: Ateneo de Manila University Press.

Jeanjean, Henri. 1990. *De l'Utopie au pragmatisme? Le mouvement Occitan 1976–1990.* Perpignan: Llibres del Trabucaire.

Jenks, Albert Ernest. 1905. *The Bontoc Igorot.* Manila: Bureau of Printing.

Joaquín, Nick. 1952. *Prose and poems.* With an introduction by Teodoro M. Locsin. Manila Graphic House.

————. 1977. *A question of heroes: Essays in criticism on ten key figures of Philippine history.* Makati: [Filipinas Foundation].

————. 1986. *The Aquinos of Tarlac: An essay on history as three generations.* Metro Manila: Solar Publishing Corporation.

————. 1989. Culture as history. In *Culture and history, occasional notes on the process of Philippine becoming,* 1–35. Metro Manila: Solar Publishing Corporation.

————. 1991. *Prose and poems.* Makati: Bookmark.

Jocano, Felipe Landa. 1968. *Sulod society: A study in the kinship system and social organization of a mountain people of central Panay.* Quezon City: University of the Philippines Press.

Jolly, Clifford and Fred Plog. 1978. *Introduction to physical anthropology and archeology.* New York: Alfred A. Knopf.

————. 1982. *Physical anthropology and archeology.* New York: Alfred A. Knopf.

Jones, E. L. 1991. A framework for the history of economic growth in Southeast Asia. *Australian Economic History Review* 31:5–19.

Jones, Prudence and Nigel Pennick. 1994. *A history of pagan Europe.* London: Routledge.

Jose, Regalado Trota. 2003. Settling down and building in old Bohol. In *Tubod: The heart of Bohol.* Edited by Ramon N. Villegas. Manila: National Commission for Culture and the Arts.

Junker, Laura Lee. 1993. Craft goods specialization and prestige goods exchange in Philippine chiefdoms of the fifteenth and sixteenth centuries. *Asian Perspectives* 32, no. 1:1–35.

————. 2000. *Raiding, trading and feasting. The political economy of Philippine chiefdoms.* Quezon City: Ateneo de Manila University Press.

Kahn, Joel S. and Josep R. Llobera. 1981. *The anthropology of pre-capitalist societies.* London: Macmillan.

Kearney, Michael. 1995. The local and the global: The anthropology of globalization and transnationalization. *Annual Review of Anthropology,* 24:547–65.

Keesing, Felix Maxwell. 1962. *Ethnohistory of northern Luzon.* Stanford: University Press.

Keiji, Nagahara. 1990. The medieval peasant. In *The Cambridge history of Japan.* Vol. 3. Translated by Suzanne Gay. Edited by Kozo Yamamura. United Kingdom: Cambridge University Press.

Kennett, Frances with Caroline MacDonald-Haig. 1994. *World dress.* London: Mitchell Beazley.

Keyes, Charles. 1987. Southeast Asian religion: Mainland cultures. *Encyclopedia of Religion,* 13:513–20. Mircea Eliade, editor in chief. New York: Macmillan Publishing Company.

Keyfitz, Nathan. 1961. The ecology of Indonesian cities. *The American Journal of Sociology* 66, no. 4:348–54.

Khan, Hasan-Uddin. 1995. *Contemporary Asian architects.* Los Angeles: Taschen America.

Kiefer, Thomas. 1972. *The Tausug: Violence and law in a Philippine Moslem society.* New York: Holt, Rinehart and Winston.

Kikuchi, Yasushi. 1984. *Mindoro highlanders: The life of the swidden agriculturists.* Quezon City: New Day Publishers.

—————. 1989. The concept of corporate group in cognatic societies: Dynamic aspect in the Philippines. In *Philippine kinship and society.* Edited by Yasushi Kikuchi. Quezon City: New Day Publishers.

King, Damaso. 1991. Parish church and cathedral of St. Paul—Vigan. *The Ilocos Review* 23:2–32.

Koentjaraningrat. 1986. Local genius' dalam Kebudayaan. In *Kepribadian budaya bangsa (Local genius),* 80–90. Edited by Ayatrohaedi. Jakarta: Pustaka Jaya.

Kottak, Conrad Philip. 2000. *Anthropology: The exploration of human diversity.* Boston: McGraw-Hill.

Krader, Lawrence. 1968. *Formation of the state.* Englewood Cliffs, New Jersey: Prentice-Hall.

La Gironière, Paul Proust de. [1855]1962. *Twenty years in the Philippines.* With a preface by Alejandro R. Roces and an introduction by Benito Legarda y Fernandez. Manila: Filipiniana Book Guild.

Lafaye, Jacques. 1976. *Quetzalcoatl and Guadalupe.* With a foreword by Octavio Paz, translation by Benjamin Keen. Chicago: The University of Chicago Press.

Lamberg-Karlovsky, C. C. and Jeremy A. Sabloff, eds. 1974. Introductory remarks. *The rise and fall of civilizations: Modern archaeological approaches to ancient cultures.* Menlo Park, California: Cummings Publishing Company.

Larkin, John A. 1972. *The Pampangans: Colonial society in a Philippine province.* Berkeley: University of California Press.

Lasker, Bruno. 1950. *Human bondage in Southeast Asia.* Chapel Hill: University of North Carolina Press.

Lavenda, Robert H. and Emily A. Schultz. 1987. *Cultural anthropology: A perspective on the human condition.* St. Paul: West Publishing Company.

Le Gentil de la Galaisière, Guillaume Joseph Hyacinthe Jean Baptiste. [1779–1781] 1964. *A voyage to the Indian seas.* With an introduction by William Alain Burke Miailhe. Translation by Frederick C. Fischer. Manila: Filipiniana Book Guild.

Le, Thanh Khoi. 1955. *Le Viet-Nam: Histoire et civilisation.* Paris: Les Editions de Minuit.

Lebar, Frank, ed. and com. 1972–1975. *Ethnic groups of Insular Southeast Asia.* Vol. 2: *Philippines and Formosa.* New Haven, Connecticut: Human Relations Area Files Press.

Legarda y Fernandez, Benito. 1999. *After the galleons: Foreign trade, economic change and entrepreneurship in the nineteenth-century Philippines.* Quezon City: Ateneo de Manila University Press.

Lempériere, Annick. 1998. La belle epoque en la ciudad de México. *Artes de México, México-Francia: Fascinaciones mutuas,* no. 43:40–45.

Lévi-Strauss, Claude. 1966. *The savage mind.* Translation of *La pensée sauvage.* Chicago: The University of Chicago Press.

Lincoln, Bruce. 1987. Indo-European religions. *Encyclopedia of Religion,* 7:198–204. Mircea Eliade, editor in chief. New York: Macmillan Publishing Company.

Loarca, Miguel de. [1582]1973. Relación de las Yslas Filipinas. In B and R, 5:34–187.

Locsin, Leandro. 1992. Architect and National Artist. Manila. Personal communication.

Lopez Jaéna, Graciano. 1951. *Discursos y artículos varios.* Nueva edición revisada y edicionada con escritos no incluidos en la primera. Notas y comentarios por Jaime C. de Veyra. Manila: Bureau of Printing.

Lopez, Leslie. 2002. Sociologist at the Ateneo de Manila University. Personal communication.

López, Manuel Torres. 1985. Las invasiones y los reinos germánicos de España (años 409–711). In *Historia de España.* Vol. 3: *España Visigoda (414–711 de J. C.),* 3–140. Ramon Menendez Pidal, founder and director. Madrid: Espasa-Calpe, S.A.

Loyzaga, Jorge. 1996. Personal communication.

Lumbera, Bienvenido. 1986. *Tagalog poetry 1570–1898: Tradition and influences in its development.* Quezon City: Ateneo de Manila University Press.

Lynch, Frank, S.J. 1963. *An mga aswang: A Bicol belief.* Field reports and analyses. Naga City: Ateneo de Naga, Bicol Area Survey.

Macedo, Luis Ortiz. 1994. *Los palacios nobiliarios de la nueva España.* Prologue by Eloisa Vargaslugo. Mexico: Seminario de Cultura Mexicana.

Magos, Alice. 1986. The ideological basis and social context of Ma-aram practice in a Kiniray-a society. Ph.D. dissertation, University of the Philippines, Quezon City.

Mahajani, Usha. 1971. *Philippine nationalism: External challenge and Filipino response, 1565–1946.* Queensland: University of Queensland Press.

Maher, Robert F. Archaeological investigation in Central Ifugao. 1974. *Asian Perspectives* 16, no. 1:39–70.

Majul, Cesar Adib. 1960. *Mabini and the Philippine Revolution.* Quezon City: University of the Philippines.

———. 1994. So far from God, so near the monastery. *Filipinas* 3, no. 31:18–19.

Mallat de Bassilan, Jean Baptiste. 1846. *Les Philippines.* 2 vols. Paris: Bertrand.

Manrique, Jorge Alberto. 1976. Del barroco a la ilustración. In *Historia general de México,* 2:357–446. México, D.F.: SEP/El Colegio de México.

Manuel, E. Arsenio. 1973. *Manuvu' social organization.* Quezon City: Community Development Research Council, University of the Philippines.

Marsden, William. [1811]1966. *The history of Sumatra.* A reprint of the 3d ed. Introduced by John Bastin. Kuala Lumpur: Oxford University Press.

Martel, Tonette. 1997. Solo: Lorrie Reynoso, "My taste buds will always be Filipino." *Philippine Star,* 31 Dec. Section L, 1–3.

Martinez de Zuñiga, Joaquín, OSA. [1803–1805]1897. *Estadismo de las Islas Filipinas ó mis viajes por este país.* 2 vols. Annotations by Wenceslao E. Retana. Madrid: Imprenta de la Viuda de M. Minuesa de los Rios.

Marx, Karl. [1845–1846]1972. The German ideology. In Tucker 1972, *MER.*

———. [1848a] 1972. The Communist manifesto. In Tucker 1972, *MER.*

———. [1848b] 1986. La bourgeoisie et la contre révolution. In Furet 1986, *MRF.* With texts by Karl Marx, compiled, presented, and translated by Lucien Calvie. Paris: Flammarion.

———. [1850] 1972. Tactics of social democracy. In Tucker 1972, *MER.*

———. [1852] 1972. The eighteenth Brumaire of Louis Philippe. In Tucker 1972, *MER.*

————. [1864] 1972. Critique of Gotha Program. In Tucker 1972, *MER.*

————. [1867] 1972. Das capital. In Tucker 1972, *MER.*

————. [1871] 1972. The civil war in France. In Tucker 1972, *MER.*

————. [1894] 1967. *Das Kapital: Kritik der politischen Oekonomie.* 3 vols. Edited by Friedrich Engels (1820–1895). [n.p.]: Europaische Verlagsanstalt.

————. [1894]1978. *Capital: A critique of political economy.* Introduced by Ernest Mandel. Translated by David Fernbach. New York: Vintage Books/ Random House.

Marx, Karl and Friedrich Engels. [1846a]1969. *Deutsche Ideologie: Karl Marx und Friedrich Engels: Werke.* Vol. 3. Berlin: Dietz Verlag for the Institut fuer Marxismus-Leninismus beim ZK der Sed.

————. [1846b]1994. The German ideology. In *Karl Marx: Selected writings.* Edited by Lawrence H. Simon. Indianapolis: Hackett Publishing Company.

————. [1857–1858]1973. *Grundrisse: Foundations of the critique of political economy.* Translated with a foreword by Martin Nicolaus. New York: Vintage Books.

Maxwell, Robyn. 1990. *Textiles of Southeast Asia: Tradition, trade and transformation.* Oxford: University Press.

May, Glenn. 1993. *Battle for Batangas, a Philippine province at war.* Quezon City: New Day Publishers.

————. 1997. Personal communication.

Mayer, Theodore. 1960. The historical foundation of the German constitution. In *Medieval Germany 911–1250,* 1–33. Edited by Geoffrey Barraclough. Oxford: Basil Blackwell.

McCloud, Donald G. 1986. *System and process in Southeast Asia: The evolution of a region.* Boulder, Colorado: Westview Press.

McCrea, Joan Marie. 1971. Corvee. *Enyclopedia Britannica* 6:560–61. Chicago: Encyclopedia Britannica.

Medina, Juan Eulogio Alejandrino. 1997. Personal communication.

Mednick, Melvin. 1965. Encampment on the lake: The social organization of a Moslem-Philippine (Moro) people. Chicago: Philippine Studies Program, Department of Anthropology, University of Chicago.

Mehmet, Ozay. 1990. *Islamic identity and development: Studies of the Islamic periphery.* Kuala Lumpur: Forum.

Merino, Luis, OSA. 1987. *Arquitectura y urbanismo en el siglo XIX: Introducción general y monografía, estudios sobre el municipio de Manila.* Vol. 2. Manila: Centro Cultural de España and the Intramuros Administration.

Michener, James. 1988. *Iberia: Spanish travels and reflection.* New York: Random House.

Mickunas, Algis. 1994. Cultural logics and the search for national identities. In *Phenomenology of the cultural disciplines.* Edited by Mano Daniel and Lester Embree. Dordrecht: Kluwer Academic Publishers.

Miquel, Pierre. 1976. *Histoire de la France.* Paris: Fayard.

Mondadori, Arnoldo. 1988. *The history of art.* Translated by Geoffrey Culverwell et al. Leicester: Blitz Editions.

Morga, Antonio. [1609]1910. *Sucesos de las Islas Filipinas.* Edited and with commentary by Wenceslao E. Retana. Madrid: Librería General de Victoriano Suárez.

————. [1609]1961. *Sucesos de las Islas Filipinas.* Annotations by José Rizal and prologue by Ferdinand Blumentritt (1890). Manila: Comisión Nacional del Centenario de José Rizal.

Mozo, Antonio. 1763. *Noticia histórico-natural de los gloriosos triumphos y felices adelantamientos conseguidos en el presente siglo por los religiosos del orden de N.P.S. Agustín en las missiones que tienen a su cargo en las islas Philipinas, y en el grande imperio de la China.* Madrid: Andrés Ortega.

Much, Rudolf. 1959. *Die Germania des Tacitus.* Heidelberg: Carl Winter Universitaetsverlag.

Muñoz Perez, José. 1988. La consolidacìon de la sociedad indiana. La población de la America Hispana en el Siglo XVI. *Historia de las Americas* 2:627–59. Coordinated by Luis Navarro Garcia. Madrid: Alhambra Longman, Universidad de Sevilla, Secretariado de Publicaciones, Sociedad Estatal para el Quinto Centenario.

————. 1988. La sociedad encomendera. *Historia de las Americas* 2:233–61. Coordinated by Luis Navarro Garcia. Madrid: Alhambra Longman, Universidad de Sevilla, Secretariado de Publicaciones, Sociedad Estatal para el Quinto Centenario.

Myrdal, Gunnar. 1968. *Asian drama: An inquiry into the poverty of nations.* Vol. 3. William J. Bander et al., principal assistants. New York: Pantheon.

Nakane, Chie. 1967. *Kinship and economic organization in rural Japan.* New York: University of London, the Athlone Press.

Needham, Joseph. 1954. *Science and civilization in China.* Vol. 3. With the research assistance of Wang Ling. Cambridge, England: University Press.

Nelson, Henry and Robert Jurmain. 1985. *Introduction to physical anthropology.* St. Paul, Minnesota: West Publishing Company.

Newsweek. 1997. Interview: A taste for duck eggs. 14 July, 58.

Nolasco, Clarita. 1969. The creoles in Spanish Philippines. M.A. thesis, Far Eastern University, Manila.

Novo, Salvador. 1998. Incursión gastronómica francesa en México. *Artes de México, México-Francia: Fascinaciones mutuas,* 43:48.

Nuñez, Alfredo Jimenez. 1989. Los habitantes, mestizaje, población actual. *Gran Enciclopedia de España y América.* Vol. 2. Madrid: Gela S. A., Espasa-Calpe/Argantonio.

Nutini, Hugo G. 1972. The Latin-American city: A cultural-historical approach. In *The anthropology of urban environments,* 89–95. Edited by Thomas Weaver and Douglas White. Boulder, Colorado: The Society for Applied Anthropology Monograph Series No. 11.

Nydegger, William F. and Corinne Nydegger. 1966. *Tarong: An Ilocos barrio in the Philippines.* New York: Wiley.

O'Callaghan, Joseph F. 1975. *A history of medieval Spain.* Ithaca: Cornell University Press.

O'Connor, Stanley J. 1988. Southeast Asian sculpture. *Encyclopedia of Asian History.* Vol. 3:401–3. Ainslie T. Embree, editor in chief. New York: Charles Scribner's Sons.

O'Harrow, Stephen. 1983. Men of Hu, men of Han, men of the Hundred Man: The conceptualization of early Vietnamese society. Personal manuscript. Submitted to and accepted by the *Bulletin de l'Ecole Française d'Extrême Orient.*

Ofreneo, Rene E. 1980. *Capitalism in Philippine agriculture.* Quezon City: Foundation for Nationalist Studies.

Ortega, Francisco de, OSA. [1573]1903. Letter to the viceroy of Nueva España, Manila. 6 June 1573. In B and R, 34:256–72.

Osborne, Milton. 1983. *Southeast Asia: An introductory history.* London: George Allen and Unwin.

Owen, Francis. 1960. *The Germanic people: Their origin, expansion and culture.* New York: Bookman Associates.

Palazon, Juan. 1964. *Majayjay (How a town came into being).* Manila: Historical Conservation Society.

Pallesen, A. Kemp. 1985. *Culture contact and language convergence.* Manila: Linguistic Society of the Philippines.

Parker, Henry Banford. 1966. *A history of Mexico.* Boston: Houghton Mifflin Company.

Patanñe, Eufemio P. 1996. *The Philippines in the sixth to sixteenth centuries.* San Juan, Metro Manila: LSA Press, Inc.

Paz, Octavio. 1994. Posiciones y contraposiciones: México y Estados Unidos. In *El peregrino en su patria: Historia y politica de México,* 437–53. Edited by Octavio Paz. Mexico. D.F.: Circulo de Lectores/Fondo de Cultura Económica.

Pertierra, Raul. 1988. *Religion, politics and rationality in a Philippine community.* Quezon City: Ateneo de Manila University Press.

Peters, Jens. 1997. *Lonely planet guidebooks: Philippines.* Hawthorn, Victoria: Lonely Planet Publications.

Pfister, Christian. 1913a. The Franks before Clovis. In *The Cambridge medieval history* 2: *Foundation of the western empire,* 292–303. John Bagnell Bury, planner, and H. M. Gwatkin, editor. Cambridge University Press.

———. 1913b. Gaul under the Merovingian Franks: Narrative of events, institutions. In *The Cambridge medieval history* 2: *Foundation of the western empire,* 109–58. J. B. Bury, planner, and H. M. Gwatkin, editor. Cambridge University Press.

Philippine Panorama. 2004. Editorial. *Philippine Panorama, Sunday Magazine of Manila Bulletin,* 25 January, 3.

Pike, Kenneth. 1954. *Language in relation to a unified theory of the structure of human behavior.* Vol. 1. Glendale: Summer Institute of Linguistics.

Pires, Tomé [ca. 1468–ca. 1540]1971. In *Travel accounts of the islands (1513–1787).* Edited by Filipiniana Book Guild. Manila: Filipiniana Book Guild.

Pitkin, D. 1963. Mediterranean Europe. *Anthropology Quarterly* 36:120–29.

Plasencia, Juan de. [1589a]1910 (wrongly dated as 1598). Untitled. In the notes of Wenceslao E. Retana, ed. *Sucesos de las Islas Filipinas,* 471–75. See Morga 1609.

———. [1589b] 1973. Las costumbres de los indios tagalos de Filipinas. B and R, 7:173–96.

Postma, Antoon. 1992. The Laguna copper-plate inscription: Text and commentary. *Philippine Studies* 40, no. 2:183–203.

Prill-Brett, June. 1987. *Pechen: The Bontok peace pact institution.* Baguio: Cordillera Studies Center, University of the Philippines College Baguio.

———. 1992. Ibaloy customary law on land resources. Cordillera Studies Center Working Paper 19. Cordillera Studies Center, University of the Philippines College Baguio.

Quesada, Eugenio C. 1956. *Paete: Being an informal narrative of the life, joys and sufferings of the people.* Manila: [s.n.].

Quezon, Manuel Luis. 1946. *The good fight.* Introduction by Gen. Douglas MacArthur. New York: D. Appleton-Century Company.

Quilis, Antonio. 1984. La lengua española en las Islas Filipinas. *Cuadernos del Centro Cultural de la Embajada de España* 11:1–22.

Quirino, Carlos 1958. The manners, customs and beliefs of the Philippine inhabitants of long ago. Being chapters of "A late sixteenth century

Manila manuscript." Transcribed, translated and annotated by Carlos Quirino and Mauro Garcia. *The Philippine Journal of Science* 87, no. 4:325–453.

―――. 1978. Prophet of deliverance. In *Filipino Heritage: The making of a nation* 6:1513–17. Alfredo Roces, editor in chief. Lahing Pilipino Publishing, Inc.

Rada, Martín de. [1577]1978. Carta al P. Alonso de la Veracruz, OSA, dándole noticias de las costumbres, ritos, y clases de esclavitud que hay en las Filipinas, con otras informaciones importantes de las Islas. Vol. 14. In *Historia de la provincia Agustiniana del Smo. Nombre de Jesús.* Edited by Isacio Rodríguez. Manila: Convento de San Agustín.

Ramos, Angie. 1996. They'll wear what once was a symbol of inferiority. *Manila Bulletin*, 20 Nov., 11.

Ramos, Maximo. 1971. *The aswang syncrasy in Philippine folklore.* With illustrations, accounts in vernacular. Texts and translations. Foreword by F. Landa Jocano. Philippine Folklore Society, Paper No. 3.

―――. 1990. *The aswang complex in Philippine folklore.* Quezon City: Phoenix Publishing House.

Recto, Claro Mayo. 1960. Por los fueros de una herencia/For the rights of a heritage. In *The Recto valedictory and the Recto Day program 1985.* With English translation by Nick Joaquin. Manila: Claro M. Recto Memorial Foundation, Inc.

Redfield, Robert. 1953. *The primitive world and its transformation.* Ithaca, New York: Great Seal Books.

―――. 1956. *Peasant society and culture: An anthropological approach to civilization.* Chicago: University of Chicago Press.

―――. 1967. The social organization of tradition. In *Peasant society: A reader,* 25–34. Edited by Jack Potter et al. Boston: Little Brown.

Reece, Jack E. 1979. Internal colonialism: The case of Brittany. *Ethnic and Racial Studies* 2, no. 3:275–92.

Reed, Robert R. 1967. *Hispanic urbanism in the Philippines: A study of the impact of Church and state.* Manila: University of Manila.

―――. 1971. *Origins of the Philippine city: A comparative inquiry concerning indigenous Southeast Asian settlements and Spanish colonial urbanism.* Berkeley, California: University of California Press.

―――. 1978. *Colonial Manila: The context of Hispanic urbanism and process of morphogenesis.* Berkeley, California: University of California Press.

Reid, Anthony. 1988. *Southeast Asia in the age of commerce, 1450–1680.* Vol. 1: *The lands below the wind.* New Haven: Yale University Press.

Reinhard, Marcel, director. 1954. *Histoire de France: Des origines à 1715.* With the collaboration of Norbert Dufourcq. Paris: Librairie Larousse.

Relation of the voyage to Luzon . [1570]1903. June 1570. In B and R, 3:73–104.

Retana, Wenceslao. 1890. *Sinapismos: Bromitas y critiquillas.* Madrid: M. Minuesa de los Ríos.

Rios de Coronel, Hernando. [1621]1903–1909. Memorial y relacion para su Magestad. In B and R, 19:183–297.

Riquel, Fernando. [1572]1973. Relation of the conquest of the island of Luzon. In B and R, 3:141–72. (See Loarca 1582.)

Rizal, Jose. [1886] 1908. *Noli me tangere, novela tagala.* 3d ed. Manila: Librería Manila Filatélica.

———. 1886. *Noli me tangere.* Manila: Comisión Nacional del Centenario, 1961.

———. [1890]1961. Anotaciones a *Sucesos de las Islas Filipinas.* In *Sucesos de las Islas Filipinas,* by Antonio de Morga. Manila: Comisión Nacional del Centenario de José Rizal.

Roberts, Michael. 1989. A tale of resistance: The story of the arrival of the Portuguese in Sri Lanka. *Ethnos,* 54:69–82.

Robles, Eliodoro G. 1969. *The Philippines in the nineteenth century.* Quezon City: Malaya Books, Inc.

Rodriguez, Isacio R., OSA. 1976. *The Augustinian monastery of Intramuros: The people, the events that contributed to its grandeur.* Translated by Pedro G. Galende, OSA. Makati, Rizal: Colegio de San Agustín.

Rosaldo, Michelle Z. 1980. *Knowledge and passion: Ilongot notions of self and social life.* Cambridge University Press.

Rosaldo, Renato. 1980. *Ilongot headhunting, 1883–1974: A study in society and history.* Stanford, California: Stanford University Press.

Rosaldo, Renato and Michelle Rosaldo. 1972. Ilongot. In *Ethnic groups of insular Southeast Asia.* Vol. 2: *Philippines and Formosa,* 103–6. Edited by Frank Lebar. New Haven: Human Relations Area Files.

Rousseau, Jean Jacques. [1754]1990. On the origin of inequality. In *Great books of the western world,* 321–66. Mortimer J. Adler, editor in chief. Chicago: Encyclopedia Britannica, Inc.

Routledge, David. 1979. *Diego Silang and the origins of Philippine nationalism.* Diliman, Quezon City: Publications Office, Philippine Center for Advanced Studies, University of the Philippines.

Rubio y Rubio, Alfonso. 1991. Notas sobre el palacio novohispano y sus tesoros interiores. In *Los palacios de la Nueva España, sus tesoros interiores.* Jose Emilio Amores, general coordinator. Monterrey, Mexico: Museo de Monterrey and Museo Franz Mayer.

Sabau Garcia, María Luisa. 1992. *De México al mundo: Plantas.* Mexico, D.F.: Instituto de Ecología, A.C., Jardín Botánico del Instituto de Biología del UNAM, Herbolario de la Asociación Mexicana de Orquideología.

Saber, Mamitua and Mauyag M. Tamano, with Charles Warriner. 1960. The Maratabat of the Maranao. *Philippine Sociological Review* 8 (Jan.–Apr.): 10–15.

Sahlins, Marshall David. 1958. *Social stratification in Polynesia.* Seattle: University of Washington Press.

————. 1968. *Tribesmen.* Englewood Cliffs, New Jersey: Prentice-Hall.

————. 1972. *Stone age economics.* Chicago: Aldine and Atherton Inc.

Said, Edward W. 1984. *Orientalism.* London: Routledge and Kegan Paul.

Salgado, Pedro V., OP. 1988. *Social science for Filipinos.* Quezon City: R. P. Garcia Publishing.

San Buenaventura, Pedro. 1613. *Vocabulario de lengua tagala.* Pila, Laguna.

Santos, Antonia. 1997. Tondo: 1890–1897. Manuscript, History Department, Ateneo de Manila University.

————. 1999. *Revolution in the provinces,* 56–66. Edited by Bernardita Reyes-Churchill. Quezon City: Philippine National Historical Society, Inc.; Manila: National Commission on Culture and the Arts Committee on Historical Research.

Santos, Jose P. 1935. *Buhay at mga sinulat ni Emilio Jacinto.* Paunang salita ng Kgg. Rafael Palma. [Maynila].

Scharpf, Frederick, SVD. 1985. The building of the Vigan Cathedral. *The Ilocos Review* 17, 13–55.

————. 1993. A history of the diocese of Nueva Segovia (Vigan). *The Ilocos Review* 25:1–170.

Schlegel, Stuart A. 1970. *Tiruray justice: Traditional Tiruray law and morality.* Berkeley: University of California Press.

————. 1979. *Tiruray subsistence: From shifting cultivation to plow agriculture.* Quezon City: Ateneo de Manila University Press.

————. 1981. Tiruray gardens: From use right to private ownership. *Philippine Quarterly of Culture and Society* 9, no. 1:5–8.

Schoppert, Peter. 1997. *Java style.* With the collaboration of Soedarmadji Damais, photography by Tara Sosrowardoyo. Singapore: Archipelago Press.

Schumacher, John N. 1975. Philippine higher education and the origins of nationalism. *Philippine Studies* 23:53–65.

————. 1979. *Readings in Church history.* Quezon City: Loyola School of Theology, Ateneo de Manila University.

————. 1991. *The making of a nation: Essays on nineteenth-century Filipino nationalism*. Quezon City: Ateneo de Manila University Press.

Scott, William Henry. 1974. *The discovery of the Igorots: Spanish contacts with the pagans of northern Luzon*. Foreword by Harold C. Conklin. Quezon City: New Day Publishers.

—————. 1982. *Cracks in the parchment curtain and other essays in Philippine history*. Foreword by Renato Constantino. Quezon City: New Day Publishers.

—————. 1986. *Ilocano responses to American aggression 1900–01*. Foreword by Jose Maria Sison. Quezon City: New Day Publishers.

—————. 1987. *The discovery of the Igorots, Spanish contacts with the pagans of northern Luzon*. Quezon City: New Day Publishers.

—————. 1989. *Filipinos in China before 1500*. With Chinese translation by Go Bon Juan. Manila: China Studies Program, De La Salle University.

—————. 1991. *Slavery in the Spanish Philippines*. Manila: De la Salle University Press.

—————. 1992. *Looking for the pre-Hispanic Filipino*. Quezon City: New Day Publishers.

—————. 1994. *Barangay: Sixteenth-century Philippine culture and society*. Quezon City: Ateneo de Manila University Press.

Sédar Senghor, Léopold. 1964. *Liberté 1: Negritude et humanisme*. Paris: Editions de Seuil.

Sekimoto, Teruo. 1997. Professor of Anthropology, Tokyo University. Personal communication.

Senior, Clarence. 1967. Agrarian reform has brought democracy and increased production. In *The Meaning of the Mexican revolution*, 47–56. Edited by Charles Curtis Cumberland. Boston: D. C. Heath and Company.

Service, Elman Rogers. 1966. *The hunters*. Englewood Cliffs, New Jersey: Prentice-Hall Inc.

Sibeth, Adim. 1991. *The Batak: Peoples of the island of Sumatra*. London: Thames and Hudson.

Sidel, John Thayer. 1999. *Capital, coercion and crime: Bossism in the Philippines*. Stanford, California: Stanford University Press.

Sjoberg, Gideon. 1960. *The preindustrial city, past and present*. New York: Free Press.

Smith, Anthony D. 1987. *The ethnic origins of nations*. Oxford: Basil Blackwell.

Sociedad Estatal de Commemoraciones Culturales. 2004. *Filipinas Puerta de Oriente: De Legaspi a Malaspina*. San Sebastian, Spain: Sociedad Estatal de Commemoraciones Culturales, Donostiako Udala/Ayuntamiento de San Sebastian, San Telmo Museoa/Museo San Telmo, Zumarragako Udala,

Ministerio de Asuntos Exteriores, Ministerio de Educacion, Cultura y Deportes.

Soledad, Giovanni. 1997. *Pangayao*, or resistance, in a Manobo community against capitalist incursion. M.A. thesis, Ateneo de Manila University.

Sontag, Susan. 1971. Primitivism. *Enyclopedia Britannica* 18:531–32. Chicago: Enyclopedia Britannica, Inc.

Steadman, John. 1969. *The myth of Asia*. New York: Simon and Schuster.

Steward, Julian. 1955. *Theory of culture change*. Urbana: University of Illinois Press.

————. 1967. *Contemporary change in traditional societies*. Urbana: University of Illinois Press.

Suleiman, Satyawati. 1986. "Local genius" pada masa klasik. In *Kepribadian budaya bangsa (local genius)*, 152–83. Edited by Ayatrohedi. Jakarta: Pustaka Jaya.

Summers, John. 1998. Listening for historic Manila: Music and rejoicing in an international city. *Budhi: A Journal of Ideas and Culture* 2, no. 1:203–54.

Sunday Times Magazine. 1951. Three who lived.

Tacitus, P. Cornelius. [1928] 1950. *Tacitus, P. Cornelius: De Vita Iulii Agricolae and de Germania*. Original text together with an introduction, notes, appendices and index by Alfred Gudeman. Boston: Allyn and Bacon.

Taruc, Luis. 1953. *Born of the people*. New York: International Publishers.

Taylor, Keith. 1976. Madagascar in the Ancient Malayo-Polynesian myths. In *Explorations in early Southeast Asian statecraft*, 25–60. Edited by Kenneth R. Hall and John K. Whitmore. Ann Arbor: Center for South and Southeast Asian Studies, the University of Michigan.

————. 1983. *The birth of Vietnam*. Berkeley: University of California Press.

Tenbrock, Robert Hermann. 1968. *A history of Germany*. Translated by Paul J. Dine. Munich: Max Hueber.

Thompson, Edward Arthur. 1971. Germanic peoples. *Encyclopedia Britannica* 10:243–46. Chicago: Encyclopedia Britannica Inc.

Tianero, Rafael, OMI. 2002. Direct violence and Christianity among Manobo converts. M.A. thesis in Anthropology, Ateneo de Manila University.

Tilman, Robert O. 1987. *Southeast Asia and the enemy beyond: ASEAN perception of external threats*. Boulder, Colorado, and London: Westview Press.

Tiryakian, Edward A. 1973. Sociology and existential phenomenology. In *Phenomenology and social reality*, 1:187–222. Edited by Maurice Natanson. Evanston: Northwestern University Press.

Toennies, Ferdinand. 1971. *On sociology: Pure, applied and empirical; selected writings*. Edited and with an introduction by Werner J. Cahnaan and Rudolf Heberle. Chicago: University of Chicago Press.

Toynbee, Arnold. 1948–1961. *A study of history.* Vols. 1–12. London: Oxford University Press.

————. 1972. *A study of history.* Rev. and abrd. by the author and Jane Caplan. New York: Weathervane Books.

————. 1982. *A study of history.* Rev. and abrd. ed. New York: Weathervane Books.

Tucker, Robert, ed. 1972. *The Marxist-Engels reader.* New York: W. W. Norton and Company.

Tylor, Edward Burnett [1871]1958. *The origins of culture.* With an introduction by Paul Radin. New York: Harper and Row.

Unabia, Carmen Ching. 1986. The Bukidnon Batbatnon and Pamuhat: A socio-literary study 2-I:1–4. Anastacio Saway, narrator; C. C. Unabia and Danilo de la Mance, trans. Unpublished.

Urios, Saturnino. 1887. Carta del P. Saturnino Urios al P. Superior de la Misión, 20 de mayo, 1883. In *Cartas de los Pp. de la Compañía de Jesús de la Misión de Filipinas, 1877–1895.* 10 vols. Manila: Establecimiento Tipográfico de M. Perez, Hijo.

Urtula, Lucrecia and Prosperidad Arandez. 1992. *Sayaw: An essay on the Spanish influence on Philippine dance.* Manila: Cultural Center of the Philippines.

Veneracion, Jaime B. 1986. *Kasaysayan ng Bulakan.* Cologne: Bahay Saliksikan ng Kasaysayan.

————. 1987. *Agos ng dugong kayumanggi (isang kasaysayan ng Pilipinas).* Quezon City: Education Forum.

Venida, Victor S. 1996. The santo and the rural aristocracy. *Philippine Studies* 44, no. 4:500–13.

Vidal y Soler, Sebastian. 1874. *Memoria sobre el ramo de montes en las Islas Filipinas.* Madrid: Imprenta, Estereotipia y Galvanoplastia de Aribau y Cia.

Villarroel, Fidel, OP. 1971. *Father Jose Burgos, university student.* Manila: University of Santo Tomas Press.

Villoro, Luis. 1976. La revolución de independencia. *Historia general de México* 2:304–56. Mexico, D.F. SEP/El Colegio de México.

Vinogradoff, Paul. 1913. Foundations of society: Origins of feudalism. In *The Cambridge medieval history.* Vol. 2: *Foundation of the western empire,* 639–54. John Bagnell Bury, planner, and H. M. Gwatkin, ed. Cambridge University Press.

Vlekke, Bernard Hubertus Maria. 1960. *Nusantara: A history of Indonesia.* Chicago: Quarangle Books, Inc.

Voget, Fred W. 1975. *A history of ethnology.* New York: Holt, Princeton and Winston.

Von Grunebaum, Gustav E. 1955. *Islam: Essays on the nature and growth of a cultural tradition.* Menasha, Wisconsin: The American Anthropological Association.

Wagley, Charles. 1968. *The Latin American tradition: Essays on the unity and diversity of Latin American culture.* New York: Columbia University Press.

Wallace-Hadrill, J. M. 1959. *The Barbarian west: 400–1000.* London: Hutchinson University Library.

Warren, James. 1985. *The Sulu Zone 1768–1898: The dynamics of external trade, slavery and ethnicity in the transformation of a Southeast Asian maritime state.* Quezon City: New Day Publishers.

Weber, Eugen. 1976. *Peasants into Frenchmen: The modernization of rural France, 1870–1914.* Stanford: University Press.

Webber, Carolyn and Aaron Wildavsky. 1986. A *history of taxation and expenditure in the Western world.* New York: Simon and Schuster.

Wendt, Reinhard. 1998. The fiesta. *Philippine Studies* 26 (1st Quarter): 1–23.

White, Leslie. 1949. *The science of culture: A study of man and civilization.* Farrar, Straus, and Giroux.

Wicks, Robert S. 1988. Southeast Asian architecture. *Encyclopedia of Asian history* 1:86–87. Ainslie T. Embree, editor in chief. New York: Charles Scribner's Sons.

Willey, Mark V. 1994. *Filipino martial arts: Cabales, serrada, escrima.* Tokyo: Charles E. Tuttle Company, Inc. of Rutland, Vermont and Tokyo, Japan.

Winzeler, Robert L. 1976. Ecology, culture, social organization, and state formation in Southeast Asia. *Current Anthropology* 17:623–39.

Wolf, Eric R. 1967. Closed corporate peasant communities in Mesoamerica and Central Java. In *Peasant society: A reader,* 230–46. Edited by Jack M. Potter, May N. Diaz, and George M. Foster. Boston: Little and Brown.

Wolters, O. W. 1967. *Early Indonesian commerce: A study of the origins of Srivijaya.* Ithaca, New York: Cornell University Press.

————. 1982. *History, culture and religion in Southeast Asian perspectives.* Singapore: Institute of Southeast Asian Studies.

Woodside, Alexander B. 1971. *Vietnam and the Chinese model: A comparative study of Nguyen and Ch'ing civil government in the first half of the nineteenth century.* Cambridge, Massachusetts: Harvard University Press.

Wright, Henry T. 1977. Recent research on the origin of the state. *Annual Review of Anthropology* 6:379–97.

————. 1984. Prestate political formations. In *On the evolution of complex societies, essays in honor of Harry Hoijer, 1982,* 41–77. Edited by Timothy

Earle, with William Sanders, Henry Wright and Robert Adans. Malibu: Undena Publications.

Yarwood, Doreen. 1978. *The encyclopedia of world costume*. New York: Charles Scribner's Sons.

Zaide, Gregorio F. 1990. *Documentary sources of Philippine history*. Compiled, edited, and annotated by Gegorio F. Zaide. Additional notes by Sonia M. Zaide. Metro Manila: National Bookstore, Inc.

Zaragoza, Francisco. 1954. *Marella y la inquietud romántica de la revolución*. Introduction by Emilio Aguinaldo. Postscript by Claro Mayo Recto. Manila: General Printing Press.

Zialcita, Bernardo, son of Agapito Zialcita. 1997. Personal communication.

Zialcita, Fernando N. 1995. State formation, colonialism and national identity in Vietnam and the Philippines. *Philippine Quarterly of Culture and Society* 23, no. 2:77–117.

Zialcita, Fernando N. and Martin I. Tinio, Jr. 1980. *Philippine ancestral houses, 1810–1930*. Quezon City: GCF Books.

Zimmer, Heinrich. 1955. *The art of Indian Asia: Its mythology and transformations*. 2 vols. Completed and ed. by Joseph Campbell. Toronto: Pantheon Books, Inc.

Index